A TEXT BOOK OF

# ENGINEERING CHEMISTRY

## FOR

### (SEMESTER – I & II)

### FIRST YEAR DEGREE COURSE IN B. TECH.

### (COMMON FOR ALL BRANCHES)

**Strictly According to Syllabus of**

**Bharati Vidyapeeth Deemed University, Pune**

### (EFFECTIVE FROM ACADEMIC YEAR 2014)

**Dr. Manisha Y. Khaladkar**

M. Sc. (Chemistry), Ph. D.
Head of Applied Science Department,
College of Engineering,
Pune

**Dr. M. S. KADAM**

M. Sc., Ph. D.
Assistant Professor, JSPM's College of Engg.,
Hadapsar, Pune.
Formerly, Lecturer in Chemistry Deptt.
BVU's College of Engineering,
Katraj, Dhankawadi, Pune.

NIRALI PRAKASHAN
ADVANCEMENT OF KNOWLEDGE

N1057

**ENGINEERING CHEMISTRY (BHARATI VIDYAPEETH UNIVERSITY)**

**Second Edition** : **January 2015**          ISBN 978-93-5164-104-9

© : **Authors**

**Published By :**
**NIRALI PRAKASHAN**
Abhyudaya Pragati, 1312, Shivaji Nagar,
Off J.M. Road, PUNE – 411005
Tel - (020) 25512336/37/39, Fax - (020) 25511379
Email : niralipune@pragationline.com

**Printed By :**
**REPRO INDIA LTD,**
**Mumbai.**

## DISTRIBUTION CENTRES
### PUNE

**Nirali Prakashan**
119, Budhwar Peth, Jogeshwari Mandir Lane
Pune 411002, Maharashtra
Tel : (020) 2445 2044, 66022708, Fax : (020) 2445 1538
Email : bookorder@pragationline.com

**Nirali Prakashan**
S. No. 28/25, Dhyari,
Near Pari Company, Pune 411041
Tel : (020) 24690204 Fax : (020) 24690316
Email : dhyari@pragationline.com
    bookorder@pragationline.com

### MUMBAI
**Nirali Prakashan**
385, S.V.P. Road, Rasdhara Co-op. Hsg. Society Ltd.,
Girgaum, Mumbai 400004, Maharashtra
Tel : (022) 2385 6339 / 2386 9976, Fax : (022) 2386 9976
Email : niralimumbai@pragationline.com

## DISTRIBUTION BRANCHES

### NAGPUR
**Pratibha Book Distributors**
Above Maratha Mandir, Shop No. 3, First Floor,
Rani Jhanshi Square, Sitabuldi, Nagpur 440012,
Maharashtra, Tel : (0712) 254 7129

### BENGALURU
**Pragati Book House**
House No. 1, Sanjeevappa Lane, Avenue Road Cross,
Opp. Rice Church, Bengaluru – 560002.
Tel : (080) 64513344, 64513355,
Mob : 9880582331, 9845021552
Email:bharatsavla@yahoo.com

### JALGAON
**Nirali Prakashan**
34, V. V. Golani Market, Navi Peth, Jalgaon 425001,
Maharashtra, Tel : (0257) 222 0395
Mob : 94234 91860

### KOLHAPUR
**Nirali Prakashan**
New Mahadvar Road,
Kedar Plaza, 1st Floor Opp. IDBI Bank
Kolhapur 416 012, Maharashtra. Mob : 9850046155

### CHENNAI
**Pragati Books**
9/1, Montieth Road, Behind Taas Mahal, Egmore,
Chennai 600008 Tamil Nadu, Tel : (044) 6518 3535,
Mob : 94440 01782 / 98450 21552 / 98805 82331, Email : bharatsavla@yahoo.com

## RETAIL OUTLETS
### PUNE

**Pragati Book Centre**
157, Budhwar Peth, Opp. Ratan Talkies,
Pune 411002, Maharashtra
Tel : (020) 2445 8887 / 6602 2707, Fax : (020) 2445 8887
**Pragati Book Centre**
Amber Chamber, 28/A, Budhwar Peth,
Appa Balwant Chowk, Pune : 411002, Maharashtra,
Tel : (020) 20240335 / 66281669
Email : pbcpune@pragationline.com

**Pragati Book Centre**
676/B, Budhwar Peth, Opp. Jogeshwari Mandir,
Pune 411002, Maharashtra
Tel : (020) 6601 7784 / 6602 0855
**PBC Book Sellers & Stationers**
152, Budhwar Peth, Pune 411002, Maharashtra
Tel : (020) 2445 2254 / 6609 2463

### MUMBAI
**Pragati Book Corner**
Indira Niwas, 111 - A, Bhavani Shankar Road, Dadar (W), Mumbai 400028, Maharashtra
Tel : (022) 2422 3526 / 6662 5254, Email : pbcmumbai@pragationline.com

www.pragationline.com                                                    info@pragationline.com

# PREFACE TO THE SECOND EDITION

We are glad and excited to announce that the first edition of this book received an overwhelming response from the engineering student community, compelling us to release its Second edition within a very short period of time.

This thoroughly revised Second edition has been updated with additional matter, many solved problems, including solutions to all university examination problems and numerous exercises for practice.

Special care has been taken to maintain high degree of accuracy in the theory and numericals throughout the book.

We take this opportunity to express our sincere thanks to Dinesh Furia of Nirali Prakashan, a reputed pioneer in the publication field. Our special thanks to Jignesh Furia for their effective cooperation and great care in bringing out this revised edition. We also appreciate the efforts of M P Munde and the entire staff of Nirali Prakashan for bringing this book to the students in a timely manner.

We sincerely hope that this "Second Edition" will also be warmly received by all concerned as in the past.

Valuable suggestions from our esteemed readers to improve the book are most welcome and highly appreciated.

**PUNE**                                                                 **Authors**

# PREFACE TO THE FIRST EDITION

It is with great pleasure that we present the book of **"Engineering Chemistry"** for First Year Engineering Students. This text book has been prepared in accordance with the syllabus prescribed by the Bharati Vidyapeeth University.

Each chapter has been dealt within detail. Sufficient number of problems have been given and exercises have been set. Emphasis has been given to University Solved Numericals and Questions.

We take this opportunity to thank a number of colleagues and our teachers who have helped us in clearing a concept.

We are thankful to Prof. B. S. Godbole (Chemistry) for their kind help.

Our thanks are due to the Publisher Shri. Dineshbhai Furia and Co-ordinator Shri. M. P. Munde who has been instrumental in bringing out this most needed book at the most opportune time. We are thankful to the entire staff of Nirali Prakashan, Pune. Last but not the least our thanks are due to our families and friends who have also contributed in no small measure to the publishing of this book.

Constructive suggestions, criticisms and comments are always welcome from our well wishers, patrons, colleagues and students for the further improvement of this book.

**Authors**

**PUNE.**

# SYLLABUS

**UNIT I : WATER**                                                    (08 Hours)

Introduction, Hardness of water, Effect of hard water on boilers and heat exchangers : (a) Boiler corrosion, (b) Caustic embrittlement, (c) Scales and sludges, (d) Priming and foaming.

Water softening methods for industrial purposes : (a) Zeolite process, (b) Phosphate conditioning, Numericals based on the zeolite process.

**UNIT II : MATERIAL CHEMISTRY**                                      (08 Hours)

**Crystallography :** Unit cell, Laws of crystallography, Weiss indices and Miller indices, Crystal defects (point and line defects), X-ray diffraction – Bragg's law and numericals.

**Cement :** Introduction of cement, Hydraulic/Non-hydraulic cementing materials, Classification of cements, Chemistry of portland cement, Chemical composition and compound constituents of portland cement, Properties of cement and its applications.

**UNIT III : FUELS**                                                  (08 Hours)

Introduction, Classification of fuels, Calorific value of fuels, NCV and GCV, Determination of calorific values using Bomb calorimeter and Boy's gas calorimeter.

Theoretical calculation of calorific value of a fuel, Analysis of coal : (a) Proximate, (b) Ultimate analysis of coal, Numericals based on NCV, GCV.

**UNIT IV : CORROSION AND ITS PREVENTION**                            (08 Hours)

**Corrosion :** Definition, Atmospheric corrosion-mechanism, Wet corrosion-mechanism, Electrochemical and galvanic series, Factors affecting corrosion – Nature of metal, Nature of environment.

**Methods of prevention of corrosion :** Cathodic and Anodic protection, Metallic coatings, Electroplating, Hot dipping.

**UNIT V : ELECTROCHEMISTRY**                                         (08 Hours)

Introduction, Arrhenius ionic theory, Kohlrausch's law of independent migration of ions.

**Laws of Electrolysis :** Faraday's laws, Ostwald's dilution law, Acids and Bases, Concept of pH and pOH, Buffer solutions, Solubility product, Redox reactions.

Electrode potential, Electrochemical cell, Concentration cell, Reference electrodes, Overvoltage, Conductometric titrations, Fuel cells, Lead Acid storage cell and numericals based on the above articles.

**UNIT VI : STEREOCHEMISTRY**                                         (08 Hours)

Introduction, Chirality, Optical activity, Enantiomers, Diastereomers, Projection formula of tetrahedral carbon – Newman projection, Wedge projection, Fischer projection, Geometrical isomerism : cis and trans isomerism, E and Z isomers.

**Optical isomerism :** Mesoform, the number of optical isomers for chiral molecules.

**Conformations :** Conformations of ethane, conformations of n-butane.

• • •

# CONTENTS

•••

# Unit I

# WATER

## 1.1 INTRODUCTION

Water is very essential for the survival of human life, animal life and plant life. Civilization developed in the historical era near the sources of water i.e. river banks. The industrialisation started with the invention of steam engine i.e. use of one of the forms of water. With proliferation of industry, many additional uses of water have been found. Textile industries, laundries, paper industries, distillaries, food processing industries etc need water on large scale. Water is used in generating power-steam as well as hydroelectric. Thus science of water has become most important aspect for the mankind.

The earth is called blue planet because 4/5$^{th}$ of the earth's crust is covered with water. Though it is in abundance of all chemicals, the quantity available for actual use is hardly 0.3 to 0.5 % of the world's water resources that man can tap for. This is because more than 96 % water is locked in oceans which is too saline to drink or for direct use for agricultural, industrial or domestic purposes. About 2 % is locked up as polar ice caps and glaciers. From the glaciers icebergs break, but they slowly melt at sea. About 1 % is deeply underground and not accessible. Only the balance quantity of water (about 0.3 to 0.5 %) is in the form of rivers, wells, lakes and ponds - some part of which is useful for agricultural, domestic and industrial purposes.

## 1.2 SOURCES OF WATER

Water present on earth passes through a remarkable cycle of changes. Thus from sea water it forms water vapour then cloud from where it comes down as rain water and flows as mineral water, river water and finally comes again as sea water. Thus, there are various forms of natural water. The main sources are :

1. Rain water, 2. Surface water, 3. Ground water.

**1. Rain Water :** It is regarded as the purest form of naturally occurring water as it is obtained by a sort of natural distillation (evaporation and condensation). But it is not absolutely pure as it dissolves gases and carries dust particles during its passage through air. The industrial gases such as carbon-dioxide, sulphur-dioxide, nitrogen-oxides etc. contaminate rain water.

2. **Surface Water :** There are three types of surface waters viz. (i) River water, (ii) Sea water, (iii) Lake water.

   (i) **River water :** River and canal water are inland water fed by rains. This water is less pure than rain water. River water contains dissolved inorganic salts such as chlorides, sulphates, bicarbonates of calcium, magnesium and iron. It also contains organic matter derived from plants, sewage and sludges (drainages) from towns and villages. It also contains bacteria and suspended matter such as clay.

   (ii) **Sea water :** It is the most impure form of natural water. All impurities from river water are carried into the sea and thus, impurities in sea water go on accumulating. Thus, sea water becomes more and more salty. Sea water contains about 3.5 % of dissolved solid, out of which nearly 2.6 % is sodium chloride. Other impurities are magnesium chloride, magnesium sulphate, calcium sulphate, potassium chloride, magnesium bromide etc.

   (iii) **Lake water :** It is more constant in its composition. It consists of little more amount of organic matter compared with river water. The quality of water of some of the big lakes is so good that hardly any treatment is needed for its industrial uses.

3. **Ground Water :** The rain water after reaching the ground is percolated in the soil. During percolation a number of mineral salts are dissolved in it. This water is extremely clear as a result of natural filtration through the sand bed. It is also free from ammonia and organic impurities. Water from well and spring is extremely hard. Some mineral water (spring water) possesses many times medicinal value as it may contain colloidal sulphur, hydrogen sulphide, borax etc.

## 1.3 STRUCTURE OF WATER

Water is a stable compound of oxygen and hydrogen which is represented as $H_2O$ or H – O – H. Bonds between oxygen and hydrogen are covalent with some ionic character. Bond angle HOH is 104.5° and bond length O – H is 0.96 A°. Heat of formation ($\Delta H$) of water molecule is – 286 kJ/mole. It is also called hydride of oxygen. It exists as associated liquid.

(1) Electronic configuration of oxygen (At. No. 8) is $1s^2\ 2s^2\ 2p^4$. Outermost four orbitals of oxygen hybridise to form four $sp^3$ hybridised orbitals. Out of these four $sp^3$ orbitals, two orbitals are completely filled and two orbitals are partially filled. When water molecule is formed, 1s orbital of hydrogen overlaps with one of the partially filled $sp^3$ orbital of oxygen to form a covalent bond. Thus two covalent bonds are formed with two hydrogen

atoms and one common oxygen atom. Remaining two orbitals of oxygen are called non-bonding orbitals, each contains a lone pair of electrons. But due to strong repulsion between two lone pairs of electrons on non-bonding orbitals, the bond angle H – O – H is less than tetrahedral bond angle 109.5°. The actual bond angle HOH is 104.5°.

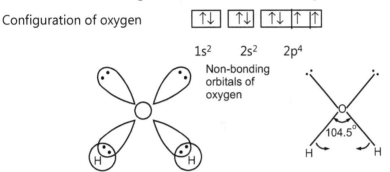

Configuration of oxygen

$1s^2$    $2s^2$    $2p^4$

Non-bonding orbitals of oxygen

104.5°

**Fig. 1.1 : Water molecule**

(2)   The covalent bonds in water molecule are polar covalent bonds. Hydrogen has electronegativity 2.1 on Pauling scale while oxygen has 3.5. As among two combining atoms, oxygen is more electronegative, electron cloud is shifted towards oxygen. Because of this oxygen acts as negative end and hydrogen atom as positive end. In such structure, centres of positive and negative charges in the molecule will not coincide. Such structure is called dipole. This dipole property makes water unique as a solvent. Water has dipole moment of 1.8 Debye units. As a general rule 'like dissolves like', ionic compounds are soluble in polar solvent like water.

**Fig. 1.2 : Water molecule as dipole**

(3)   As hydrogen atom in water molecule is bonded to a small strongly electronegative atom like oxygen, it results in strong polar molecule. The positively charged hydrogen atom of one molecule attracts the negatively charged oxygen atom of the other molecule electrostatically. This results in association of two or more molecules forming cluster of molecules. The hydrogen atom thus acts as a bridge between the two electronegative oxygen atoms. This type of bond is called hydrogen bond, which gives additional stability to the aggregate of water molecules. Because of this, water exists as associated liquid with high boiling point (100° C), while other hydrides of same group (VI A) are volatile (e.g. $H_2S$, $H_2Se$ and $H_2Te$).

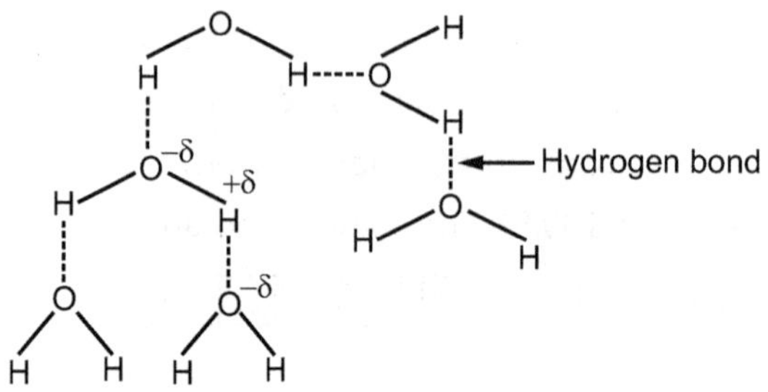

**Fig. 1.3 (a) : Cluster of water molecules**

At normal pressure (1 atm.), below 0°C, it exists in solid state above 100°C it exists in gaseous state; while from 0° C to 100° C it exists in liquid state. It can be used in all three forms for many purposes. In solid state as a coolant, in liquid state as solvent and in gaseous state for generation of power.

**Structure of Ice :**

Hydrogen bonding is observed in ice like that of in liquid water. Ice exists in seven different types of crystalline structure at very high pressure, but only one type of phase or structure is shown by ice at lower pressure. At low pressure, ice crystallises in hexagonal unit cell with each oxygen atom surrounded tetrahedrally by four others. These oxygen atoms are held together by hydrogen bonds.

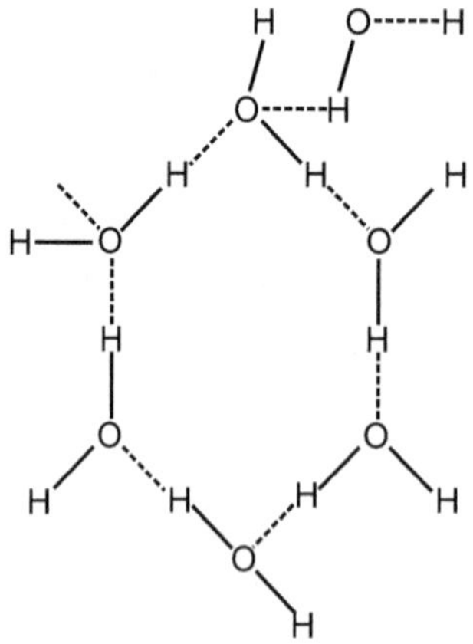

**Fig. 1.3 (b) : Hexagonal structure of ice**

O – H ... O and O ... H – O bonds are largely distributed through the solid. The resulting structure is quite open which accounts for the density of ice which is lower than that of the water at 0°C.

## 1.4 PROPERTIES OF WATER

### (1) Water as a solvent :

Ionic compounds are soluble in polar solvent like water. Solubility of ionic solids in water depends upon (i) weakening of coulombic attractive force between ions of compound (solute) by dielectric constant of water. When water is placed between two isolated electrically charged plates, the water molecules tend to orient themselves so as to reduce the potential between the plates (Fig. 1.4). This property gives water very high dielectric constant of 80 at 20°C and makes it a very good solvent for ionizable substances. It can weaken the force of attraction between ions of the ionic solute.

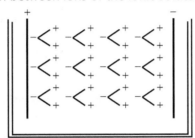

**Fig. 1.4 : Water molecules between charged plates**

e.g. Dissolution of sodium chloride, NaCl in water

$$NaCl_{(s)} \xrightarrow{H_2O} Na^{+}_{(aq)} + Cl^{-}_{(aq)} \qquad \text{... (1)}$$

$Na^{+}_{aq}$, $Cl^{-}_{aq}$ means corresponding ions in water solution. For NaCl, energy of coulombic attraction is – 497.42 kJ/mole. When dissolved in water, it decreases to –6.27 kJ/mole, which shows that oppositely charged ions are not held strongly and are thus free to move about. Hence sodium chloride dissolves easily in water.

(ii) The solvation energy released due to interaction between the ions and the solvent molecules. When ionic compound (e.g. NaCl) is in water (equation 1), water being a good dipole, each positive and negative ion of the compound is surrounded by large number of water molecules having the ion dipole interaction. Because of this electrical bond between sodium and chloride in the salt weakens to such an extent that, they can move freely in solution. Na$^+$ is fairly small, positive charge on it exerts strong attraction on the water dipoles so it is strongly hydrated. Cl$^-$ is fairly large ion, so it is weakly hydrated. Since there are large number of ions in the compound, large ion-dipole bonds are formed when ionic solid is dissolved in water. This process is called ion hydration and the energy released in the formation of such ion-dipole bonds is called hydration energy. If hydration energy overcomes the coulombic attraction energy between the ions, the compound dissolves in water.

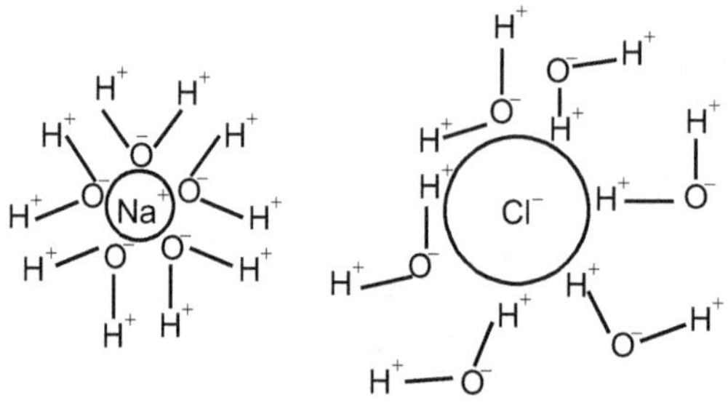

**Fig. 1.5 : Ion-dipole interaction**

Thus ionic compounds will dissolve in water because water has high dielectric constant and in most cases hydration energy exceeds lattice energy (coulombic attraction energy) of the ionic compound. Strong acids and strong bases are also soluble in water through dissociation. Most organic compounds are insoluble in water.

### (2) Conductivity :

Pure water has very low electric conductivity, but water in which some sodium chloride (or any ionic compound) is dissolved acquires electrical conductivity which is proportional to concentration of salt in water. Because of solvation of sodium and chloride ions, electrical bond between sodium and chloride is weakened to such an extent that they can move freely in solution. If an electric field is applied across the solution of such ions, the positive ions start to move towards cathode and negative ions towards anode. Because of this the solution appears to conduct an electric current.

### (3) Ionic dissociation of water :

Water is weakly dissociated through the reaction

$$H_2O_{(l)} \rightleftharpoons H^+ + OH^-$$

Applying law of mass action,

$$\frac{[H^+]\,[OH^-]}{[H_2O]} = K$$

Since water is a solvent, it's activity can be taken as unity, then we get

$$[H^+]\,[OH^-] = K = 10^{-14} \text{ at } 25^\circ C$$

Taking the logarithm we get,

$$[\log H^+] + [\log OH^-] = -14$$

As for absolutely pure water the concentration of hydrogen ions is equal to concentration of hydroxyl ions.

i.e.                    $[H^+] = [OH^-]$, which means for pure water

$$[H^+] = [OH^-] = 10^{-7}$$

∴ pH of pure water is 7, thus pure water is neutral.

**(4) The chemical stability of water :**

When liquid water is formed from its elements, 286 kJ/mol of heat energy is released. The direct reaction is explosive but it may be carried out at ordinary temperature under controlled conditions in the fuel cell. The large energy released on formation of water molecule means it is a stable molecule. Water is decomposed by alkali metals giving gaseous hydrogen and metal hydroxides. It also reacts with alkaline earth metals but with them it acts as an oxidising agent.

**(5) Phase equilibria in water :**

The freezing and boiling points of water at atmospheric pressure are the standard temperature points of the Celsius scale, 0 and 100° C. Water has a triple point at which the three phases, ice, liquid, and vapour, coexist in equilibrium, at 0.0098°C and 0.611 kN/m² pressure (Fig. 1.6). Above this pressure, equilibria are only possible between ice and liquid or between liquid and vapour. Below this pressure the only equilibrium is between ice and vapour and on heating ice under these conditions it sublimes directly to the vapour, an effect which is utilized in freeze drying.

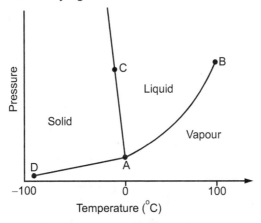

**Fig. 1.6 : Phase diagram for water. A is the triple point, AB is the liquid-vapour equilibrium (boiling point), AC is the liquid-solid equilibrium (melting point), and AD is the solid-vapour equilibrium (sublimation)**

When liquid water freezes there is an increase in volume; the density of water at 0°C is 0.9999 g/cm³ while that of ice is 0.917 g/cm³. When water is frozen under high pressure other forms of ice are obtained which have higher densities.

The latent heat of melting for ice is 335 J/g 0°C; the latent heat of evaporation of water is 2255 J/g at 100°C. The high value for the latent heat of evaporation reflects the association of water molecules in the liquid state.

**(6)** Water is a good ligand because of lone pair of electrons. It can form many stable complexes with transition metal ions.

## 1.5 COMMON IMPURITIES IN WATER

The common impurities present in the natural water may be classified as follows :

(1) Suspended impurities, (2) Dissolved impurities, (3) Colloidal impurities, (4) Biological impurities.

**1. Suspended impurities :** Water may contain the suspended impurities such as clay, mud, algae, industrial waste, organic matter etc. These remain suspended in water. They produce turbidity, colour and odour and may cause diseases.

**2. Dissolved impurities :** There may be two types of impurities viz. (a) Gases, (b) Mineral salts.

**(a) Gases :** The gases present in air such as oxygen, carbon dioxide, oxides of nitrogen, hydrogen sulphide, sulphur dioxide, are soluble in natural water.

**(b) Mineral salts :** The commonly observed salts in natural water are carbonates, bi-carbonates, sulphates and chlorides of calcium, magnesium, sodium and potassium. When salts of calcium and magnesium are present in water, it is known as hard water. Such water cannot be used for washing clothes and in boilers.

**3. Colloidal impurities :** Colloidal particles of clay, fine mud, decayed leaves, organic matter (insects and fungi) may be present in water. Such impurities neither settle down on standing nor these can be removed by filtration. Size of colloidal particle is about $10^{-4}$ cm to $10^{-7}$ cm. These are the charged particles. These become the main source of epidemic when associated with bacteria.

**4. Biological impurities :** Slime growth such as algae, micro-organism i.e. bacteria, fungi etc. are considered as pathogenic. Such impurities may be present in natural water and it may affect the efficiency of heat transfer equipment. Biological growth can also contribute to corrosion and cause odours of water which might restrict its usefulness. Such water is dangerous for human consumption and health.

## 1.6 HARD AND SOFT WATER

It is a common observation that water from some sources like well produce lather (foam) readily with soap while that from other sources like rivers, springs or even certain wells produces lather with soap only with difficulty.

Water which does not produce good *lather* with soap solution *readily* but develops *curd* (a white scum) is termed as *hard water*. Water which does not produce curd with soap solution but develops lather *readily* is known as *soft water*.

**Causes of Hardness of Water :**

Rain water absorbs carbon dioxide from air and also from decaying plants on soil. Such water when it flows over the rocks containing calcium and magnesium carbonates, reacts slowly with these substances forming bicarbonates which are much more soluble.

$$H_2O + CO_2 \longrightarrow H_2CO_3$$
$$H_2CO_3 + CaCO_3 \longrightarrow Ca(HCO_3)_2$$
$$\text{(Soluble)}$$

On the surface layer, there are also chlorides and sulphates of calcium and magnesium and these salts are soluble in water. Thus, water flowing over rocks and surface layer contains bicarbonates, chlorides and sulphates of calcium and magnesium in the dissolved state. Such water is known as *hard water*.

Soap is a mixture of sodium salts of fatty acids like stearic acid, oleic acid, palmitic acid etc. Soap (sodium salt) is soluble in water and forms lather due to which it has cleansing property. When soap is added to hard water containing calcium and magnesium salts (i.e. $Ca^{++}$ and $Mg^{++}$), insoluble calcium and magnesium salts are obtained by double decomposition. Thus

$$2C_{17}H_{35}COONa + CaCl_2 \rightarrow Ca(C_{17}H_{35}COO)_2 \downarrow + 2NaCl$$
(Soluble sodium stearate; i.e. soap)          (Insoluble calcium stearate)

$$2C_{17}H_{35}COONa + Ca(HCO_3)_2 \rightarrow Ca(C_{17}H_{35}COO)_2 \downarrow + 2NaHCO_3$$
(Insoluble calcium stearate)

$$2C_{17}H_{35}COONa + MgSO_4 \rightarrow Mg(C_{17}H_{35}COO)_2 \downarrow + Na_2SO_4$$
(Insoluble magnesium stearate)

This insolube calcium or magnesium stearate is known as curd i.e. white scum. Until all the calcium or magnesium ions are removed in this way soap will not be available for cleansing purposes. Thus, much soap is wasted in hard water. Moreover clothing washed with soap in hard water gets dingy appearance due to the adherence of sticky scum in the fabric. Detergents are better cleansing agents than soap as they are not affected by hard water.

**Types of Hardness :**

For the sake of convenience, hard water is classified as (1) Temporary hard water and (2) Permanent hard water.

**1. Temporary hard water :** Water containing bicarbonates of calcium and magnesium can be made free from these salts (i.e. softened by mere boiling and this water is known as temporary hard water. On boiling, the bicarbonate is decomposed and forms an insoluble carbonate. Carbon dioxide escapes as it is not soluble at higher temperature.

$$Ca(HCO_3)_2 \rightarrow CaCO_3 \downarrow + CO_2 \uparrow + H_2O$$
(Soluble)        (Insoluble)

$$Mg(HCO_3)_2 \rightarrow MgCO_3 \downarrow + CO_2 \uparrow + H_2O$$
(Soluble)        (Insoluble)

**2. Permanent hard water :** Water containing sulphates and chlorides of calcium and magnesium cannot be made free from these salts (i.e. cannot be softened) by mere boiling. This water is known as permanent hard water. Sometimes hardness is due to cations like ferrous, ferric, aluminium and anions like nitrates and silicates.

# 1.7 DEGREE OF HARDNESS OF WATER

Due to the presence of calcium and magnesium salts, water becomes hard. The hardness of water is expressed in terms of parts by weight of calcium carbonate. The hardness of water can be found out by chemical analysis. There are in all three systems to express the hardness of water (i) Degree Clark, (ii) French degree of hardness and (iii) Parts per million.

**1. Degree Clark :** This is a British system of expressing hardness of water. It may be defined as the *number of parts by weight of calcium carbonate present in 70,000 parts by weight of water.*

∴ 1º Clark = 1 part by wt. of $CaCO_3$/70,000 parts by weight of water.

**2. French degree of hardness :** As the name indicates it is a french system of expressing hardness of water. It is the *number of parts by weight of calcium carbonate present in 1,00,000 (or $10^5$) parts by weight of water.*

∴ 1º French = 1 part by wt. of $CaCO_3$/$10^5$ parts by weight of water.

**3. Parts per million (mg/litre) :** This is the modern system used to express the hardness of water. It is expressed as the number of parts by weight of calcium carbonate, present per million parts ($10^6$) by weight of water.

∴ 1 ppm = 1 part by wt. of $CaCO_3$/$10^6$ parts by weight of water.

**Milligrams per litre (mg/litre) :** "It is the number of milligrams of $CaCO_3$ equivalent present in one litre of water."

$$1 \text{ mg/litre} = 1 \text{ mg of } CaCO_3 \text{ equivalent in one litre}$$

But
$$1 \text{ mg} = 1 \text{ mg/1kg of water}$$
$$= 1 \text{ mg/1000 gm of water}$$
$$= 1 \text{ mg/1000} \times 1000 \text{ mg of water}$$
$$= 1 \text{ mg/}10^6 \text{ mg of water}$$

∴  | 1 mg/litre = 1 ppm |

**Relation between various units of hardness :**

1 ppm ≡ 1 mg/litre ≡ 0.1º French ≡ 0.07º Clark
1º Clark ≡ 14.3 ppm ≡ 1.43º French
1° French ≡ 10 ppm ≡ 10 mg/litre ≡ 0.7° Clark

# 1.8 CALCULATION OF DEGREE OF HARDNESS

The total hardness of water is estimated by titrating a measured volume of water, either with a standard soap solution or with EDTA (ethylene diamine tetra acetic acid) solution.

Whatever may be the salt causing hardness of water, its quantity has to be converted into the equivalent amount of calcium carbonate. For example, consider that, hardness is due to the presence of calcium bicarbonate i.e. $Ca(HCO_3)_2$.

Molecular weight of $Ca(HCO_3)_2$ is 162. Therefore, 162 parts by weight of calcium bicarbonate would react with the same quantity of soap solution as 100 parts by weight of calcium carbonate. Therefore, to get the $CaCO_3$ equivalent, the weight of $Ca(HCO_3)_2$ has to be multiplied by the factor 100/162.

Similarly, the quantities of other salts, which cause hardness, are converted into their $CaCO_3$ equivalents, by multiplying the following factors as given in Table 1.1 (a).

**Table 1.1 (a) : Calculation of CaCO₃ equivalents**

| Dissolved Salt | Molecular Weight | Multiplication Factor (for converting equivalents of CaCO₃) |
|:---:|:---:|:---:|
| $Ca(HCO_3)_2$ | 162 | 100 / 162 |
| $Mg(HCO_3)_2$ | 146 | 100 / 146 |
| $CaCl_2$ | 111 | 100 / 111 |
| $MgCl_2$ | 95 | 100 / 95 |
| $CaSO_4$ | 136 | 100 / 136 |
| $MgSO_4$ | 120 | 100 / 120 |
| $CaCO_3$ | 100 | 100 / 100 |
| $MgCO_3$ | 84 | 100 / 84 |
| $Mg(NO_3)_2$ | 148 | 100 / 148 |
| $CO_2$ | 44 | 100 / 44 |

Hard and soft water cannot be rigidly distinguished from each other. However, Table 1.1 (b) gives some classification of hard water, on the basis of ppm of $CaCO_3$.

**Table 1.1 (b) : Classification of hard water**

| ppm of CaCO₃ | Hardness of water |
|:---:|:---|
| upto 50 | Soft |
| 50 to 100 | Moderately soft |
| 100 to 150 | Slightly hard |
| 150 to 200 | Moderately hard |
| 200 to 250 | Hard |
| 250 above | Very hard |

# 1.9 EFFECTS OF HARD WATER

Hard water is unsuitable when used for domestic, industrial and steam generation purposes. The disadvantages of using hard water are given below under the three heads.

(A)  For industrial use

(B)  For domestic use

(C)  For steam generation in boilers.

### A. For industrial use :

Water finds a great use in number of industries such as paper manufacturing, dyeing, textile, sugar, etc. Water containing dissolved salts of Ca, Mg, Fe, Mn, Na etc. are harmful for various industries. The bad effects of using hard water in some of the common industries are discussed below :

**1.  Paper Industry :** During the manufacture of paper, the material like rosin size (a mixture of 70 % rosin soap + 30 % rosin acid) is added to the paper pulp to make the surface of paper smooth and glossy. If hard water is used for paper manufacturing then $Ca^{++}$ and $Mg^{+}$ ions present in it used to react with the material. Hence, the paper will not have the desired smoothness and glossiness. Moreover, due to the presence of iron and manganese impurities in water, the whiteness or colour of paper may be affected. Therefore, water used for this industry should be free from the impurities such as Ca, Mg, Fe, Mn, etc.

**2.  Dyeing Industry :** Hard water is also harmful to use in dyeing industry. Dye is a colouring matter used for colouration of textile cloth, wool, silk, synthetic fibres and plastics, etc. The dissolved salts of Ca, Mg, and Fe may react with dyes to form undesirable precipitates due to which impure shades of dyes are produced on the fibres. If iron is also present in water, it produces spots or yellow stains on the clothes. Hence, water used for this industry should be free from Ca, Mg and Fe impurities.

**3.  Textile Industry :** If hard water is used for this industry then large quantity of soap is wasted while washing the yarn. This is because in hard water soap cannot produce good quantity of lather. At the same time undesirable precipitate of insoluble calcium and magnesium salts of higher fatty acids, is formed. This precipitate may adhere to the fabrics while dyeing them and the exact shades of the colour are not obtained. Iron and manganese, may cause spots on fabrics if such water is used for textile industry. Therefore water used for this industry should be at least free from calcium, magnesium, iron and manganese salts.

**4.  Sugar Industry :** If water used in sugar industry contains the impurities like sulphate, alkali carbonate, nitrate and bacteria, then the sugar may not crystallise well and it may be deliquescent. The sugar may be decomposed while keeping in storage.

**B. For domestic use :**

For domestic purposes, lot of quantity of water is used. Water is mainly used for (1) Washing, (2) Cooking, (3) Bathing, and (4) Drinking.

**1.  Washing :** Hard water is unsuitable for washing because it does not give lather freely with soap. Due to this, large quantity of soap is wasted. Hard water forms the sticky precipitate of insoluble calcium and magnesium stearate and it may adhere on the fabric. Due to this, spots and streaks are produced on the clothes, which becomes prominent on ironing. Presence of iron may redden the water and due to which yellow stains may be produced on the clothes.

**2.  Cooking :** Since impurities are present in water, the boiling point of water is elevated. Hence, the pulses and vegetables may not cook well, so more time and more fuel are required when such water is used for cooking. The salts of calcium and magnesium get deposited on the inner walls of the water-heating vessels and cooking utensils when hard water is used for cooking. Secondly, due to overheating of utensils and vessels, their life is reduced.

**3. Bathing :** Hard water is undesirable for bathing. Since a good lather is not formed by using such water, the cleaning quality of soap is depressed and it is wasted. Insoluble residue is formed with soap if hard water is used, and is adsorbed on our body, due to which our skin becomes dry and dark.

**4. Drinking :** We need large quantity of water for drinking purposes. Hard water is undesirable for drinking because presence of impurities may cause bad effect on digestion process. Similarly, possibility of formation of calcium oxalate crystals may be increased. In favourable conditions, these crystals may be accumulated either in kidney or bladder to form kidney stones.

**C. For steam generation in boilers :**

The manufacturing industries need water for a great variety of purposes, out of which steam generation is the most important one. Water containing dissolved salts of sulphates, bicarbonates, chlorides of calcium and magnesium, iron salts has adverse effect on steam boilers. Hence, water for raising steam in boilers must be soft and must not contain too much dissolved or suspended matter; so as to avoid the troubles of (i) Corrosion, (ii) Caustic embrittlement, (iii) Priming and foaming, (iv) Scale and sludge formation.

# 1.9.1 Boiler Corrosion

The most serious problem, created by the use of unsuitable water in boilers, is corrosion. *"Corrosion can be defined as the decaying of metals by a chemical or electro-chemical reaction with their environment"*. Water containing various types of impurities cause corrosion of the inner surface of the boiler. Corrosion in boiler is due to the following reasons viz. (i) Dissolved gases, (ii) Dissolved salts and (iii) Acidity or alkalinity of water.

(i) **Dissolved gases :** Among the dissolved gases, oxygen is the most corroding impurity. Water contains about 8 ml of oxygen per litre at about 10°C. Dissolved oxygen in presence of water and under prevailing high temperature attacks material of boiler.

$$4\ Fe + 4\ H_2O + 2\ O_2\ \rightarrow\ 4Fe(OH)_2$$
$$4Fe(OH)_2 + O_2\ \rightarrow\ 2\ (Fe_2O_3 \cdot 2H_2O\ )$$
Ferrous hydroxide          Rust

Dissolved oxygen can be removed by adding calculated quantity of sodium sulphite or hydrazine or sodium sulphide. Recently, Azamina - 8001 – RD (polyvalent organic compound) is used to remove dissolved oxygen in minimum time.

Water also contains small amount of dissolved carbon dioxide. If hard water is used for steam generation then the dissolved bicarbonates of calcium or magnesium are decomposed to produce carbon dioxide.

$$Mg(HCO_3)_2 \rightarrow MgCO_3 + H_2O + CO_2\uparrow$$

Carbon-dioxide when dissolved in water forms a weak acid (carbonic acid).

$$H_2O + CO_2 \rightarrow H_2CO_3\ (carbonic\ acid)$$

This carbonic acid slowly attacks over the metal of the boiler.

Carbon dioxide and oxygen can be removed by mechanical deaeration. Carbon-dioxide may be removed by adding calculated quantity of ammonia.

$$2NH_4OH + CO_2 \rightarrow (NH_4)_2CO_3 + H_2O$$

**(ii) Dissolved salts :** If in a hard water, impurity such as magnesium chloride is present, it hydrolyses to produce hydrochloric acid.

$$MgCl_2 + 2H_2O \rightarrow Mg(OH)_2 \downarrow + 2\ HCl$$

The liberated acid reacts with iron material of the boiler like a chain reaction producing hydrochloric acid again and again.

$$Fe \quad + \quad 2HCl \quad \rightarrow \quad FeCl_2 + H_2\uparrow$$
$$FeCl_2 \quad + \quad 2H_2O \quad \rightarrow \quad Fe(OH)_2 + 2HCl$$

Hence, presence of even a small amount of $MgCl_2$ will cause corrosion of boiler to a large extent. Therefore, it is necessary to neutralise the acidity of water by adding alkaline salts or even ammonia.

**(iii) Acidity or Alkalinity of water :** If water used in boiler is acidic (pH < 7), it causes corrosion of iron to a large extent. On the other hand, if water is alkaline (pH = 7 to 9.5) it may restrict corrosion of iron to some extent. But if water is too alkaline (pH = 11 to 14) then corrosion of iron will be to a greater extent.

# 1.9.2 Caustic Embrittlement (or Caustic Corrosion)

This is a type of boiler corrosion, caused by using highly alkaline water in boiler. This type of corrosion is generally observed in the boiler which operates under high pressure. During water softening process, small quantity of sodium carbonate ($Na_2CO_3$) is added. In high pressure boilers, sodium carbonate decomposes to give sodium hydroxide and carbon dioxide.

$$Na_2CO_3 + H_2O \rightarrow 2\ NaOH + CO_2\uparrow$$

Due to the formation of sodium hydroxide (caustic soda), water becomes more alkaline. A number of minute cracks are observed on the inner lining of boiler. This alkaline water flows into such minute cracks by capillary action. Here water evaporates and the dissolved caustic soda is left behind. The amount of caustic soda goes on increasing due to progressive evaporation. The alkaline action of caustic soda attacks the surrounding areas of cracks thereby dissolving iron material of the boiler. This causes embrittlement of boiler parts, particularly, at stressed parts like rivets, bends, joints etc. causing even failure of the boiler.

Caustic embrittlement can be avoided by

(i)  using sodium phosphate instead of sodium carbonate for softening water,

(ii)  by adding tannin or lignin as additives to the boiler water, since these block the minute cracks thereby preventing infiltration of caustic soda solution,

(iii)  by adjusting the alkalinity of water to optimum level (pH – 7 to 9).

### 1.9.3 Priming and Foaming

When a boiler is steaming rapidly, some particles of liquid water are mixed with the steam and pass from the boiler along with steam. This process is known as *priming*. The cause of priming is due to dissolved solids particularly the suspended solid or high steam velocities or improper boiler design.

Foaming is the production of persistent foam or bubbles in boilers, which do not break easily. Foaming occurring particularly at the water surface is due to presence of large quantity of dissolved matter in water, by which the surface tension of water is lowered. This is responsible for the phenomenon of foaming.

There are some disadvantages of priming process :

(i) The actual height of water in boiler is not judged.

(ii) To adjust the steam pressure in the boiler, more heat is required. Therefore, efficiency of the process is decreased.

(iii) Water and dissolved salts may enter the parts of machinery which decreases the life of machinery.

Priming can be avoided by using mechanical steam purifier, maintaining low levels in boilers, avoiding rapid changes in steaming rate and using pure water. Foaming can be avoided by blowdown operations to predetermined intervals, adding castor oil or anti-foaming agents.

### 1.9.4 Scale and Sludge Formation in Boiler

By continuous evaporation of water in the boiler increases the concentration of dissolved salts. When their concentration reaches to the saturation point, they are thrown out of the water in the form of precipitates on the inner walls of the boiler. If the precipitate is loose and slimy, it is known as *'sludge.'* On the other hand, if the precipitated matter forms a hard adhering coating on the inner walls of the boiler, it is known as *'scale.'*

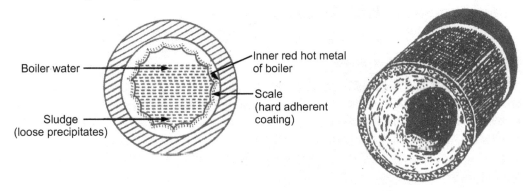

Boiler water

Inner red hot metal of boiler

Scale (hard adherent coating)

Sludge (loose precipitates)

**Fig. 1.7 (a) : Scale and sludge in boilers  Fig. 1.7 (b) : Boiler scale in a hot-water pipe**

**Scale formation in Boilers :** *"The precipitated matter forms a hard adhering coating on the inner surface of the boiler are called boiler scales."* Scales are so hard and adherent that it is difficult to remove them, even with the help of hammer or chisel. The scales are bad conductors of heat and are more troublesome. Scales are of following types : (i) Carbonate, (ii) Sulphates, (iii) Silicates, (iv) Phosphates, and (v) Oxides.

The hardness of scale depends upon the nature of impurities present in the water. The most troublesome scales are formed due to the presence of sulphates and silicates of calcium and magnesium. Such scales are non-porous, hard, more adherent and non-conductor of heat, hence these cause overheating of the boiler material. Calcium carbonate forms a non-adherent scale and can be easily removed by blowing off or washing out. Magnesium chloride, if present in the scale will bring about corrosion of tubes and boiler plates.

**Sludge formation in Boilers :** *"When a soft, loose slimy deposits are formed inside the boiler and do not stick up permanently are known as sludges."* Sludges are generally, formed, at comparatively cooler parts of the boiler, and they collect in areas of the system, where the flow rate is slow or at bends in the line. In such parts they build up a deposit which choke the steam pipes. "Sludges are formed by substances which have greater solubilities in hot water than in cold water e.g. $CaCl_2$, $MgCl_2$, $MgSO_4$, $MgCO_3$ etc.

Sludges are poor conductors of heat, so they tend to waste a portion of heat generated. The formation of sludge is not a major problem, because it can be removed by frequent blow-down operation or simply by brushing. Many times sludges are formed along with the scales, then these two are mixed and both get deposited as scales. Sometimes, excess of sludge formation disturbs the working of the boiler.

**Difference between Scales and Sludges :**

|   | Scales | Sludges |
|---|---|---|
| 1. | Form an adherent coating within the boiler which cannot be removed even by mechanical means. | Form slimy or less adherent coating within the boiler which can be removed by mechanical means. |
| 2. | Scales are harder and more permeable. | Sludges are soft and less permeable. |
| 3. | Scales are bad conductors of heat. | Sludges are poor conductors of heat. |
| 4. | These are formed throughout the metal surface in contact with water. | These are formed at comparatively cooler portions of the boiler. (e.g. in bends of lines). |

# 1.10 TREATMENT OF WATER

To obtain water suitable for industrial and domestic purposes, certain treatment should be given to the water. For domestic purpose, the water used must be hygenically pure, i.e. free from germs and bacteria.

It should not be hard. On the other hand, water used in the industries should be free from dissolved mineral salts, dissolved gases. The acidity or alkalinity of water must be adjusted as per requirement of the industry. Water is treated mainly for two purposes : (i) for industrial purposes and (ii) for domestic purposes.

## 1.11 METHODS OF SOFTENING HARD WATER

*The process of removing soluble calcium and magnesium salts from hard water is called softening the water.* During the process of softening of hard water, the soluble salts are converted into the insoluble salts. These insoluble salts can be removed by filtration and soft water can be obtained. The methods of softening hard water depend upon the fact that whether the hardness is temporary or permanent.

**[A] Methods for softening temporary hard water :**

**1. Boiling :** Temporary hard water can be softened by mere boiling as explained earlier. Carbon dioxide escapes and a carbonate settles down. The upper layer of water is pumped off.

$$Ca(HCO_3)_2 \rightarrow CaCO_3 \downarrow + CO_2 \uparrow + H_2O$$

This method cannot be used on large scale, but the process can be used on small scale only.

**2. Clark's Method :** This method is also used to soften temporary hard water which is very hard. In this method, a calculated quantity of slaked lime is added to hard water. Soluble bicarbonates are converted into insoluble carbonates which are removed by filtration.

$$Ca(HCO_3)_2 + Ca(OH)_2 \rightarrow 2\ CaCO_3 \downarrow + 2H_2O$$
$$Mg(HCO_3)_2 + Ca(OH)_2 \rightarrow CaCO_3 \downarrow + MgCO_3 \downarrow + 2H_2O$$

It should be noted that only proper quantity of lime should be used. If too much quantity of lime is used then excess of lime will remain in the solution and thus retain the hardness of water.

**[B] Methods of softening permanent hard water :**

Permanent hard water contains sulphates and chlorides of calcium and magnesium and this water cannot be softened by mere boiling or adding slaked lime. The methods used to soften such water are :

1. Soda-ash process.    2. Lime-soda process.
3. Permutit process.    4. Ion-exchange process.

## 1.11.1 Soda–Ash Process

By adding soda-ash [i.e. sodium carbonate ($Na_2CO_3$)] it is possible to remove permanent as well as temporary hardness of water. In this method calculated quantity of soda-ash is added to hard water. So that bicarbonates, sulphates and chlorides of calcium and magnesium are converted into insoluble carbonates and hence, water becomes softer.

$$Ca(HCO_3)_2 \quad + \ Na_2CO_3 \ \rightarrow \ CaCO_3 \downarrow + 2NaHCO_3$$
$$CaCl_2 \quad\quad\quad + \ Na_2CO_3 \ \rightarrow \ CaCO_3 \downarrow + 2\ NaCl$$
$$MgSO_4 \quad\quad\ + \ Na_2CO_3 \ \rightarrow \ MgCO_3 \downarrow + Na_2\ SO_4$$

## 1.11.2 Lime-Soda Process

In this process, both lime $Ca(OH)_2$ (calcium hydroxide) and soda $Na_2CO_3$ (sodium carbonate) are used to soften the water. It means this process is the combination of Clark's method and soda-ash method. By this method, both temporary and permanent hardness of water can be removed. Bicarbonates and carbonates are removed by lime while sulphates and chlorides are removed by soda.

$$Ca(HCO_3)_2 + Ca(OH)_2 \rightarrow 2\,CaCO_3 \downarrow + 2H_2O$$

$$Mg(HCO_3)_2 + Ca(OH)_2 \rightarrow CaCO_3 \downarrow + MgCO_3 \downarrow + 2H_2O$$

$$MgCO_3 + Ca(OH)_2 \rightarrow CaCO_3 \downarrow + Mg(OH)_2$$

If water contains sulphates and chlorides of magnesium then both soda and lime are required.

$$MgSO_4 + Na_2CO_3 + Ca(OH)_2 \rightarrow Mg(OH)_2 + CaCO_3 + Na_2SO_4$$

$$MgCl_2 + Na_2CO_3 + Ca(OH)_2 \rightarrow Mg(OH)_2 + CaCO_3 + 2NaCl$$

On the other hand, if the sulphates and chlorides of calcium are present then only soda-ash is required.

$$CaSO_4 + Na_2CO_3 \rightarrow CaCO_3 \downarrow + Na_2SO_4$$

$$CaCl_2 + Na_2CO_3 \rightarrow CaCO_3 \downarrow + 2NaCl$$

Lime soda process can be carried out either in cold water or in hot water. If the process is carried out in cold water, it is called as *cold-lime soda* process. If it is carried out in hot water then, it is known as *hot-lime soda* process.

**1. Cold-Lime Soda Process :** In this method, calculated quantity of lime and soda are mixed with water at room temperature. The precipitate obtained is finely divided and to coagulate the precipitate, small quantity of coagulant such as alum should be used. Removal of precipitate by filtration gives soft water. The process can be carried out by two methods viz., batch process and continuous process.

**(a) Batch Process :** A calculated quantity of lime and soda-ash is added to water in a large tank made up of steel plates. It is provided with a mechanical stirrer for stirring or agitating the mixture. (Fig. 1.8).

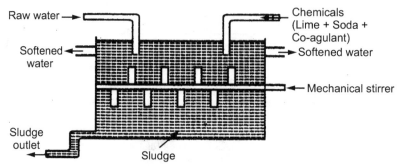

**Fig. 1.8 : Batch cold-lime soda process**

After thorough mixing, the mechanical stirring is stopped and small quantity of coagulant (alum) is added to coagulate the precipitate of the impurities.

$$Al_2(SO_4)_3 + 3\ Ca(HCO_3)_2 \rightarrow 2Al(OH)_3 \downarrow + 3CaSO_4 + 6CO_2 \uparrow$$

The precipitated impurities i.e. sludge are formed at the bottom of the tank. The water is pumped out and allowed to pass through a filter unit of sand and coal. After filtration the soft water is obtained. To complete the process, 2 to 3 hours are required. After removal of sludges the tank is washed with water. The same procedure described above is repeated again to soften more quantity of hard water.

**(b) Continuous Process :** This process is a continuous process and therefore, time is not wasted during the operations. In cold lime-soda process, hard water and calculated quantity of chemicals (lime + soda + coagulant) are fed from the top into the inner vertical circular chamber fitted with a vertical rotating shaft carrying a number of paddles (Fig. 1.9).

As the hard water and chemicals flow down, there is a vigorous stirring and continuous mixing takes place. The softened water, as it comes into the outer co-axial chamber, rises upwards. The heavy sludge (or precipitated flock) settles down in the outer chamber by the time the softened water rushes up. The softened water then passes through a filtering medium (usually made of wood fibres to ensure complete removal of sludge). Filtered soft water finally flows out continuously through the outlet nearly at the top. The sludges at the bottom are removed through sludge outlet occasionally. This process provides water containing hardness of 50 to 60 ppm.

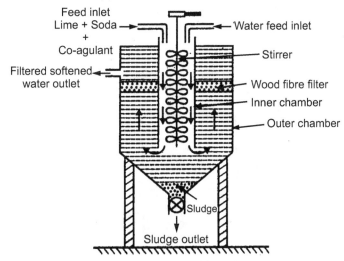

**Fig. 1.9 : Continuous cold-lime soda process**

**2.  Hot lime-soda process :** In this process, hard water is treated with lime-soda at a temperature of 80 to 150°C. Since the process carried out at elevated temperature, the speed of the reaction increases and the process is completed in 15 minutes. There are certain advantages of hot-lime soda process over cold lime soda process.

(i)    The rate of precipitating reaction is faster at elevated temperature, hence, the reaction is completed in a short time of 15 minutes.

(ii)   The coagulant is not needed for precipitation, because the precipitate settles rapidly.

(iii)  The dissolved gases such as $CO_2$ are removed at higher temperature.

(iv)   The water obtained by this process is much softer as compared with cold lime soda process.

(v)    The process of filtration becomes much faster and easier.

(vi)   The softening capacity of this process is much higher than the cold-lime soda process.

**(a)  Batch Process :** Hard water is taken in a rectangular tank made up of steel plates, which is provided by heating coils. Calculated quantity of lime and soda is added to the tank. By increasing the temperature of water at about 150ºC, the speed of the reaction can be increased. Within 15 minutes the process is completed. By using water pump the clear and soft water is pumped and allowed to pass through a filter unit. Sludges are removed from the tank. The tank is washed thoroughly and the same procedure is repeated again.

**(b)  Continuous Process :** The apparatus consists of a tank with two concentric cylindrical chambers. The lower end of the inner chamber is funnel-shaped and consists of three inlets (Fig. 1.10). The outer chamber is big with larger cross section at the top than at the bottom. This facilitates rise of water from the bottom. The hard water and chemicals are added through the left side inlets and from the third inlet, steam is allowed to pass to increase the temperature of the water. The precipitate formed settles at the bottom and soft clear water is withdrawn from the top of the outer chamber. The hardness of the water is reduced to 25 ppm from this method.

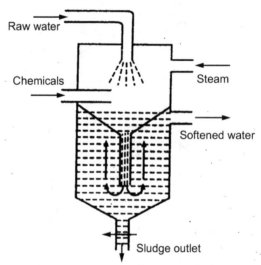

**Fig. 1.10 : Continuous hot-lime soda process**

## 1.11.3 Permutit or Zeolite Process

This is the modern process used for removing both temporary and permanent hardness of water. *Permutit or zeolites are complex silicates of several metallic and non-metallic oxides. They have approximate chemical formula ($Na_2Al_2Si_2O_8 \cdot 6 H_2O$).* These silicates hold sodium ions loosely hence, these are called as *sodium permutit* ($Na_2P$) or sodium zeolite ($Na_2Z$) where permutit and zeolite stands for $Al_2Si_2O_8 \cdot 6H_2O$.

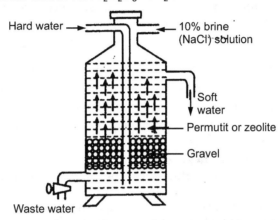

Hard water — 10% brine (NaCl) solution
Soft water
Permutit or zeolite
Gravel
Waste water

**Fig. 1.11 : Permutit's process of softening of hard water**

The remarkable property of sodium permutit ($Na_2P$) is that when it comes in contact with hard water, it exchanges its $Na^+$ ions with $Ca^{++}$ and $Mg^{++}$ ions to form insoluble calcium permutit (CaP) and magnesium permutit (MgP).

Sodium permutit is placed in a suitable container and hard water is allowed to pass through it (Fig. 1.11). The calcium and magnesium salts react with it forming insoluble calcium and magnesium permutits. These salts are retained in the filter bed and water after reaction is therefore, free from calcium and magnesium salts. Only the harmless sodium salts are left in the water. The following reactions take place in the process :

For temporary hardness :

$$Ca(HCO_3)_2 \quad + \quad Na_2P \quad \rightarrow \quad CaP \downarrow + 2NaHCO_3$$
$$Mg(HCO_3)_2 \quad + \quad Na_2P \quad \rightarrow \quad MgP \downarrow + 2NaHCO_3$$

For permanent hardness :

$$CaCl_2 \quad + \quad Na_2P \quad \rightarrow \quad CaP \downarrow + 2NaCl$$
$$MgCl_2 \quad + \quad Na_2P \quad \rightarrow \quad MgP \downarrow + 2NaCl$$
$$CaSO_4 \quad + \quad Na_2P \quad \rightarrow \quad CaP \downarrow + Na_2SO_4$$
$$MgSO_4 \quad + \quad Na_2P \quad \rightarrow \quad MgP \downarrow + Na_2SO_4$$

When the process is continued for about 12 hours, all the $Na^+$ ions from the permutit are replaced by $Ca^{++}$ and $Mg^{++}$ ions and it is found that the permutit stops working and water is no more softened.

When the permutit is exhausted (i.e. it is completely converted into CaP and MgP), it is regenerated by treating wih 10 % brine (NaCl) solution for few minutes, sodium permutit

(Na$_2$P) is formed and can again be used for softening of more hard water. The reactions in regeneration can be shown as follows :

$$CaP \quad + \quad 2NaCl \quad \rightarrow \quad Na_2P \quad + \quad CaCl_2$$
$$MgP \quad + \quad 2NaCl \quad \rightarrow \quad Na_2P \quad + \quad MgCl_2$$

## Limitations of Permutit or Zeolite Process :

(i)    If hard water contains large quantities of coloured ions like manganese ions ($Mn^{++}$) or ferrous ions ($Fe^{++}$) then these ions formed manganese or iron permutit. Such permutit cannot be regenerated easily.

(ii)   If hard water contains mineral acids then it may destroy permutits. Moreover, in zeolite process only cations like $Ca^{++}$, $Mg^{++}$ are replaced but anions like $CO_3^{--}$, $HCO_3^{-}$ etc. remain in water. Such water cannot be used in boilers as $CO_2$ is released from it and is extremely corrosive to boiler material.

(iii)  If hard water is turbid then turbidity may clog (or block) the pores of permutit and it restricts the flow of water.

## Advantages of Permutit or Zeolite Process :

(i)    The water having zero hardness can be obtained i.e. it removes the hardness completely.

(ii)   The equipment used is compact thus occupying small space.

(iii)  It is a clean process as no impurities are precipitated and hence, there is no sludge formation.

(iv)   The process automatically adjusts itself for different hardness of incoming water.

(v)    It requires less time.

## Difference between Lime-Soda and Permutit Process :

| Lime Soda Process | Permutit Process |
|---|---|
| 1. The plant occupies more space. | The plant occupies less space. |
| 2. Capital cost is lower, but the operational expenses are high. | Capital cost is higher, but the operational expenses are low. |
| 3. It can be used for softening acidic water. | It cannot be used for softening acidic water because acids destroy permutits (zeolites). |
| 4. It can be used for the raw water having turbidity (suspended-impurities). | It can not be used for water having suspended impurities because the impurities block the pores of the zeolites. |
| 5. It cannot operate under pressure. | It can operate under pressure and can be made fully automatic. |
| 6. It involves difficult steps like coagulation, setting and filtration. | It does not involve these steps. |
| 7. This process removes cations as well as anions. | This process removes only the cations like $Ca^{++}$ and $Mg^{++}$. |
| 8. Treated water contains lesser amounts of sodium salts than the hard water. | Treated water contains larger amount of sodium salts than the hard water. |
| 9. Water obtained is not perfectly pure; it contains about 15–50 ppm hardness | Water of zero hardness is obtained. |

# 1.11.4 Ion-Exchange (or Deionisation or Demineralisation) Process

This is the modern development in water softening method. Certain organic compounds possess a property like zeolite i.e. they are capable of exchanging ions. Such organic synthetic compounds are known as resins. There are two types of resins : (1) Cation exchange resins, (2) Anion exchange resins.

**(a) Cation exchange resins :** These resins are capable of exchanging rapidly cations by $H^+$ ions. Cation exchange resins can be represented as $RH_2$, so their exchange reaction with cations (e.g. $Ca^{++}$) is :

$$RH_2 + Ca^{++} \rightarrow RCa + 2H^+$$

**(b) Anion exchange resins :** These resins are capable of exchanging rapidly anions by $OH^-$ ions. Anion exchange resin can be represented as $R'(OH)_2$, so their exchange reaction with anions (e.g. $SO_4^{--}$) is :

$$R'(OH)_2 + SO_4^{--} \rightarrow R'SO_4 + 2OH^-$$

From the above it is clear that, if hard water is passed first through cation exchanger and then through anion exchanger, the resulting water will be free from both cations and anions and water is said to be *'deionised'* or *'demineralised.'*

**Process :** It consists of two cylindrical towers, out of which the first tower consists of 'cation exchanger' ($RH_2$) and the another one consists of 'anion exchanger' [$R'(OH)_2$] (Fig. 1.12). Hard (or impure) water is first allowed to pass through a tower containing cation exchanger, which removes all the cations like $Ca^{++}$, $Mg^{++}$, $Na^+$, $Fe^{++}$ etc. and releases $H^+$ ions.

$$RH_2 \quad + \quad Ca^{++} \quad \rightarrow \quad RCa \quad + \quad 2H^+$$
$$RH_2 \quad + \quad Mg^{++} \quad \rightarrow \quad RMg \quad + \quad 2H^+$$
$$RH_2 \quad + \quad 2Na^+ \quad \rightarrow \quad RNa_2 \quad + \quad 2H^+$$

Thus, the anions like chlorides, sulphates and bicarbonates are converted into corresponding acids HCl, $H_2SO_4$ and $H_2CO_3$. In other words, water from cation exchanger is free from all cations, but it is acidic.

This acidic water is then, passed through another tower containing an anion exchanger, where acids are converted into water.

$$R'(OH)_2 \quad + \quad 2HCl \quad \rightarrow \quad R'Cl_2 \quad + \quad 2H_2O$$
$$R'(OH)_2 \quad + \quad H_2SO_4 \quad \rightarrow \quad R'SO_4 \quad + \quad 2H_2O$$
$$R'(OH)_2 \quad + \quad H_2CO_3 \quad \rightarrow \quad R'CO_3 \quad + \quad 2H_2O$$

Consequently, water thus produced is free from all ions (cations and anions) and is virtually distilled water.

The water is finally freed from dissolved gases like $CO_2$, etc. by passing it through a 'degasifier', which is a tower whose sides are heated and which is connected to a vacuum pump. High temperature and low pressure reduces the quantity of dissolved $CO_2$ and $O_2$ in water. Such softened water can be used for industrial purposes.

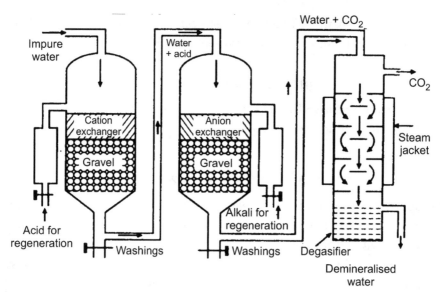

**Fig. 1.12 : Demineralisation by ion exchangers**

**Regeneration :** When the resins get exhausted (i.e. when their capacity to exchange $H^+$ and $OH^-$ ions is lost), they are regenerated. The exhausted cation exchanger is then regenerated by passing a dilute solution of acid through the first tower (e.g. dil. HCl or dil. $H_2SO_4$).

$$RCa \quad + \quad 2HCl \quad \rightarrow \quad RH_2 \quad + \quad CaCl_2$$
$$RMg \quad + \quad 2HCl \quad \rightarrow \quad RH_2 \quad + \quad MgCl_2$$

The washing containing $CaCl_2$, $MgCl_2$ (or $CaSO_4$, $MgSO_4$) etc. is passed to drain.

Similarly, the exhausted anion exchanger is regenerated by passing dilute solution of alkali through the second tower (e.g. dil NaOH or KOH).

$$R'Cl_2 \quad + \quad 2NaOH \quad \rightarrow \quad R'(OH)_2 \quad + \quad 2NaCl$$
$$R'SO_4 \quad + \quad 2NaOH \quad \rightarrow \quad R'(OH)_2 \quad + \quad Na_2SO_4$$

Thus washings containing NaCl, $Na_2SO_4$ etc. is also passed to drain. The regenerated resins are then used again.

**Comparison of Lime soda, Zeolite and Ion exchange methods**

| Point of comparison | Lime soda | Zeolite | Ion exchange |
|---|---|---|---|
| 1. Equipment | Occupies large space. Need permanent construction. Costly | Compact and portable. <br><br> Cheap | Compact and portable. |
| 2. Reagent | Cheaper and easily available. | Costly | Cheap |
| 3. Labour | Needs skilled labour | No restriction | No restriction |
| 4. Bi-products | Large amount of sludge | Nil | Nil |
| 5. Residual hardness | 15 (Hot), to 50 (Cold) ppm | 2-10 ppm | 0-2 ppm |
| 6. Reduction in dissolved salts | Slightly reduced | Not reduced | Almost reduced |
| 7. Restriction on water quality | No restriction | Free from suspended solids, acids and Fe, Mn, ions. | Free from suspended solids. |

# 1.12 CALCULATIONS OF REAGENTS REQUIRED FOR SOFTENING HARD WATER

A general method for the calculation of reagents required for removing hardness due to $Ca(HCO_3)_2$, $Mg(HCO_3)_2$, $CaCl_2$, $CaSO_4$, $MgCl_2$ and $MgSO_4$ is as follows :

(1)  For $Ca(HCO_3)_2$ only lime is required.

$$Ca(HCO_3)_2 \;+\; Ca(OH)_2 \;\rightarrow 2\,CaCO_3 \downarrow + 2\,H_2O$$

$$\underset{=\,162}{40 + (1 + 12 + 48) \times 2} \quad \underset{=\,74}{40 + (16 + 1) \times 2}$$

Thus for 162 parts by weight of $Ca(HCO_3)_2$ require 74 parts by weight of $Ca(OH)_2$. Hardness is given in ppm or mg/lit. Let calcium bicarbonate hardness be $y_1$ mg/lit., then for treating 1 litre of such water

$$\text{Lime required} = \left\{ \frac{y_1 \times 74}{162} \right\} mg$$

(2)  For $Mg(HCO_3)_2$ only lime is required.

$$Mg(HCO_3)_2 + 2\,Ca(OH)_2 \rightarrow Mg(OH)_2 \downarrow + CaCO_3 \downarrow + 2\,H_2O$$

$$\underset{=\,146}{24 + (1 + 12 + 48) \times 2} \quad 2 \times 74 = 148$$

Thus for 146 parts by weight of magnesium bicarbonate requires 148 parts by weight of $Ca(OH)_2$. So for $y_2$ mg of $Mg(HCO_3)_2$ [e.g. hardness is $y_2$ mg/lit]

$$\text{Lime required} = \left\{ \frac{y_2 \times 148}{146} \right\} = \frac{2y_2 \times 74}{146} \text{ mg per litre}$$

(3)  For $CaCl_2$ only $Na_2CO_3$ is required :

$$CaCl_2 \quad + \quad Na_2CO_3 \quad \rightarrow CaCO_3 + 2\ NaCl$$

$$\underset{=\ 111}{40 + 35.5 \times 2}\ \underset{=\ 106}{23 \times 2 + 12 + 48}$$

Thus for 111 parts by weight of $CaCl_2$ needs 106 parts by weight of $Na_2CO_3$.

∴   For $y_3$ mg/lit of $CaCl_2$ will require $= \dfrac{y_3 \times 106}{111}$ mg/lit of $Na_2CO_3$.

(4)  For $CaSO_4$ only $Na_2CO_3$ is required.

$$CaSO_4 + Na_2CO_3 \rightarrow CaCO_3 + Na_2SO_4$$

$$\quad\ 136 \qquad\quad 106$$

Thus 136 parts by weight of $CaSO_4$ require 106 parts by weight of $Na_2CO_3$, so $y_4$ mg/lit. of $CaSO_4$ will need $= \dfrac{y_4 \times 106}{136}$ mg/lit.

(5)  For $MgCl_2$ both lime and soda are required.

$$MgCl_2 + Na_2CO_3 + Ca(OH)_2 \rightarrow Mg(OH)_2 + CaCO_3 + 2\ NaCl$$

$$\quad 95 \qquad\quad 106 \qquad\qquad\quad 74$$

Thus 95 parts by weight of $MgCl_2$ need 106 parts by weight of $Na_2CO_3$ and 74 parts by weight of $Ca(OH)_2$. So for $y_5$ mg/lit. of $MgCl_2$,

$$Na_2CO_3 \text{ required} = \left\{ \frac{y_5 \times 106}{95} \right\} \text{mg/lit.}$$

and

$$Ca(OH)_2 = \left\{ \frac{y_5 \times 74}{95} \right\} \text{mg/lit.}$$

(6)  For $MgSO_4$ both lime and soda are required.

$$MgSO_4 + Na_2CO_3 + Ca(OH)_2 \rightarrow Mg(OH)_2 + CaCO_3 + Na_2CO_3$$

$$\quad 120 \qquad\quad 106 \qquad\qquad\quad 74$$

Thus for 120 parts by weight of $MgSO_4$; 106 parts by weight of $Na_2CO_3$ and 74 parts by weight of $Ca(OH)_2$ are required. Therefore, for $y_6$ mg/lit. of $MgSO_4$ requires

$$Na_2CO_3 = \left\{ \frac{y_6 \times 106}{120} \right\} \text{mg/}l$$

and

$$Ca(OH)_2 = \left\{ \frac{y_6 \times 74}{120} \right\} \text{mg/}l$$

In numerical problems, above calculations are done only for those salts which are present in water and the total quantities of lime and soda are obtained. Thus

*For temporary hardness,*

$$\text{Lime required} = 74 \left\{ \frac{y_1}{162} + \frac{2y_2}{146} \right\} \text{ and no soda is required.}$$

*For permanent hardness,*

(i)     $$\text{Lime required} = 74 \left\{ \frac{y_5}{95} + \frac{y_6}{120} \right\} \text{mg/}l$$

(ii)    $$\text{Soda required} = 106 \left\{ \frac{y_3}{111} + \frac{y_4}{136} + \frac{y_5}{95} + \frac{y_6}{120} \right\} \text{mg/}l.$$

## SOLVED PROBLEMS

### Problem 1.1 :

*Calculate the quantity of lime and soda required for softening 50,000 litres of water containing the following salts per litre :*

(1)  $Ca(HCO_3)_2 = 8.1$ mg,     (2)  $Mg(HCO_3)_2 = 7.3$ mg,     (3)  $CaSO_4 = 13.6$ mg,

(4)  $MgSO_4 = 12.0$ mg,     (5)  $NaCl = 4.6$ mg.

### Solution :

*Calculation of lime :* Lime is required for $Ca(HCO_3)_2$, $Mg(HCO_3)_2$ and $MgSO_4$.

$$\text{Quantity of lime per litre} = 74 \left\{ \frac{8.1}{162} + \frac{2 \times 7.3}{146} + \frac{12}{120} \right\} = 18.5 \text{ mg}$$

So quantity of lime for 50,000 litres = $18.5 \times 50,000 = 925000$ mg = 925 g

### Calculation of soda :

Soda is required for $CaSO_4$ and $MgSO_4$

∴     $$\text{Quantity of soda per litre} = 106 \left\{ \frac{13.6}{136} + \frac{12}{120} \right\} = 21.2 \text{ mg}$$

∴     For 50,000 litres soda required = $21.2 \times 50,000 = 1060000$ mg = 1060 g

The presence of NaCl neither causes any hardness nor it reacts chemically with lime or soda, hence no consideration is taken for its presence.

### Problem 1.2 :

*500 litres of a sample of water containing magnesium bicarbonate required 20 g of $Ca(OH)_2$ to soften it. What is the hardness of the sample of water in ppm ?*

**Solution :**

500 litres of water need 20 g of $Ca(OH)_2$.

∴    1 litre of water will need $= \dfrac{20 \times 1}{500} = 0.04$ g of $Ca(OH)_2$

Let x g of $Mg(HCO_3)_2$ be present in water sample (1 litre)

∴                              $\dfrac{2x \times 74}{146} = 0.04$

∴                              $x = \dfrac{0.04 \times 146}{2 \times 74} = 0.03947$ g $= 39.47$ mg.

So hardness of water sample is 39.47 ppm.

## Problem 1.3 :

The hardness of 10,000 litres of a sample of hard water is completely removed by passing it through a zeolite softener. The exhausted softener required 10 litres of brine solution containing 100 gm/l of NaCl for regeneration. Calculate the hardness of the sample of water.

**Solution :**

10 litres of brine solution contains

$$= 10 \times 100 = 1000 \text{ g of NaCl}$$

Now 10,000 litres of hard water $\equiv$ 1000 g of NaCl

∵ Equivalent weight of NaCl is 58.5 and of $CaCO_3$ is 50.

Therefore 1000 g of NaCl $\equiv \left\{\dfrac{1000 \times 50}{58.5}\right\}$ g of $CaCO_3$ equivalent hardness.

∴         1 litre of hard water $\equiv \left\{\dfrac{1000 \times 50}{58.5 \times 10,000}\right\}$

$$= \dfrac{5}{58.5} \text{ g of CaCO}_3 \text{ equivalent.}$$

i.e.         $\dfrac{5 \times 1000}{58.5} = 85.5$ mg of $CaCO_3$ equivalent hardness.

Hence, the hardness of sample water = 85.5 mg/lit or 85.5 ppm.

## Problem 1.4 :

A completely exhausted zeolite softener needs 120 litres of 10 % brine solution for regeneration. How many litres of hard water of hardness 500 ppm can be softened by this softner ?

**Solution :**

120 litres of brine solution contain $(120 \times 100)$ g of NaCl which is

$$\equiv \frac{120 \times 100 \times 50}{58.5}$$

$$= 10256 \text{ g of } CaCO_3 \text{ eq. hardness.}$$

The hardness of given sample of water is 500 ppm i.e. 500 mg/lit.

It means 500 mg or 0.5 g of $CaCO_3 \equiv 1$ litre of water. So 10256 g of $CaCO_3$ equivalent hardness $\equiv \dfrac{10256}{0.5} \equiv 21,120$ litres.

Hence the softner has the capacity to soften 21,120 litres of the given sample of hard water.

# EXERCISE

1.  (a)  What are the natural sources of water ?

    (b)  What makes water an universal solvent ? Write the general chemical reaction of water with metal oxides.

2.  Describe the common impurities present in natural water.

3.  (a)  What is hard water ? What are its disadvantages ?

    (b)  What principle is applied to remove hardness of water ?

4.  (a)  What are the causes of hardness of water ? How will you distinguish between temporary and permanent hard water ?

    (b)  Distinguish between hard and soft water.

5.  What is degree of hardness ? How it is expressed ? State the relation of the systems used to express the hardness of water.

6.  (a)  Discuss the bad effects of using hard water in the following industries :

    (i)  Paper industry, (ii) Dyeing industry, (iii) Textile industry ?

    (b)  Why the hard water is not suitable for washing and cooking ?

    (c)  Give bad effects of using hard water for drinking and cooking.

7.  Discuss the effects, if hard water is used for domestic purposes.

8.  Why is hard water unfit for use in boiler ?

9.  (a) Write notes on : (i) Priming and foaming, (ii) Caustic embrittlement.

    (b) What troubles are created by the presence of sodium carbonate in high pressure boilers ?

    (c) Write the chemical reactions in Lime-soda process.

    (d) Write at least two chemical reactions occurring in softening temporary and permanent hard water.

    (e) Write chemical reactions occurring in Lime-soda process when hard water contains magnesium salts.

10. (a) What are scales and sludges ? What are their disadvantages in boilers ? How are these prevented ?

    (b) Define boiler scales, permanent hard water, soft water. Explain disadvantages of hard water in paper and dyeing industries.

11. Describe the methods used for softening the temporary hard water.

12. (a) What are the causes of hardness of water ? Explain the chemical reactions involved in the lime-soda process.

    (b) Explain any two limitations of Permutit's or ion exchange process. How alum helps in sedimentation ? Explain.

13. What is permutit or zeolite ? Describe Permutit's process of softening of hard water. Give the reactions in regeneration of the permutit.

14. What is the principle of Permutit's process ? Describe in brief the Permutit's process of removing temporary and permanent hardness of water. How is the permutit regenerated when it is exhausted in the process ?

15. Describe in brief Permutit's process of softening of hard water. Give the limitations and advantages of the Permutit's process.

16. (a) What is demineralisation ? Describe in brief the ion-exchange process of hard water with labelled diagram.

    (b) Write principle of ion exchange process. Draw neat labelled diagram of Permutit's process.

17. (a) What are boiler scales ? Explain the causes of the formation of boiler scales.

    (b) Discuss the effects of using hard water for steam generation.

18. Explain the effects of using hard water for paper industry and textile industry.

19.(a) Explain the importance of pH to prevent corrosion of bridges and in the treatment of effluents.

(b) What is meant by zeolites ? Give their functions in the Permutit's process.

20. Write a simple test to identify soft water and hard water. State the chemical equation.

21. (a) What are boiler scales and sludges ? Explain their formation due to decomposition of bicarbonates with chemical reactions.

(b) List the problems due to formation of scales and sludges in boiler.

OR

Explain any four disadvantages of hard water in boilers due to scale formation.

22 What are the causes of temporary hardness of water ? Explain the principle applied to remove the type of hardness with chemical reaction.

23. (a) Explain the effects of *'boiler scales'* on boilers.

(b) Write the disadvantages of sludge formation in boilers.

24. Explain with chemical reactions, what happens when hard water is treated with soap. Mention two different problems arising by the use of hard water in boilers.

25. (a) A sample of permanent hard water contains micro-organisms. Name one method each to remove hardness and micro-organisms.

(b) Write principles of soda-ash process. State how water can be made potable.

26. Explain the Permutit's process with the help of labelled diagram. Write main reactions occurring in the process.

OR Give principle of ion exchange process. Draw the diagram. Give two chemical reactions in regeneration of ion exchangers.

27. What are the purposes of the following processes in purification of water ?

(i) Sedimentation

(ii) Coagulation

(iii) Filtration

(iv) Sterilisation

28. What are cation exchange resins and anion exchange resins ? How are these regenerated in ion-exchange process ?

29. (a)  Define soft water and hard water.

    (b)  Give two chemical equations for chemical reactions occurring in chlorination or chloramination.

30. Write at least two chemical reactions occurring in softening of temporary and permanent hard water.

31. Define sedimentation. Explain process of coagulation.

32. Explain any four disadvantages of hard water in domestic use.

33. Define scales. Explain any three disadvantages of scale formation in boilers.

34. Define soft water. Explain any three disadvantages of hard water in domestic applications.

35. Label the parts of diagram for ion exchange process and write the chemical equations involved in the removal of permanent hardness of water.

36. Explain the toxic effect of arsenic.

37. Explain the toxic effect of cadmium.

38. Explain the toxic effect of lead.

39. Explain the toxic effect of mercury.

# Unit II

# MATERIAL CHEMISTRY

## (A) CRYSTALLOGRAPHY

## 2.1 INTRODUCTION

It is very important to study solid state chemistry and material science from technology point of view. Solid state chemistry plays important role in civil engineering as civil engineers have to deal with various materials important for construction work. Mechanical engineers have to deal with metals, alloys and their properties. Semiconductor materials are extremely important in electronic engineering. In addition to this digital waste management can be done efficiently if the properties of the material used as known. The important crystals used are metals, semiconductors, diamonds, silicates etc. for engineering and technological developments.

Crystals are the solids composed of atoms/ions/molecules arranged in a fixed pattern which repeats themselves in a three-dimensional space. The shape and size of the crystal depend on the conditions under which the crystal is grown.

Crystallization is a process in which amorphous substances are converted to their crystalline state by maintaining proper conditions.

Crystallization can be done by (1) slowly solidifying the molten substance, (2) slowly solidifying a substance from its saturated solution at room temperature, (3) directly from the solid state chemical reactions.

## 2.2 IMPORTANT TERMINOLOGIES IN CRYSTALLOGRAPHY

### (i) Crystallography :

It is a branch of chemistry which deals with the geometry, properties and structure of crystalline substances.

### (ii) Lattice points :

The atoms/ions/molecules located either at the corners or at the faces of crystals and repeat themselves in three-dimensional space to form a crystalline structure. These can be presented by dots or points as shown in Fig. 2.1. These points are called as lattice points.

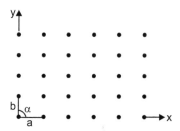

**Fig. 2.1 : Lattice points and two-dimensional space lattice**

### (iii) Space lattice or crystal lattice :

The crystalline structure which has infinite array of lattice points in three dimensions where every point is surrounded by identical and fixed number of points is called as space lattice or crystal lattice.

The two-dimensional array of points in a space lattice is shown in Fig. 2.1.

### (iv) Unit cell :

Unit cell is the smallest three-dimensional unit in space which repeats itself to form a three-dimensional space lattice or crystal. Unit cell has all properties of crystal as a whole.

The unit cell results from the joining of closest neighbouring lattice points in space lattice.

### Lattice Parameters of a Unit Cell :

(a) **Crystallographic axes :** The lines drawn parallel to the lines of intersection of any three faces that do not lie in the same plane are called **crystallographic axes**.

(b) **Primitives :** The distance of first lattice points from the origin of crystallographic axes is called as primitives. In Fig. 2.2 distances a, b and c represent the distance of first lattice points along x, y and z axes respectively from the origin. The distances a, b and c define the dimensions of unit cell. These distances are known as **primitives**. The magnitude of primitives determines the size of unit cell.

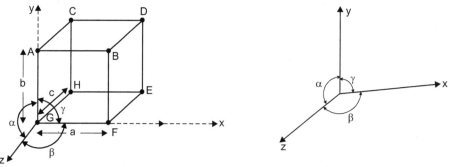

**Fig. 2.2 : Basic lattice parameters of a unit cell**

(c) **Interfacial angles** : The angles between three crystallographic axes are known as **interfacial angles**. Conventionally the angle between b and c (i.e. y and z axes) is $\alpha$, the angle between c and a (i.e. z and x axes) is $\beta$, whereas the angle between a and c (i.e. x and y axes) is $\gamma$. These angles define the shape of the crystals.

Collectively, the primitives a, b and c and interfacial angles $\alpha$, $\beta$ and $\gamma$ are called as basic **lattice parameters**.

Fig. 2.2 shows a unit cell of a cubical crystal. It has **eight** points situated at corners (denoted by A, B, C, D, E, F, G and H), **twelve edges** (AB, CD, AC, BD, GF, HE, GH, FE, AG, BF, CH and ED) and **six faces** (ABCD, EFGH, ACHG, BDEF, ABGF and CDEH).

**(v) Isotropy and anisotropy :**

Due to regular arrangement of lattice points, certain properties like conductivity, rate of dissolution, tensile strength, refractive index, brittleness etc. are same in all directions in a crystal. This phenomenon is called as **isotropy**.

If these properties are different in solid (for example in amorphous solids where there is no regular arrangement of lattice points) in different direction, then the phenomenon is called as **anisotropy**.

## 2.3 LAWS OF CRYSTALLOGRAPHY

There are three fundamental laws in crystallography. These laws give the important information on structure and position of lattice points in crystal. The laws are

(i)    Law of constancy of interfacial angles (Steno's law),

(ii)   Law of constant elements of symmetry,

(iii)  Law of rational indices.

## 2.3.1 Law of Constancy of Interfacial Angles

Law of constancy of interfacial angles states that, "For a crystalline solid substance, the interfacial angle always remains constant irrespective of size of crystal".

The size of the crystal changes with conditions of crystallization, but according to this law, for a crystalline substance the angles between faces of the crystal do not change. This means that the basic geometry of the crystal will not change with crystallization conditions.

e.g. **(1) NaCl :** It is observed that the shape of NaCl crystal is cubic. Let us take NaCl crystals of two different sizes. [Fig. 2.3 (a)]. Although the sizes are different, the interfacial angle $\theta$ is same.

(2) **Graphite :** Graphite has a hexagonal unit cell. The interfacial angle is always 120° irrespective of size.

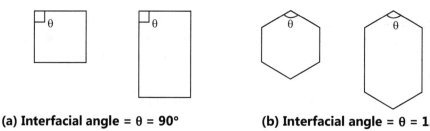

**(a) Interfacial angle = θ = 90°**
**e.g. NaCl, Sugar**

**(b) Interfacial angle = θ = 120°**
**e.g. Graphite**

**Fig. 2.3**

## 2.3.2 Elements of Symmetry

- The most important characteristic of crystals is that, they are symmetric in nature.
- Crystals are formed by repetitive arrays of lattice points. Therefore, there exist symmetry in all crystals. Symmetry can be defined with respect to elements of symmetry.
- There are three elements of symmetry. Element of symmetry is a geometrical entity such as a line (or axis), plane or a point with respect to which one or more symmetry operations may be carried out. The elements of symmetry are :

  (A) Plane of symmetry,  (B) Axes of symmetry, and (C) Centre of symmetry.

  **The elements of symmetry for a cubical crystal :**

  **(A) Plane of Symmetry :** It is an imaginary plane passing through crystal which divides the crystal into two halves in such a way that one half is superimposable mirror image of the other. A cubic crystal has two types of plane of symmetry.

  **(i) Rectangular Plane of Symmetry :** These are the planes situated midway and parallel to the opposite faces. Since a cubic crystal has six faces, i.e. three pairs of opposite faces, it has three rectangular planes of symmetry each passing through opposite faces as shown in Fig. 2.4 (a).

They are called as rectangular planes of symmetry because they cut the cube in two identical rectangles.

**Rectangular Planes of Symmetry :**

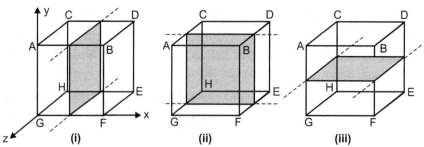

**(i) Passing through faces ABCD and EFGH, (ii) Passing through faces ACGH and BDFE,**
**(iii) Passing through faces ABGF and BDEF**

**Fig. 2.4 (a) : The three planes of symmetry parallel to the faces of a cube**

**(ii)** **Diagonal Plane of Symmetry :** These are the planes passing through the opposite edges. As they lie on the diagonals of the opposite faces, they are termed as diagonal planes of symmetry.

Since there are 12 edges or six pairs of opposite edges in a cubic crystal, as much as six diagonal planes of symmetry are possible in a cubic crystal. Planes passing diagonally through the cubic crystal is shown in Fig. 2.4 (b).

In a cubic crystal, there are 3 (Rectangular) + 6 (Diagonal) = 9 planes of symmetry.

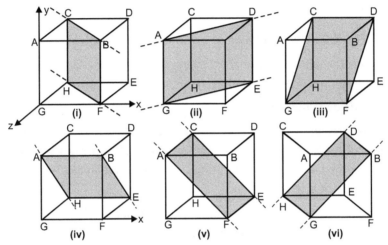

**(i) Passing through edges CB and HF, (ii) Passing through edges AD and GE,**
**(iii) Passing through edges CD and GF, (iv) Passing through edges AB and HE,**
**(v) Passing through edges AC and EF, (vi) Passing through edges BD and GH**
**Fig. 2.4 (b) : Six diagonal planes of symmetry in a cube**

**(B) Axis of Symmetry :**

"It is an imaginary line (an axis) passing through crystal about which if crystal is rotated through 360° gives an identical appearance more than once."

In cubical crystal, there are three types of axes of symmetry.

(i)   Two-fold axis of symmetry,

(ii)  Three-fold axis of symmetry, and

(iii) Four-fold axis of symmetry.

**(i) Two-Fold Axis of Symmetry (Diad) :**

Imagine a line passing through the centres of two diagonally opposite **edges** of a cube. On rotating the cube about this line, the identical appearance of the cube occurs **two times** during the course of rotation through 360°. Such an axis is called as an **axis of two-fold symmetry or a diad axis**. This axis is shown in Fig. 2.5.

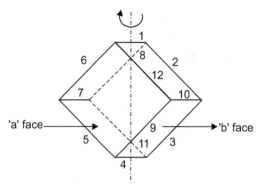

**Fig. 2.5 : Two-fold axis of symmetry for a cubical crystal**

It is clear from the above figure that, there are 12 edges. So there will be **six axes** (e.g. axis passing through edges 1 and 4) each passing through opposite edges.

**(ii) Three-Fold Axis of Symmetry :**

Imagine a line passing through the opposite points of a cube along the body diagonal. On rotating the cube about this line as axis, the identical appearance of the cube occurs **three times** during the course of rotation through 360°. Such an axis is said to be an axis of **three-fold symmetry or a triad axis**.

Now, since there are eight points or four such body diagonally opposite pairs of corners in a cubic crystal, **4 such axes** are possible.

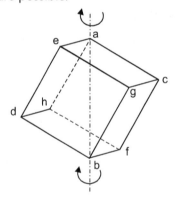

**Fig. 2.6 : Three-fold axis of rotation for a cubical crystal**

For a cubical crystal, three fold axis of symmetry are :

(i)    passing through a and b,

(ii)   passing through c and d,

(iii)  passing through e and f,

(iv)  passing through g and h.

### (iii) Four-Fold Axis of Symmetry :

Imagine a line passing through the centres of two opposite faces of a cube. On rotating the cube about this line, the identical appearance of the cube occurs four times during the course of rotation through 360°, i.e. the original appearance is repeated four times as a result of rotation by 90°. Such an axis is said to be **four-fold axis** of symmetry or a tetrad axis.

Now, since there are six such opposite faces or three pairs of opposite pairs, there will be three such axes at right angles to each other for a cubical crystal.

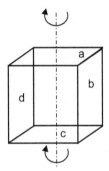

**Fig. 2.7 : Four fold axis of rotation for a cubical crystal**

### (C) Centre of Symmetry :

It is an imaginary point located at the centre of crystal in such a way that if a line is drawn through this point, it cuts the opposite faces at same distance.

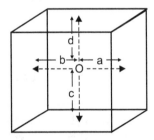

**Fig. 2.8 : Centre of symmetry,**
**Distance a = b = c = d, 'O' is centre of symmetry**

Each cubical crystal has one centre of symmetry.

**It should be noted that, the planes and axis of symmetry for a crystal always passes through centre of symmetry.**

**Elements of Symmetry for a Cubical Crystal :** The total number of symmetry elements for a cubical crystal are :

(A)  Planes of symmetry

|     | (i) | Rectangular planes of symmetry | = | 03 |
|---|---|---|---|---|
|     | (ii) | Diagonal planes of symmetry | = | 06 |

(B)  Axes of symmetry

|     | (i) | Two-fold axis of symmetry | = | 06 |
|---|---|---|---|---|
|     | (ii) | Three-fold axis of symmetry | = | 04 |
|     | (iii) | Four-fold axis of symmetry | = | 03 |

(C)  Centre of symmetry                                          =   01

**Total number of elements of symmetry for a cubical crystal**      **23**

# 2.3.3 Law of Constant Elements of Symmetry : Statement

This law states that "for all the crystals of same substance, the total number of symmetry elements always remain constant irrespective of size of the crystals."

# 2.3.4 Law of Rational Indices

Since a crystal has a fixed geometry, any lattice point inside or on the surface of the crystal can be located by simply defining the dimensions of the point on the crystallographic axes.

The law of rational indices describes the orientation of a plane in the crystal in which the point of interest is located.

The orientations of a plane in a crystal can be described by specifying simple indices that are simple rational numbers.

**Statement :**

The law of rational indices states that "the ratio of intercepts of a lattice plane on the crystallographic axis can be expressed in terms of rational number."

Consider an example of cubical crystal. Let the distance of X' from origin O is 'a', the distance Y' from origin be 'b' and distance Z' be 'c'. For a perfectly cubical crystal, the lengths a, b and c are equal but this is not a case in crystals of different sizes. [Fig. 2.9 (a)]. If the planes are located inside the crystal, then they can be described using simple rational numbers.

It can be understood from the above statement that the ratio of three intercepts of any plane in a crystal can be given by ma : nb : oc where a, b and c are the intercepts on the axes X, Y and Z respectively and m, n and o are the integers. [See Fig. 2.9 (a)]

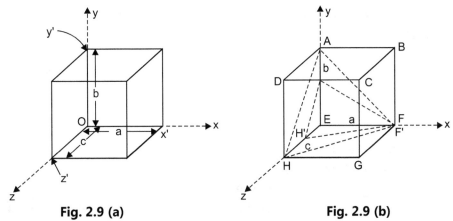

**Fig. 2.9 (a)**                          **Fig. 2.9 (b)**

Suppose that the plane AFH [Fig. 2.9 (b)] present inside the cubical crystal is to be described. It can be seen from the figure that the plane cuts the X-axis at distance 'a' and axes Y and Z at distances 'b' and 'c' respectively. Since this crystal is perfectly cubical and the distances are equal (i.e. a = b = c) then the ratios are 1 : 1 : 1. Hence this plane can be simply described by integer number ratio i.e. 1 : 1 : 1. In crystallography, it is written as [1 1 1].

Let us consider the plane H'A'F'. Here the length EH' = EA' = 2EF'. Therefore, the coefficients are 1, 1 and 2. Then in crystallography this plane is indicated as [1, 1, 2] indices.

# 2.4 DESIGNATION OF LATTICE PLANES IN CRYSTALLOGRAPHY

There are two ways by which the lattice planes are designated or indexed in crystallography : (i) Weiss indices. (ii) Miller's indices.

## 2.4.1 Weiss Indices

Weiss used integers to index the planes by considering the intercepts made by a plane on the axis. In Fig. 2.9 (b), ABCDEFGH is a unit cell. EX, EY and EZ are the vectors representing crystallographic axes. The unit cell lengths are a, b and c respectively. i.e. EF = a, EH = c and EA = b. A plane AFH passes through the lattice and cuts X-axis at a distance a, Y-axis at a distance b and Z-axis at a distance c. As the lengths of intercepts in terms of a, b and c are one unit from origin, the Weiss indices of this plane are 1, 1, 1.

However, to use Weiss indices, we have to consider the intercepts at infinity many times for indicating planes parallel to a axis, they also include fractions and that is rather inconvenient. Consequently they are replaced by Miller's indices.

## 2.4.2 Miller's Indices

The Miller's indices of a plane are obtained by taking the reciprocals of the Weiss co-efficients and multiplying through by the smallest number that will express all reciprocals as integers. Thus if a plane cuts axes at distances a, b and 2c, the Weiss indices will be 1, 1, 2. Then its reciprocals will be 1, 1, $\frac{1}{2}$ and after multiplying by 2, we will get Miller's indices as 2, 2, 1 and plane is called 2, 2, 1 plane.

**Procedure for finding Miller's Indices :**

(a) Find the intercept of the desired plane on the three co-ordinate axes. Let these intercepts be pa, qb and rc on X, Y and Z axes respectively.

(b) Express the coefficients of intercepts as the multiples of the unit cell dimensions i.e. p, q and r. These are called Weiss indices.

(c) Take the reciprocals of Weiss indices $\left(\dfrac{1}{p}, \dfrac{1}{q} \text{ and } \dfrac{1}{r}\right)$.

(d) Convert these reciprocals into whole numbers. These whole numbers are Miller's indices. They are denoted by h, k, l.

**Table 2.1**

| Cuts on axes | Weiss indices | Miller's indices |
|:---:|:---:|:---:|
| a, b, c | 1 1 1 | 1 1 1 |
| 2a, 2b, 2c | 2 2 2 | 1 1 1 |
| a, ∞, ∞ | 1 ∞ ∞ | 1 0 0 |
| a, ∞, $\frac{1}{2}$ c | 1 ∞ $\frac{1}{2}$ | 1 0 2 |

When enclosed by parenthesis e.g. (100), the Miller's indices refer to a single specific plane and when enclosed by braces e.g. {100}, they denote all planes of the form. Examples of various planes in cubic system labeled with their appropriate indices are shown in Fig. 2.10.

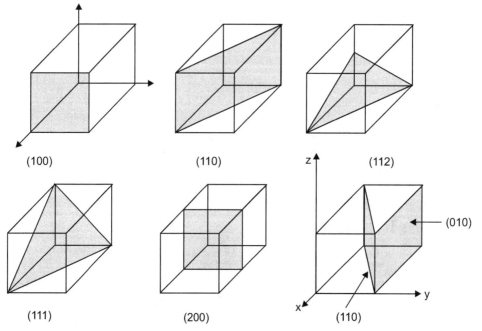

**Fig. 2.10 : Prominent planes of the cubic system**

**Table 2.2 : Weiss indices and Miller's indices of few representative intercepts of the planes**

| Intercept | Coefficients of intercepts (Weiss indices) [p, q, r] | Reciprocal of Weiss indices (1/p, 1/q, 1/r) | Whole numbers (Miller's indices) [h, k, l] |
|---|---|---|---|
| a, b, c | 1, 1, 1 | 1, 1, 1 | (1 1 1) |
| a, b, 2c | 1, 1, 2 | 1, 1, 1/2 | (2 2 1) |
| a, α, 2c | 1, α, 2 | 1, 0, 1/2 | (2, 0, 1) |
| −a, b, c | −1, 1, 1 | −1, 1, 1 | ($\bar{1}$, 1, 1) |
| 3a, −b, c | 3, −1, 1 | 1/3, −1, 1 | (1, $\bar{3}$, 3) |

## SOLVED PROBLEMS ON WEISS AND MILLER'S INDICES

**Problem 1 :**

*Obtain Miller's indices of a plane which intercepts at a, b/2 and 3c in a simple cubic unit cell. Draw a neat diagram showing the plane.*

**Solution :**

| Intercepts | Coefficients (Weiss indices) [p, q, r] | Reciprocals | Miller's indices [h, k, l] |
|---|---|---|---|
| $a, \dfrac{b}{2}, 3c$ | $1, \dfrac{1}{2}, 3$ | $1, 2, \dfrac{1}{3}$ | 3, 6, 1 |

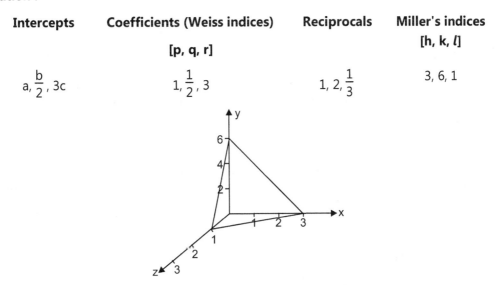

**Fig. 2.11 : Miller's indices of intercepts a, b/2 and 3c of a simple cubic unit cell**

**Problem 2 :**

*Sketch the following planes with a cubic unit cell. The Miller's indices of the planes are (001), (120), (211).*

**Solution :**

Here Miller's indices are given, follow the reverse procedure to obtain the intercepts and then the planes.

| Miller's indices | Reciprocals | Weiss indices | Intercepts |
|---|---|---|---|
| 001 | $\alpha, \alpha, 1$ | $\alpha, \alpha, 1$ | $\alpha a, \alpha b, 1$ |
| 120 | $1, \dfrac{1}{2}, \alpha$ | $1, \dfrac{1}{2}, \alpha$ | $1a, \dfrac{1}{2}b, \alpha c$ |

**Case 1 :** $\alpha a$, $\alpha b$ means the plane is parallel to X and Y axes where it has one unit intercept on Z-axis. This curve can be drawn as

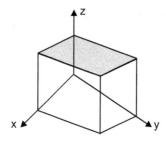 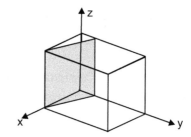

**Fig. 2.12**

## 2.5 CRYSTAL SYSTEMS

It is seen in the previous sections that, a unit cell of a crystal can be completely described if the intercepts on the X, Y and Z axes (a, b and c) i.e. primitives and the interfacial angles ($\alpha$, $\beta$ and $\gamma$) are known. In short, shape and size of the crystal depend on the magnitude of a, b and c and the angles $\alpha$, $\beta$ and $\gamma$.

If various combinations of these lattice parameters are made, then theoretically many types of crystal system are possible but in nature only seven types of crystal systems are present. All the crystals in the nature fit in any one of the following crystal systems. These crystal systems are called as fundamental crystal systems, these are :

(1) Simple cubic,      (2) Orthorhombic,      (3) Tetragonal,

(4) Monoclinic,      (5) Triclinic,      (6) Hexagonal,

(7) Trigonal.

All these crystal systems are sketched in Fig. 2.13.

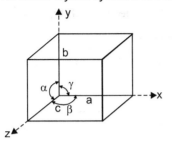

a = b = c

α = β = γ = 90°

**Simple cubic**

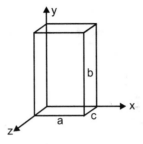

a ≠ b ≠ c

α = β = γ = 90°

**Orthorhombic**

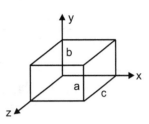

a = b ≠ c

α = β = γ = 90°

**Tetragonal**

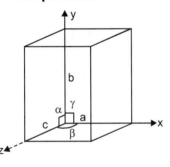

a ≠ b ≠ c

α = γ = 90°, β ≠ 90°

**Monoclinic**

a ≠ b ≠ c

α ≠ β ≠ γ ≠ 90°

**Triclinic**

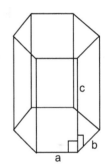

a = b ≠ c

α = β = 90°, γ = 120°

**Hexagonal**

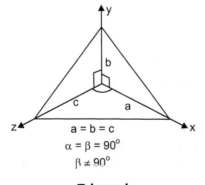

a = b = c

α = β = 90°

β ≠ 90°

**Trigonal**

**Fig. 2.13**

Following table gives the names of crystal structure, description of lattice parameters, total number of symmetry elements along with the suitable examples of each type.

### Table 2.3 : Fundamental crystal systems in nature

| System | Lattice parameters of unit cell | | Elements of symmetry | Examples |
|---|---|---|---|---|
| | Lengths | Angles | | |
| 1. Cubic | $a = b = c$ | $\alpha = \beta = \gamma = 90°$ | 9 planes + 13 axes + 1 centre = 23 | NaCl, KCl, ZnS, Diamond |
| 2. Orthorhombic | $a \neq b \neq c$ | $\alpha = \beta = \gamma = 90°$ | 3 planes + 3 axes + 1 centre = 07 | $KNO_3$, $K_2SO_4$, S, $BaSO_4$, $PbSO_4$ |
| 3. Tetragonal | $a = b \neq c$ | $\alpha = \beta = \gamma = 90°$ | 5 planes + 5 axes + 1 centre = 11 | $SiO_2$, $ZnO_2$, $TiO_2$, White Sn |
| 4. Monoclinic | $a \neq b \neq c$ | $\alpha = \gamma = 90°$, $\beta \neq 90°$ | 1 plane + 1 axis + 1 centre = 03 | S, $Na_2SO_4 \cdot 10H_2O$, $Na_2B_4O_7 \cdot 10H_2O$ |
| 5. Triclinic | $a \neq b \neq c$ | $\alpha \neq \beta \neq \gamma \neq 90°$ | No plane, No axis, 1 centre = 01 | $K_2Cr_2O_7$, $H_3BO_3$ |
| 6. Hexagonal | $a = b \neq c$ | $\alpha = \beta = 90°$, $\gamma = 120°$ | 7 planes + 7 axes + 1 centre = 15 | ZnO, $PbS_2$, CdS, HgS, Ice, Graphite |
| 7. Trigonal | $a = b = c$ | $\alpha = \gamma = 90°$, $\beta \neq 190°$ | 7 planes + 7 axes + 1 centre = 15 | $NaNO_3$, $CaSO_4$, Quartz, Calcite |

## 2.6 BRAVAIS LATTICES

The crystal systems described in the above section give the information about shape and size of the crystals along with the elements of symmetry. But they do not describe the position of lattice points which may be present either on the faces or in the centre or at the corners of crystal.

The lattice points (the atoms/ions/molecules present at corners/faces/centre) are important because they determine the chemical and some physical properties of the crystalline substances.

If the description regarding position of lattice points is added to the crystal system along with lattice parameters (i.e. the elements of symmetry) then the crystal system is called as **Bravais lattice**. Bravais lattices describe the crystal system totally. i.e. chemical as well as physical properties of crystals.

Depending on position of lattice points in the crystal systems, the unit cells can be described as (a) Primitive, (b) Face centered and (c) Body centered unit cells.

## 2.6.1 Primitive Unit Cells (P)

When lattice points (atoms/molecules/ions) are present **only at the corners** of the unit cell, then it is called as primitive or simple unit cell. Generally, such unit cells are denoted by P.

e.g. Following figure shows the primitive unit cells of cubical and orthorhombic crystals.

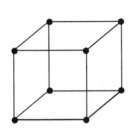  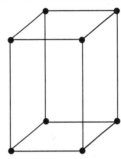

**(a) Simple or primitive cube (SC)**      **(b) Primitive unit cell of orthorhombic crystal**

**Fig. 2.14 : Two examples of primitive unit cells**

## 2.6.2 Face Centered Unit Cells (F)

When the lattice points are present at the **corners as well as on the faces** of unit cell, then it is called as face centred unit cell. Generally, it is denoted by F.

e.g. Following figure shows the face centered unit cells of cubical and orthorhombic crystals.

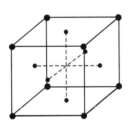  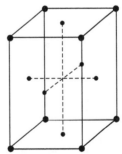

**(a) Face centered cubic unit cell (FCC)**      **(b) Face centered orthorhombic unit cell**

**Fig. 2.15 : Two examples of face centered unit cells**

## 2.6.3 Body Centered Unit Cells (B)

When the lattice points are present at the **corners and at the centre of the unit cell**, then they are called as body centered unit cells. Generally body centered unit cells are denoted by B.

e.g. Following figure shows the body centered unit cells of cubical and orthorhombic crystals.

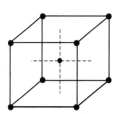    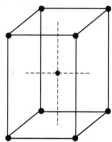

**(a) Body centered cubical unit cell (BCC)    (b) Body centered orthorhombic unit cell**

**Fig. 2.16 : Two examples of body centered unit cell**

It is observed that, for the seven natural fundamental crystal systems, only 14 Bravais lattices are observed. These 14 types of Bravais lattices for the crystal systems are described in the following table.

**Table 2.4 : Seven crystal systems and fourteen Bravais lattices**

| Crystal system | Primitive (P) | Body centered (I) | Face centered (F) | Side centered (C) |
|---|---|---|---|---|
| Cubic<br>$a = b = c$<br>$\alpha = \beta = \gamma$<br>$= 90°$ | | | | |
| Tetrahedral<br>$a = b \neq c$<br>$\alpha = \beta = \gamma$<br>$= 90°$ | | | | |
| Ortho-rhombic<br>$a \neq b \neq c$<br>$\alpha = \beta = \gamma$<br>$= 90°$ | | | | |

*... Contd.*

| | | | | |
|---|---|---|---|---|
| Hexagonal<br>$a = b \neq c$<br>$\alpha = \beta = 90°$<br>$\gamma = 120°$ | | | | |
| Trigonal<br>$a = b = c$<br>$\alpha = \beta = \gamma$<br>$\neq 90°$ | | | | |
| Monoclinic<br>$a \neq b \neq c$<br>$\alpha = \gamma = 90°$<br>$\neq \beta$ | | | | |
| Triclinic<br>$a \neq b \neq c$<br>$\alpha \neq \beta \neq \gamma$<br>$\neq 90°$ | | | | |

## 2.7 ELEMENTS OF SYMMETRY FOR CUBIC CRYSTAL

Focus in this section will be on study of cubical crystal system. Since the bravais lattices of cubic crystals are simple, well understood and the concepts can be extended to bravais lattices of other crystal systems.

For a cubical crystal, the intercepts on the three axes (primitives) are of equal in length i.e. $a = b = c$ and the interfacial angles $\alpha = \beta = \gamma = 90°$.

There are three bravais lattices for a cubical crystal : (As shown in Table 2.4)

(i)    Simple or primitive cubical crystal (SC),

(ii)   Face centered cubical crystal (FCC) and

(iii)  Body centered cubical crystal (BCC).

## 2.7.1 Number of Lattice Points per Unit Cell in a Cubical Crystal

### (i) Simple or Primitive Cubical Cell (SC) :

For calculating the number of lattice points per unit cell, the lattice points are considered to be spheres.

In a simple cubic crystal unit cell, the lattice points are present only at the corners of the cube. So there are eight lattice points present at the eight corners of a unit cell.

But a crystal as a whole does not contain only one unit cell. The unit cells repeat themselves in a regular manner to form a large three dimensional crystal. It can be understood that, lattice point present at each corner in a unit cell is shared by eight lattice points from **other unit cells**.

Then contribution of that lattice point to the unit cell of interest = 1/8.

Since there are eight lattice points, the net contribution = $\frac{1}{8} \times 8 = 1$.

Hence, if lattice points are considered to be atoms, we can conveniently say that for a **simple cubic unit cell**, only **one atom** is present per unit cell.

### (ii) Face centered cubical cell (FCC) :

In a face centered cubical cell, lattice points are present at the 8 corners of unit cell and one lattice point is present on the face of cell.

The contribution of lattice points from the corners = $\frac{1}{8} \times 8 = 1$.

There are total six faces for cubical cell. The contribution of lattice points = $\frac{1}{2} \times 6 = 3$ as each lattice point on the face is shared by face of other unit cell.

If atoms are considered to be lattice point, then total number of atoms in the unit cell = $\left(\frac{1}{8} \times 8\right) + \left(\frac{1}{2} \times 6\right) = 1 + 3 = 4$.

Hence, for a face centered cubical crystal, **four atoms** are present in a unit cell.

### (iii) Body centered cubical cell (BCC) :

In a body centered cubical cell, lattice points are present at the corners of unit cell and one lattice point is present '**inside the body**' of unit cell.

Contribution of lattice points from corners = $\frac{1}{8} \times 8 = 1$.

The contribution from lattice point, present inside the cell = 1 as it is not shared by any other unit cell (since it is present inside the unit cell).

If the atoms are considered to be lattice points, then total number of atoms in the unit cell $= \left(\dfrac{1}{8} \times 8\right) + 1 = 1 + 1 = 2$.

Hence, for body centered cubical crystal, **two atoms** are present in a unit cell.

## 2.7.2 Atomic Radius of Cubical Unit Cells

The distance between the centres of two nearest neighbouring atoms is called as nearest neighbour distance. It is denoted by 'a'.

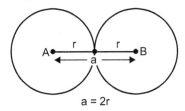

a = 2r

**Fig. 2.17 : Nearest neighbour distance**

If 'r' is considered to be radius of atom, then a = 2r i.e. the nearest neighbour distance is twice of the radius of atoms.

Let us calculate the radii of different Bravais lattices of a cubical crystal.

**(i) Simple Cube Cell :**

A simple cube cell in two-dimensional space can be represented as -

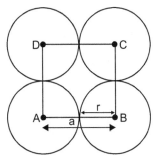

**Fig. 2.18 : Radius of simple cube unit cell**

a = 2r

$$\boxed{r = \dfrac{a}{2}}$$

Hence for a simple or primitive cube unit cell, the radius of the atom is half of the distance between centres of the two nearest neighbouring atoms.

**(ii) Face Centered Cubic Cell (FCC) :**

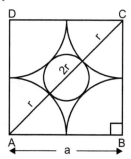

**Fig. 2.19 : Radius of face centered cubical unit cell**

Consider the right angled triangle ABC.

$$AC^2 = AB^2 + BC^2$$

$$(r + 2r + r)^2 = a^2 + a^2$$

$$(4r)^2 = 2a^2$$

$$16r^2 = 2a^2$$

$$r^2 = \frac{2a^2}{16}$$

∴

$$\boxed{r = \frac{a\sqrt{2}}{4}}$$

**(iii) Body Centered Cubic Cell (BCC) :**

In a body centered cubical unit cell, one of the atoms is present inside the unit cell, so it can be shown in Fig. 2.20. It should be noted that the line BC passes through the atom that is present at the centre of the unit cell.

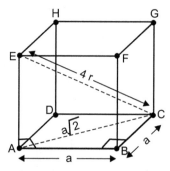

**Fig. 2.20 : Radius of body centered cubical unit cell**

Consider right angled $\triangle$ ABC, $\angle$ ABC = 90°

$$\therefore \quad AC^2 = AB^2 + BC^2$$

$$= a^2 + a^2$$

$$= 2a^2$$

$$AC = a\sqrt{2} \qquad \qquad \ldots (1)$$

Consider right angled $\triangle$ EAC, $\angle$ EAC = 90°

$$\therefore \quad EC^2 = AE^2 + AC^2 \qquad \qquad \ldots (2)$$

Substituting equation (1) in (2),

$$(4r)^2 = a^2 + (a\sqrt{2})^2$$

$$16r^2 = a^2 + 2a^2$$

$$16r^2 = 3a^2$$

$$\boxed{r = \frac{a\sqrt{3}}{4}}$$

# 2.8 PACKING OF ATOMS IN METALS

Many properties of metal such as electrical conductivity, ductility, malleability, density, colour etc. depend on the arrangement of atoms in the bulk of metal.

During crystallization atoms try to arrange themselves in the bulk in such a way that, they occupy maximum space and no free spaces (voids) are left. While doing so, the result is minimization of energy and hence maximum stability is achieved.

Packing of the atoms in metal gives information about the arrangement and position of atoms in the bulk.

While describing the packing of atoms in a metal, it is assumed that, the atoms are hard and spherical.

Depending on nature of metals, they are crystallized in one of the following three forms.

(a)   The Hexagonal Close Packing (HCP),

(b)   Cubic Close Packing or Face Centered Close Packing (CCP or FCP) and

(c)   Body Centered Close Packing. (BCC)

While studying these close packing arrangements, it should be noted that the atoms in a metal are arranged as one layer over other layer.

## 2.8.1 Hexagonal Close Packing

Fig. 2.21 shows the hexagonal close packing of atoms in metals.

Let us consider that the first layer be denoted by 'A' and has six atoms arranged in a fashion shown below. The layer 'B' contains three atoms as shown below.

The two layers are arranged in the sequence B – A – B – A – B …… and so on in such a way that the three atoms in layer B are in the open space below layer 'A' so that the maximum open space is filled. In this packing, each atom is surrounded by 12 atoms i.e. six in the same plane, three below plane and three above plane.

e.g. Zn, Mg, Mn, etc.

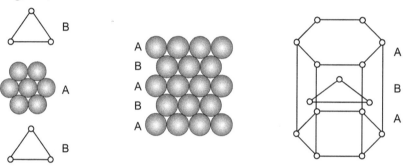

**Fig. 2.21 : Hexagonal close packed structure (HCP)**

## 2.8.2 Cubic Close Packing or Face Centered Close Packing (CCP or FCP)

In cubic close packing, there are three layers instead of two. The third layer is denoted by 'C' and it also contains three atoms, but the arrangement of atoms in 'C' is different from that of 'B'. The arrangement is shown in the following figure.

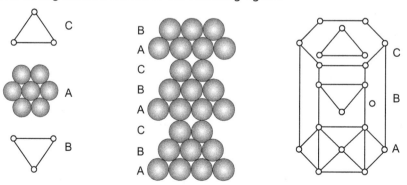

**Fig. 2.22 : Cubic close packing (CCP)**

The layers are arranged over one another in such a way that, the next layer is fitted in the gap formed by previous layer. The arrangement of layers is – B – A – C – B – A – C – B – ....... Such a packing is known as cubic close packing. This arrangement is shown in Fig. 2.22.

In such type of packing, each atom in layer A is surrounded by 12 atoms i.e. six in the same plane, three from each plane present below and above.

e.g. Al, Ag, Au, Cu, etc.

### 2.8.3 Body Centered Close Packing (BCP)

Compared to above two types, close packing of atoms is less in the third type - *body centered cubic structure*. In this type of packing, spheres lie at the corners of cube as well as at the centre of the cube. Thus, each sphere touches eight spheres of equal size, packing factor is 0.68 of the available space. Alkali metals i.e. sodium, potassium crystallize in body centered cubic structure. (See Fig. 2.23).

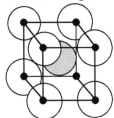 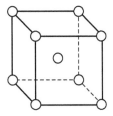

**Fig. 2.23 : Body centered cubic structure (BCC)**

## 2.9 ATOMIC PACKING FACTOR (APF)

Atomic packing factor is related to the packing of atoms in the metal during formation of crystals. It can be understood that higher magnitude of APF means the closest packing of atoms i.e. higher packing efficiency. Higher packing factor indicates that, more number of atoms are arranged/present in a small volume. Hence APF can have effect on many physical properties such as density, conductivity, dissolution as well as chemical properties.

APF is defined as, "the ratio of volume occupied by the atoms in the unit cell to that of volume of unit cell itself".

It should be noted that, all volume of the unit cell is not equal to the volume of atoms present in the unit cell as there are free spaces present (voids) in the crystal.

Therefore, maximum number of atoms per unit cell results in maximum A.P.F.

From definition of A.P.F.,

$$A.P.F. = \frac{\text{Volume of atoms in unit cell}}{\text{Volume of unit cell}}$$

Let us calculate the A.P.F. for various bravais lattices that are studied previously for a cubical unit cell. While calculating A.P.F., it is assumed that the lattice points are hand spheres.

**(1) A.P.F. of simple or primitive cube unit cell :**

**Given :** Number of atoms per unit cell for simple cubic unit cell = 1.

$$\text{Radius of atom simple cube } = \text{ r} = \frac{a}{2}$$

where a = Edge length or distance between centres of gwo neighbouring atoms.

Since atoms are considered to be spheres,

$$\text{Volume of atom } = \frac{4}{3}\pi r^3$$

$$\therefore \qquad \text{A.P.F. } = \frac{\text{Volume of atoms in unit cell}}{\text{Volume of unit cell}}$$

$$= \frac{\text{No. of atoms} \times \text{Volume of (atom) sphere}}{\text{Volume of a cubical unit cell}}$$

$$= \frac{1 \times \frac{4}{3}\pi r^3}{a^3} = \frac{1 \times \frac{4}{3}\pi \left(\frac{a}{2}\right)^3}{a^3}$$

$$= \frac{4\pi a^3}{3 \times 8 \times a^3} = \frac{\pi}{6} = 0.52$$

$$\text{Packing efficiency } = \text{A.P.F.} \times 100 = 0.52 \times 100$$

$$= 52\%$$

The A.P.F. for simple cube is 0.52 or packing efficiency is 52%. This indicates that only 52% of total volume of unit cell is occupied by atoms in the unit cell and remaining is empty.

**(2) A.P.F. of face centered cubic structure (FCC) :**

**Given :** The number of atoms per unit cell for FCC = 4.

$$\text{Radius of atoms in FCC} = \frac{a\sqrt{2}}{4}$$

$$\text{A.P.F. } = \frac{\text{Volume of atom} \times \text{No. of atoms}}{\text{Volume of unit cell}}$$

$$= \frac{\frac{4}{3}\pi r^3 \times 4}{a^3} = \frac{\frac{16}{3} \times \pi \times \left(\frac{a\sqrt{2}}{4}\right)^3}{a^3}$$

$$= \frac{\frac{16}{3}\pi \times \frac{2\sqrt{2}}{64} \cdot a^3}{a^3} = \frac{16\pi \cdot 2\sqrt{2}}{3 \times 64 \times a^3} \cdot a^3$$

$$= \frac{\pi}{3\sqrt{2}} = 0.74$$

The A.P.F. of FCC structure is found to be 0.74 i.e. packing efficiency is of 74%. This indicates that 74% space in the unit cell will be occupied by atoms. This can be called as a close packing.

**(3) A.P.F. of body centered cubic structure (BCC) :**

**Given :** Number of atoms/unit cell for BCC = 2

Radius of atoms in unit cell $= \dfrac{a\sqrt{3}}{4}$

$$\text{A.P.F.} = \frac{\text{No. of atoms} \times \text{Volume of atom}}{\text{Volume of unit cell}} = \frac{2 \times \dfrac{4}{3}\pi r^3}{a^3}$$

$$= \frac{2 \times \dfrac{4}{3}\pi \left(\dfrac{a\sqrt{3}}{4}\right)^3}{a^3} = \frac{8}{3}\pi \cdot \frac{a^3 \cdot 3\sqrt{3}}{64 \cdot a^3}$$

$$= \frac{\pi\sqrt{3}}{8} = 0.68$$

The A.P.F. of BCC structure is found to be 0.68 i.e. packing efficiency = 68%. This indicates that 68% space in the unit cell will be occupied by the atoms in unit cell.

For the above calculations it is clear that the packing efficiency of FCC structure is maximum (74%) followed by BCC structure (68%). However, packing efficiency of simple cube structure is only about 52%.

## 2.10 CO-ORDINATION NUMBER OF CUBIC LATTICE

**Definition :** The total number of nearest neighbour atoms of a particular atom is called as co-ordination number.

The co-ordination number depends on the nature of substance. The co-ordination numbers of simple cube, face centered cube and body centered cube are described below.

(i)  **Simple Cube Cell (SC) :** From Fig. 2.24, it can be seen that, for $Cl^-$ or $Na^+$ ions there are two nearest atoms along X-axis one along +X-axis and other along –X-axis. Similarly, there are two nearest neighbours along ±Y axis and two along ± Z axis. Thus, in all, there are 2 + 2 + 2 = 6 nearest neighbours. Hence, the co-ordination number is six.

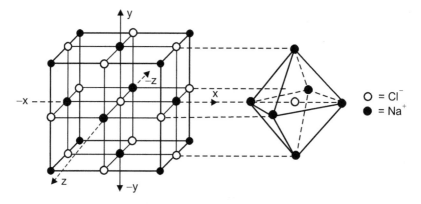

**Fig. 2.24 : Simple cubic cell**

(ii) **Face Centered Cubic Cell (FCC) :** For face centered cubic (FCC) unit cell, the co-ordination number is 12. Consider atom O located at the centre of face ABCD in Fig. 2.25. This atom has four neighbours at the corners in the same plane (lattice points ABCD). This atom also has four more neighbouring atoms that are present on the faces on the left hand side in the same unit cell denoted by EFGH respectively and four more neighbouring atoms will be present in the faces second unit cell which is present on the right hand side. (The second adjacent unit cell is not shown in Fig. 2.25).

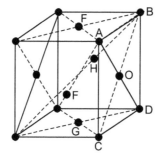

**Fig. 2.25 : Face centered cubic or Tetrahedral cubic**

The co-ordination number of hexagonal close packed crystal is same as FCC and equals 12.

(iii) **Body Centered Cell (BCC) :** In this, an atom in the centre (or body) of the cell has all the eight corner atoms as its close neighbours. Hence, the co-ordination number is eight.

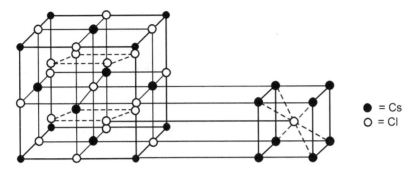

**Fig. 2.26 : Body centered cubic cell**

Following table summarizes the characteristics of all the bravais lattice of cubical crystal system.

**Table 2.5 : Characteristics of cubical crystal system**

| Property | Simple Cube (S.C.) | Face Centered Cube (FCC) | Body Centered Cube (BCC) |
|---|---|---|---|
| 1. Number of atoms per unit cell | 01 | 04 | 02 |
| 2. Atomic radius (r) | $r = \dfrac{a}{2}$ | $r = \dfrac{a\sqrt{2}}{4}$ | $r = \dfrac{a\sqrt{3}}{4}$ |
| 3. Atomic packing factor (APF) | 0.52 | 0.74 | 0.68 |
| 4. Co-ordination number | 06 | 12 | 08 |

## 2.11 DIFFRACTION OF X-RAYS BY CRYSTAL PLANES

Bending of light in the geometrical shadow of object is called as diffraction. Diffraction of X-rays from a crystal surface gives an important information about its structure. X-rays are used for this purpose because X-ray wavelengths are comparable to that of interplanar distances in crystals.

The phenomenon of diffraction of X-rays by crystal planes explains the structure of crystal which in turn can explain the properties of chemical substances observed at molecular level.

It is observed that the interplaner distances in a crystal are comparable with that of wavelength of X-rays. This means that a crystal can be regarded as a grating and the planes containing lattice points can be regarded as large number of lines grooved. So diffraction pattern is observed.

## 2.11.1 Bragg's Law

Bragg's law states that "If the path difference between two parallel X-rays falling on the crystal planes is equal to integral multiple of wavelength of incident wavelength, then diffraction takes place constructively."

i.e.        Path difference  =  n$\lambda$  for constructive diffraction.                     ... (1)

where n = 1, 2, 3, 4, …… and  $\lambda$ = wavelength of incident X-rays.

**Derivation of Bragg's Equation :**

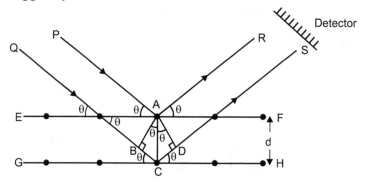

**Fig. 2.27 : Bragg's law**

- Let us consider two parallel X-ray beams P and Q are falling on crystal planes EF and GH respectively.

- Let A and C be the points on the planes EF and GH respectively where the X-rays touch them.

- Let 'd' be the distance between two planes EF and GH (i.e. interplaner distance).

- Let $\theta$ be the angle of glancing of two X-rays on the two planes in the crystal. Once the X-rays incident on the plane, then they will undergo reflection. It is known that angle of incidence is equal to angle of reflection. (See Fig. 2.27). The reflected beams of X-ray are R and S respectively for P and Q.

- The angle $\theta$ is called as glancing angle (It should be noted that it is not the angle of incidence).

        Glancing angle  = 90° – Angle of incidence

**Construction :** Draw line AC whose length is equal to 'd' i.e. interplanar distance. Also construct lines AB and AD in such a way that AB $\perp$ QC and AD $\perp$ CS to calculate path difference.

**Derivation :** Path difference is an extra distance travelled by X-ray Q as compared to X-ray P when it reaches the detector. The extra distance travelled by Q is calculated as

$$\text{Path difference} = (QC + CS) - (PA + AR)$$

$$= (QB + BC) + (CD + DS) - (PA + AR)$$

But QB = PA and DS = AR as AB $\perp$ QC, AD $\perp$ CS and X-rays P and Q are parallel.

$\therefore$ $\qquad$ Path difference = PA + BC + CD + AR – PA – AR

$\therefore$ $\qquad$ Path difference = BC + CD $\hspace{5cm}$ ... (2)

Now consider right angled $\triangle$ ABC, $\angle$ ABC = 90°

$$\sin \theta = \frac{BC}{AC}$$

$\therefore$ $\qquad\qquad$ BC = AC sin θ

$\qquad\qquad\qquad$ = d sin θ $\hspace{5cm}$ ... (3)

Consider right angled $\triangle$ ACD, $\angle$ ADC = 90°

$$\sin \theta = \frac{CD}{AC}$$

$\therefore$ $\qquad\qquad$ CD = AC sin θ

$\qquad\qquad\qquad$ = d sin θ $\hspace{5cm}$ ... (4)

Substitute (3) and (4) in (2),

$\therefore$ $\qquad$ Path difference = d sin θ + d sin θ

$\qquad\qquad\qquad$ = 2d sin θ $\hspace{5cm}$ ... (5)

According to Bragg's law for constructive diffraction, (Equation 1)

$\qquad$ Path difference = nλ

Comparing equations (5) and (1),

$\therefore$ $\hspace{4cm}$ nλ = 2d sin θ

This equation is called as Bragg's equation, n is called as order of reflection.

When n = 1, 2, ......, etc., it is called as first order, second order diffraction, etc. respectively.

If the angle 'θ', the wavelength of incident X-ray 'λ' and the order of reflection 'n' is known, then the interplanar distance 'd' can be calculated using Bragg's equation. This quantity plays important role in the crystal structure because if the Miller's indices [h, k, $l$] for a plane and the interplanar distance 'd' is known, then nearest neighbour distance 'a' [See Section 2.7.2] can be calculated as :

$$d = \frac{a}{\sqrt{h^2 + k^2 + l^2}}$$

From nearest neighbour distance, the atomic radii in the crystal can be calculated by using for formulae given in the section 2.7.2.

## 2.12 CRYSTAL DEFECTS OR IMPERFECTIONS

- Ideally, crystal is a solid which has repetitive and regular arrangement of its constituents i.e. lattice points.

- Real crystalline systems should obey the third law of thermodynamics, which states that, "Entropy of pure and perfectly crystalline substance at absolute zero (–273°C) temperature is zero".

- This means that, at absolute zero temperature, there is no entropy in the crystal i.e. there is no disorder but as temperature increases (say room temperature, 25°C), the entropy in the crystal system increases, i.e. the disorders in the crystal increase.

- Hence at room temperature, the crystals have defects i.e. imperfections.

  "The departure from perfectly regular arrangement of lattice points (atoms/ions/molecules) in a crystal system is called as crystal defect".

- Generally, crystals are grown at room temperature and special expertise is needed for growing crystals.

- There are many reasons that may lead to imperfections in a crystal. Few common reasons are listed below.

**(1) Rate of crystallization :** The crystallization should be done slowly from the saturated solution of substance to be crystallized or from its melt. If the rate of solvent evaporation is not maintained, imperfections occur in crystals.

**(2) Working conditions during crystallization :** The crystallization should be done slowly at room temperature and the saturated solution or melt should not be disturbed (such as by stirring) once the crystallization process starts. If these conditions are not maintained, they lead to imperfections.

**(3) Purity of the substance :** The substance to be crystallized should be taken in the purest form. If impurity is present in the substance then this impurity gets trapped in the crystal structure leading to defects or imperfections.

Following flow-chart shows the commonly observed defects in the crystal structure.

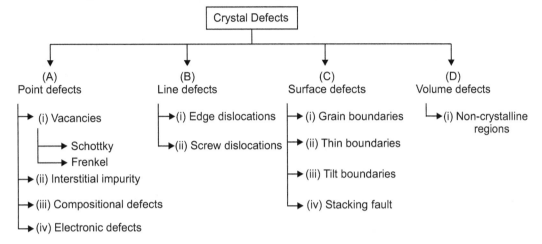

- As far as scope of this book is concerned, the first two types of defects i.e. point defects and line defects will be studied in detail.

## (A) Point Defects :

- The point defects refer to point like imperfect regions in the crystal structure. The point defects have diameter of 1-2 atoms only, hence they are also sometimes called as zero dimension defects.

- As shown in the above flow-chart, there are four types of point defects :

(1)  Vacancies (empty space) in crystal structure.

(2)  Interstitial movement of atoms or ions.

(3)  Compositional defects.

(4)  Interstitial impurity. (See Fig. 2.28)

### (1)  Vacancies (empty spaces) in crystal structure (Schottky defect) :

Consider Fig. 2.28. It is a crystal lattice of general ionic compound $A^+ B^-$. Fig. 2.28 (a) shows the perfect crystal structure where no defects/imperfections are present. But sometimes during crystallization, it may happen that, one ion pair (cation and anion) is completely missing from its position (Fig. 2.28 b).

This creates an empty space or vacancy in the crystal structure. Although the ratio of cations and anions in perfect and imperfect crystal is not changed, overall crystal remains neutral as unit positive and unit negative charge is missing.

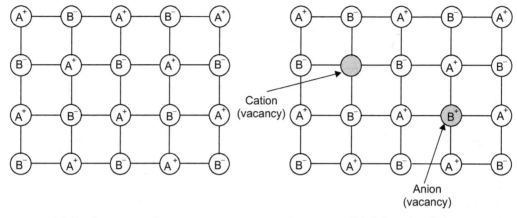

**(a) Perfect crystal**                                    **(b) Schottky defect**

**Fig. 2.28**

The defects in which such empty spaces or vacancies are present are called as **Schottky defects**. If Schottky defects are present in the crystal, then its density decreases.

e.g. Alkali halides (NaCl, KBr, KCl etc.)

**(2)  Interstitial movements of atoms/ions (Frenkel defect) :**

•     Consider Fig. 2.29 (a) and (b). Fig. 2.29 (a) shows a perfect ionic crystal however in Fig. 2.29 (b), it can be observed that one of the ions (either anion or cation) or both are moved in a interstitial position (empty space or void) in the crystal.

•     Overall charge on the crystal is neutral but such movements of ions/atoms lead to drastic changes in the physical, chemical and mechanical properties of a crystal.

•     Such types of defects are called as **Frenkel defects**.

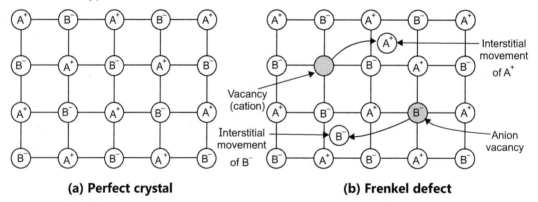

**(a) Perfect crystal**                                    **(b) Frenkel defect**

**Fig. 2.29**

e.g. Imperfections in AgBr, AgCl, $CaF_2$ etc.

**Differences between Schottky and Frenkel defects :**

| Schottky Defects | Frenkel Defects |
|---|---|
| 1. It arises due to vacancy at a cation site and anion site in crystal structure. | 1. It arises due to movement of ions or atoms in the structure in the interstitial position. |
| 2. Overall charge on the crystal is maintained. | 2. Overall charge on the crystal is maintained, however, charge distribution is altered. |
| 3. Generally, it occurs in compounds of high co-ordination number. | 3. Generally, it occurs in the compounds of low co-ordination number. |
| 4. It occurs when cations and anions in the ionic crystal are of same size. | 4. It occurs in the ionic crystals when there are differences in the ionic sizes. |
| 5. Since porosity of the crystal increases, it leads to decrease in the crystal density. | 5. Crystal density remains unaltered. |
| 6. Electrical conductivity increases since there are holes present in the crystal structure. | 6. No much difference in the electrical conductivity is observed. |
| 7. e.g. NaCl, CsCl etc. | 7. e.g. $CaF_2$, ZnS etc. |

### (3) Compositional defects :

- If the impurities are present in the substance, then during crystallization, generally it happens that these impurity atoms/ions enter the crystal lattice. This leads to change in the composition of the crystal and such defects are called as compositional defects.

- Consider Fig. 2.30 (a), an impurity (foreign) atom has occupied the position of matrix atom. Such compositional defects by replacements occur when the size of impurity atom is nearly same to that of size of matrix atoms.

- Consider Fig. 2.30 (b), an impurity atom has not replaced the matrix atom but it has occupied the free space (or void) present in the crystal lattice.

- Such defects are possible only when size of the impurity atom entering the crystal lattice is much smaller than that of the matrix atom but it is enough to fit in the void present in the crystal lattice. Such types of defects are called as interstitial impurity defects.

For example, carbon is an interstitial impurity in iron. It occupies octahedral voids at high temperature. FCC structure of iron because atomic radius of iron is 2.29 A° whereas that of carbon is only 0.71 A°.

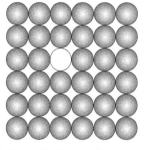

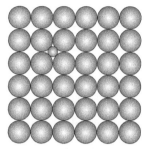

**(a) Substitutional impurity**                **(b) Interstitial impurity**

**Fig. 2.30**

**Effects of point defects on the properties of crystals :**

**(1)** **Formation of colour centres :** When electrons get trapped in the anion vacancies then formation of colour centres or f-centres take place.

**(2)** **Diffusion :** If there is vacancy or movement of atoms taking place in a crystal structure, then diffusion pattern in the crystal changes.

**(3)** Point defects lead to changes in the mechanical properties of the crystal.

**(4)** Electrical and thermal conductivity of crystal changes due to presence of point defects.

**(B) Line Defects :**

If a part of a line of atoms is missing from its regular site, then this missing row of atoms is called as dislocation. The distortion is centered along a line and hence the line defect is called as dislocation. Movement of dislocation is necessary for plastic deformation. The dislocation is a boundary between the slipped region and the unslipped region and lies in the slip plane. The structure and behaviour of dislocations affect properties of engineering materials.

**Types of dislocations :** There are two basic types of dislocations. They are :

   (i)    Edge dislocations and (ii) Screw dislocations.

**(i)  Edge dislocation :**

Consider a crystal in which extra line of atoms (half plane) is introduced from the upper portion of the crystal and this extra half plane of atoms terminates in the middle of the crystal. This type of imperfection along a line of the crystal is called as Edge dislocation or line imperfection. Fig. 2.31 shows an edge dislocation and is represented as $\perp$ i.e. positive dislocation, when the extra half plane is introduced from above the crystal while it is negative dislocation, if the extra half plane is introduced from below the crystal and is represented as T.

A line drawn through the dislocated region is called as the dislocation line. In positive dislocation, the atoms lying above the dislocation line are compressed, whereas the atoms lying below the dislocation line exhibit tension and vice versa for negative dislocation.

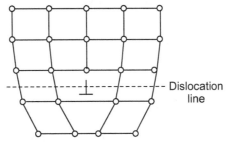

**Fig. 2.31 : Edge dislocation**

## (ii) Screw dislocation :

A screw dislocation can be imagined as being produced by cutting the crystal partway through with a knife and then shearing one part of the crystal with respect to the other parallel to the cut. The name screw dislocation is given, because it transforms successive atomic planes into the surface of a helix. A circular arrow represents the screw dislocation.

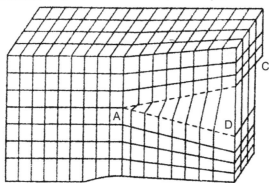

**Fig. 2.32 : Screw dislocation**

In general, dislocations are more complicated. However, they can be resolved to obtain their edge and screw components. Dislocations come into the materials during the solidification or by mechanical processing of metals. The number of dislocations is expressed by dislocation density which is the total length of dislocations per unit volume (lines in $cm/cm^3$) or is the number of dislocations intersecting a unit cross-sectional area (lines/$cm^2$). Dislocation lines can end at the surface of a crystal and at grain boundaries, but never inside a crystal. Dislocations have a strong effect on deformation characteristics and mechanical properties. They also influence the recrystallization temperature, phase transformation characteristics, electrical properties and corrosion resistance of materials.

**Effects of line defects on the properties of crystals :**

1. **Deformation :** If line defects are present in the crystal, then the crystal becomes mechanically weak and application of stress leads to permanent deformation in the crystal

2. **Crystal size :** Because of line defects, the crystal size can be increased during crystal formation. The deformation can become site of deposition.

3. **Chemical reactivity :** Chemical reactivity of the crystal increases because of the presence of line defects since these can provide site of attack for other reactant.

4. If such deformations are present in alloys, then mechanical strength of the alloys increases as compared to pure metals.

## SOLVED PROBLEMS

### Problem 1 :

*At what glancing angle would the first order diffraction from (100) plane of KCl is observed using X-ray of wavelength 154 pm ? The distance of unit cell is 315 pm.*

**Solution :**

**Given :** n = 1, hkl = 100, $\lambda$ = 154 pm, d = 315 pm.

We know that, $\quad\quad n\lambda = 2d \sin \theta$

$$\sin \theta = \frac{\lambda}{2d} = \frac{154}{2 \times 315} = 0.244$$

$$\sin \theta = 0.244$$

$$\theta = 14.1°$$

∴   The glancing angle for the incident X-ray = 14.1°.

### Problem 2 :

*A first order X-ray ($\lambda$ = 154 pm) reflection maximum from a set of (200) planes of BCC cubic lattice was observed at 16° - 6'. Calculate the length of the edge of the unit cell.*

**Solution :**

**Given :** n = 1, $\lambda$ = 154 pm, hkl = 200, $\theta$ = 16° - 6', a = ?

$$n\lambda = 2d \sin \theta$$

$$d = \frac{n\lambda}{2 \sin \theta} = \frac{1 \times 154}{2 \times \sin 16° \text{ - } 6'} = 277.67 \text{ pm}$$

$$d = \frac{a}{\sqrt{h^2 + k^2 + l^2}}$$

$$a = d \times \sqrt{h^2 + k^2 + l^2} = 277.67 \times \sqrt{2^2 + 0^2 + 0^2}$$

$$= 277.67 \times 2 = 555.3 \text{ pm}$$

∴   The length of the edge for the crystal = 555.3 pm.

## Problem 3 :

Calculate the distance between (100) planes of crystal which exhibits first order reflection at an incidence angle at 30° with X-rays of wavelength $2 \times 10^{-10}$ m.

## Solution :

**Given :** hkl = 100, n = 1, θ = 30°, λ = $2 \times 10^{-10}$ m, d = ?

∴                    $n\lambda = 2d \sin \theta$

$$d = \frac{\lambda}{2 \sin \theta} = \frac{2 \times 10^{-10}}{2 \times \sin 30} = \frac{2 \times 10^{-10}}{2 \times 0.5} = 2 \times 10^{-10} \text{ m}$$

∴   The interplanar distance is $2 \times 10^{-10}$ m.

## Problem 4 :

At what glancing angle would the first order diffraction from (110) plane of KCl observed using X-ray of wavelength 150 pm ? The dimension of unit cell is 305 pm.

## Solution :

**Given :** hkl = 110, n = 1, λ = 150 pm, a = 305 pm

$$d_{hkl} = \frac{a}{\sqrt{h^2 + k^2 + l^2}} = \frac{305}{\sqrt{1 + 1 + 0}} = \frac{305}{\sqrt{2}} = 215.67 \text{ pm}$$

$$n\lambda = 2d \sin \theta$$

$$\sin \theta = \frac{n\lambda}{2d} = \frac{1 \times 150}{2 \times 215.67} = 0.348$$

$$\theta = 20.35°$$

∴   The glancing angle for incident X-ray is 20.35°

## Problem 5 :

211 planes in a cubic lattice of edge length 5 A°, produces first order reflection maxima with X-rays of wavelength 0.8 A°. Find the glancing angle.

**Solution :**

**Given :** d = $5 \times 10^{-10}$ meters, $\lambda = 0.8 \times 10^{-10}$ meters, $\theta$ = ?, n = 1.

**Formula :**

$$n\lambda = 2d \sin \theta$$

$$\sin \theta = \frac{n\lambda}{2d}$$

$$\sin \theta = \frac{1 \times 0.8 \times 10^{-10}}{2 \times 5 \times 10^{-10}}$$

$$\sin \theta = \frac{0.8}{10}$$

$$\theta = 4.588°$$

# (B) CEMENT

## 2.13 INTRODUCTION

Concrete is a composite material formed by the combination of (a) cement, (b) aggregate and (c) water, in a particular proportion in such a way that concrete produced meets the need of the job on hand, particularly as regards its workability, strength, durability and economy.

Hence, it is necessary to understand the details of the above materials.

## 2.14 CEMENT

Cement in general can be defined as 'a material which possesses very good adhesive and cohesive properties which make it possible to bond with other materials to form a compact mass'. That is, cement is a material which possesses cementatious properties. Cement is the most important and costliest ingredient of concrete. It was invented by Joseph Aspdin of U. K. in 1824. He named it Portland Cement because the hardened concrete made out of the cement, fine aggregates, coarse aggregates and water in definite proportions resembled the natural stone occurring at portland in England. The materials which set and harden in the presence of water are said to possess hydraulic properties. As cement gets strength due to the chemical action between cement and water and its ability to harden under water, it is also known as *hydraulic cement.*

## 2.15 MANUFACTURE OF PORTLAND CEMENT

The manufacture of cement involves three distinct operations as shown in Fig. 2.33.

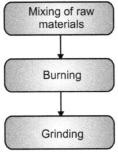

**Fig. 2.33**

### 2.15.1 Mixing of Raw Materials

The raw materials used in the manufacture of cement are: (a) Agrillaceous materials – consisting of silicates of alumina in the form of clays and shales, and (b) Calcareous materials – in the form of limestone, chalk and marl, which is a mixture of clay and calcium carbonate. These materials are mixed thoroughly. The mixing of raw materials can be done in two ways as shown in Fig. 2.34.

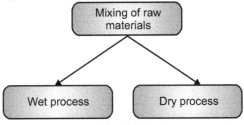

**Fig. 2.34**

### 2.15.2 Wet Process

In the earlier part of the century i.e. from 1913 to 1960, the wet process was popular for the manufacture of cement. This was because of the possibility of more accurate control in mixing of the raw materials. The techniques of intimate mixing of raw materials were not available then. Later, with the development of the technique of dry mixing of powdered materials using compressed air, the dry process gained momentum.

The dry process requires much less fuel as the materials are already in a dry state, whereas in the wet process the slurry contains 35% to 50% water. To dry the slurry, more fuel is required. In the wet process, the calcareous materials such as limestone are crushed and stored in silos or storage tanks. The algrillaceous material such as clay is thoroughly mixed with water in a wash mill. The washed clay is then stored in basins. Now, the crushed limestone from the silos and wet clay from basins are mixed together in a wet grinding mill to make slurry. The slurry is led to the correcting basin where it is constantly stirred. At this stage, the chemical composition of the slurry is tested and adjusted as necessary. The corrected slurry is stored in storage tanks and kept ready to serve as feed for a rotary kiln.

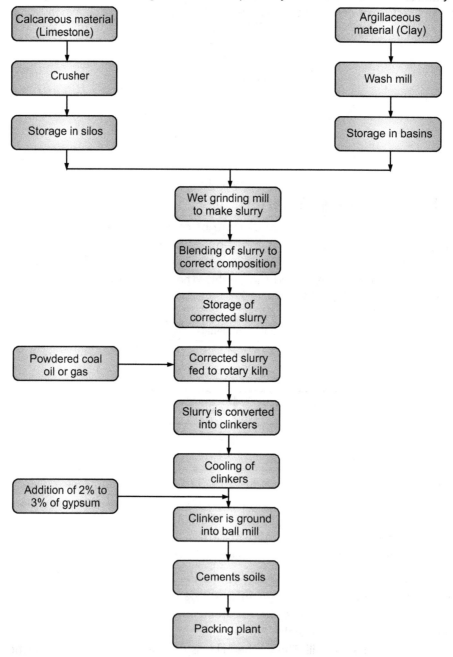

**Fig. 2.35 : Wet Process of Cement Manufacturing**

## 2.15.3 Dry Process

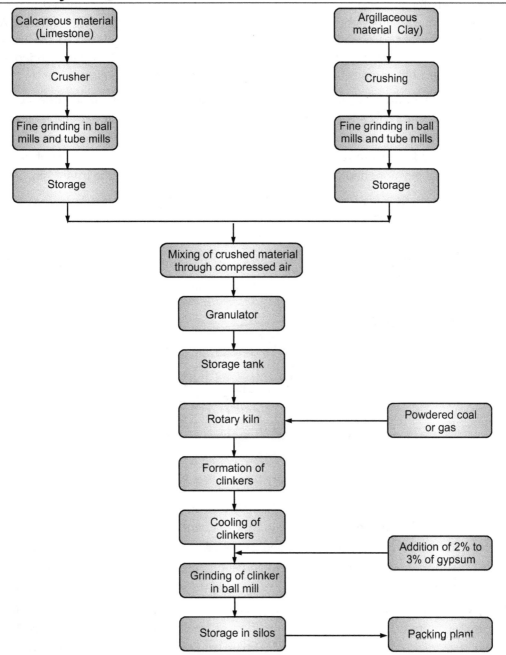

**Fig. 2.36 : Dry Process of Manufacturing of Cement**

The boulders of limestones upto 1.2 m size are transported in huge dumpers and dumped into the hoopers of the crusher. The limestone is now crushed to a size of 75 mm.

The crushed limestone is moved from the crusher by a series of conveyors for stacking. The argillaceous material is also crushed and stacked like the limestone. The crushed materials are checked for calcium carbonate, lime, alumina, ferrous oxide and silica contents. Any material found short, is added separately. The materials are then ground to the desired degree of fineness. The dry powder, called the raw meal, is then further blended and corrected for its right composition and mixed by means of compressed air.

The aerated powder tends to behave almost like liquid and in about one hour of aeration, a uniform mixture is obtained. The blended meal is further sieved and feed into a rotating disc called *granulator*. A small quantity of water, about 12% by weight, is added to make the blended meal into pellets. This is done to permit air flow for exchange of heat for further chemical reactions and conversion for the same into clinkers in the rotary kiln.

## 2.15.4 Burning

Burning is carried out in a rotary kiln. Rotary kiln for a wet process is shown in Fig. 2.37.

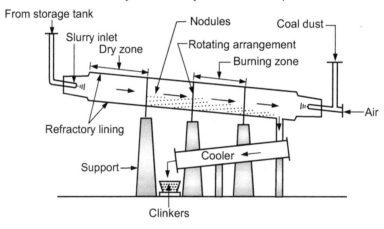

**Fig. 2.37 : Rotary Kiln for Wet Process**

The rotary kiln is so arranged that it rotates at about one to three revolutions per minute, about its longitudinal axis. It is laid at a gradient of about 1 in 25 to 1 in 30. The corrected slurry is injected at the upper end of the kiln and hot gases or flames are forced through the lower end. The portion of the kiln near its upper end is known as the *dry zone*. In this zone, the water of the slurry is evaporated. As the slurry gradually descends, there is an increase in temperature and in the next section of the kiln, carbon-di-oxide from the slurry is evaporated. This leads to the formation of small lumps known as *nodules*. These nodules then gradually roll down to the burning zone, where the temperature is about 1400°C to 1500°C. In the burning zone, the nodules are calcined and formation of small, hard, dark greenish-blue balls known as *clinkers* take place.

In the dry process, coal brought from coal fields is pulverised in vertical coal mill and is stored in silo. It is pumped with required quantity of air through the burners. The preheated raw materials roll down the kiln and get heated to such extent that carbon-dioxide is expelled along with other combustion gases. The material is then heated to a temperature of 1400°C to 1500°C and the formation of clinckers take place.

The size of the clinkers varies from 3 mm to 20 mm. The temperature of the clinkers coming out of the burning zone of the kiln is as high as 1000°C. A rotary kiln of small size is provided to cool down the hot clinkers. Cooled clinkers, having temperature of about 95°C, are collected in containers of suitable sizes.

## 2.15.5 Grinding

The clinkers, so obtained from the rotary kiln, are ground to the required degree of fineness in a ball mill or a tube mill. During grinding, a small quantity of gypsum (about 3% to 4%) is added. Gypsum controls the initial setting time of cement. If gypsum is not added, the cement would set soon as water is added to it. Thus, gypsum acts as a retarder, and delays the initial setting action of cement.

## 2.16 BASIC CHEMISTRY OF CEMENT

The chief chemical constituents of portland cement are lime, silica, alumina, iron oxide, magnesium oxide and little amount of sulpher trioxide and soda etc. Their chemical composition is as follows:

1. **Lime (CaO):** Lime is the most important ingredient of cement. Its proportion in a good cement is generally in the range of 60% to 67%. However, lime in excess causes the cement to expand and disintegrate. On the other hand, if lime is in deficiency, the strength of cement is decreased and it also causes the cement to set quickly.

2. **Silica ($SiO_2$):** Silica is also an important ingredient of cement. Its proportion in a good cement is generally in the range of 17% to 25%. It imparts strength of the cement due to the formation of dicalcium and tricalcium silicates. If silica is present in excess, though the strength of the cement increases but at the same time its setting time is also increased.

3. **Alumina ($Al_2O_3$):** Alumina imparts quick setting property to the cement. It acts as a flux and lower down the clinkering temperature. However, high temperature is essential for the formation of a suitable type of cement and hence, alumina should not be present in excess, as it weakens the cement. In a good cement, the content of alumina is confined to 3% to 8%.

4. **Calcium sulphate ($CaSO_4$):** Calcium sulphate is in the form of gypsum. Its function is to increase the initial setting time of cement. In a good cement, the content of calcium sulphate is confined to 3% to 4%.

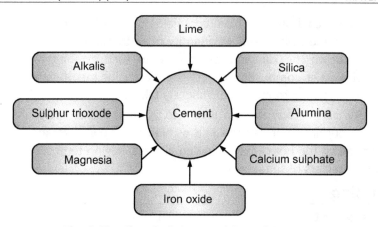

**Fig. 2.38 : Chemical Composition of Cement**

5. **Iron oxide ($Fe_2O_3$):** Iron oxide imparts colour, hardness and strength to the cement. A good cement should have 3% to 4% of iron oxide.

6. **Magnesia (MgO):** Magnesia, if present in small amount, imparts hardness and colour to the cement. However, a high content of magnesia makes the cement unsound. Therefore, an ideal concentration of magnesia is between 0.5% to 4%.

7. **Sulphur trioxide ($SO_3$):** A very small amount of sulphur is present in the form of sulphur trioxide. It is useful in making the cement sound. However, if it is in excess, the cement becomes unsound. Therefore, sulphur trioxide should be present in the range of 1% to 2%.

8. **Alkalies:** Most of the alkalies present in raw materials are carried away by the flue gases during heating and the cement contains generally $Na_2O$ and $K_2O$. It should be tried that the presence of these alkalies should be as low as possible (not more than 1%). If they are present in excess, they cause a lot of problems such as alkali-aggregate reaction, efflorescence etc.

## 2.17 HYDRATION OF CEMENT

When the water is added to cement, a chemical reaction starts which is exothermic in nature and produces a significant amount of heat. This is known as *hydration* and the liberated heat is called the *heat of hydration*. The process of hydration is not an instantaneous. It is faster in the early periods and continues indefinitely at slower rate. In about a month's time, 85 to 90% of the cement hydrates and the cement attains almost its full strength. The hydration still continues and cement grows stronger with time. The process of hydration may be explained as follows:

In a cement paste i.e. a thorough mixture of cement and water, chemical reaction soon starts and after a lapse of some time, the paste consists of hydrates of various compounds, collectively called gel, unhydrate cement, water and residue of the water-filled spaces in the fresh paste. These voids are called *capillary pores*. The cementing gel consists of thin fibrous crystals which is porous in nature. These pores are called gel-pores. About 23% of water by mass of cement is required for chemical reaction of cement with water and is known as bound water. About 15% of water by mass of cement is required to fill the gel-pores and is known as gel-water. Thus, a total of 38% of water by mass of cement is required for complete hydration. In this discussion, it is assumed that the reaction takes place in a sealed container. The remaining water mixed with cement causes undesirable capillary cavities. If only 38% of water is added, the capillary cavities can be eliminated. The products of hydration are colloidal and because of this, during hydration the surface area of solid phase increases enormously. This absorbs a large amount of free water. If water added is 38%, all the colloids are not sufficiently saturated which decreases the relative humidity of the paste.

This leads to a lower hydration as the gel can be formed only in water filled space. This requires a minimum of 50% of water by mass of cement or in other words, a water-cement ratio in excess of 0.5 is sufficient for hydration. In actual conditions, the reaction does not take place in a sealed container and with lower percentage of water, the concrete mix would not be workable. A mix is workable if it can be easily mixed, placed and compacted at the required place. Usually about 50 to 60% of water by mass of cement is added to manufacture the concrete. The rate of hydration is mainly influenced by:

1. **The temperature at which hydration takes place:** At high temperatures the reaction is rapid. Only 10 to 15 minutes of hydration at higher temperature is equivalent to 10 to 12 hours of hydration at lower temperatures. It is for this reason that in cold weather, sometimes the aggregates are heated before they are used for making concrete.

2. **The fineness of cement:** The finer the cement, the more rapid is the reaction. As the hydration starts at the surface of the cement particles, the larger the available surface area, the more rapid is the hydration. Finer cements have larger surface areas and therefore the hydration is rapid. However, a very fine ground cement is susceptible to air-set and deteriorates earlier.

3. **The ingredients of cement:** The reaction can be made rapid or slow by changing the properties of the ingredients of the cement.

## 2.18 CLASSIFICATION OF CEMENT

Portland cements are classified under the American Society for Testing Materials (A.S.T.M.) standards. As per ASTM, cement is designated as Type I, Type II, Type III, Type IV, Type V and other minor types like Type IS and Type IP etc.

**Type I: Normal portland cement:** This is the general purpose cement suitable for all uses when the special properties of the other types are not required.

**Type II: Modified portland cement:** This cement has a lower heat of hydration than type I and generates heat at a slower rate. It also has improved resistance to sulphate attack.

**Type III: High early strength portland cement:** This cement is used where high strengths are desired at very early periods.

**Type IV: Low heat portland cement:** This is a special cement for use where the amount and rate of heat generated must be kept to a minimum. The development of strength is also at a slower rate. It is intended for use only in large masses of concrete such as large gravity dams where temperature rise resulting from the heat generated during hardening is a critical factor.

**Type V: Sulphate resistant portland cement:** This is a special cement intended for use only in structures exposed to severe sulphate action, such as in soils, and waters of high alkali content. It has a slower rate of hardening than normal portland cement.

## 2.19 TYPES OF CEMENTS

By changing slightly the chemical composition, it is possible to obtain cement exhibiting different properties. Hence, cement can be manufactured to suit the desired properties. The following are the types of cement.

(a)   Ordinary portland cement (OPC).

(b)   Rapid hardening portland cement (RHPC)

(c)   Extra-rapid hardening portland cement.

(d)   Portland blast-furnace cement.

(e)   Low heat portland cement.

(f)   Sulphate resisting portland cement.

(g)   White portland cement.

(h)   Coloured portland cement.

(i)   Super-sulphate cement.

(j)   Masonry cement.

(k)   Expansive cement.

(l)   Oil-wet cement.

(m)  Hydrophobic cement.

(n)   Pozzolana cement.

(o)   High-Alumina cement.

(p)   High-strength cement.

(q)   Acid-resisting cement.

(r)   Quick setting cement.

(s)   Blended cement.

Some of them are described below:

**Ordinary Portland Cement :**

It is a widely used cement for most of the works. It is suitable for general construction works when there is no exposure to sulphates in the soil or in the ground water. The manufacturing of cement as discussed in Article 2.15, pertains to the ordinary portland cement.

For using the portland cement to produce high strength concrete (M35 and above) for specialized works; high strength cement is required. The Bureau of Indian Standards has therefore introduced three different grades of ordinary portland cement. Consequently, ordinary portland cement is now available in three different grades as follows:

1.  Grade 33 (IS : 269 – 1989)

2.  Grade 43 (IS : 8112 – 1987)

3.  Grade 53 (IS : 12269 – 1987)

The grade indicates the compressive strength of cement at 28 days. Testing according to IS : 4031 (Methods of physical tests for hydraulic cement). Higher strength of cement (grade 43 and grade 53) is achieved by:

1.  Selecting good quality of limestone as a raw material.

2.  Using low ash coal firing as the coal ash is detrimental to the quality of clinker.

3.  Ratio of CaO with $SiO_2$, $Al_2O_3$ and $Fe_2O_3$ is always maintained during manufacturing.

4.  At all stages of manufacturing, required quality controls are carefully exercised.

With a better quality of limestone, having higher percentage of $CaCO_3$, the cement of higher grade (even 63 grade) can be produced. In India, good quality limestone deposits are localised at Ranavav in Gujrat, Ariyalur deposits in Tamil Nadu, Gotan of Rajasthan etc.

# 2.20 CHEMICAL COMPOSITION OF PORTLAND CEMENT

The chemical properties of 33 grade, 43 grade and 53 grade cements are tabulated in Table 2.6.

**Table 2.6**

| Chemical properties | 33 grade IS : 269 - 1989 | 43 grade IS : 8112 - 1989 | 53 grade IS : 12269 - 1987 |
|---|---|---|---|
| 1.  Loss on ignition,%, maximum | 5.0 | 5.0 | 4.0 |
| 2.  Insoluble residue,%, by mass, maximum | 4.0 | 2.0 | 2.0 |
| 3.  Magnesia, (MgO),%, maximum | 6.0 | 6.0 | 6.0 |
| 4.  Sulphur,%, maximum as $SO_3$ | 2.5 | 2.5 | 2.5 |
| 5.  Tricalcium aluminate ($C_3A$), maximum | 0.66 | 0.66 | 0.66 |
| 6.  Lime saturation factor (LSF) | 0.66 to 1.02 | 0.66 to 1.02 | 0.8 to 1.02 |

### Rapid Hardening Cement (IS : 8041 – 1990):

As the name implies, it hardens and attains its strength earlier than ordinary portland cement. Three days hardening of this cement is equivalent to seven days hardening of ordinary portland cement. The rapid hardening property of this cement is achieved by a higher $C_3S$ content and by finer grinding of the cement clinker. Due to this property, early stripping of concrete formwork becomes possible.

This is advantageous where repeated use of the same shuttering is made i.e. precast works or where speedy development of strength is important. e.g. road repair works. Rapid hardening cement should not be confused with quick setting cement which sets quickly but does not harden quickly. In the early stages, this cement gives out a large quantity of heat of hydration. This cement must not be used for mass concrete or for large structural sections because due to a large quantity of heat of hydration, the temperature inside the concrete increases, leading to formation of undesirable cracks on cooling.

### Extra-rapid Hardening Portland Cement:

It is manufactured by intergrinding about 2% calcium chloride and rapid hardening portland cement. While using this cement, maximum time of 10 minutes is available for mixing, transporting and placing the concrete. Also this cement should be used within one month. This cement attains strength more rapidly than rapid hardening cement and is used for special purposes like repair works, especially in cold weather.

### Low Heat Portland Cement (IS : 12600 – 1989):

It is manufactured by reducing the percentage of $C_3S$ and $C_3A$ of ordinary portland cement. As a result, this cement gets the strength at a slower rate and the heat of hydration is less. This will require long time curing and keeping forms for a long time. This cement is particularly useful for mass concrete works. According to IS : 12600, the heat of hydration for this cement is limited to 314 kJ/kg at 28 days. Ordinary portland cement generates about 502 kJ/kg heat of hydration at 28 days.

### Sulphate Resisting Cement (IS : 12330 – 1988):

It is similar to ordinary portland cement except that it contains more silicates and less quantity of aluminates. The heat of hydration of this cement is low and it develops higher ultimate strength, although the early strength of this cement is low. It is used for underwater structures particularly exposed to alkali actions.

### Quick Setting Cement:

As the name implies, it sets quickly. This does not mean that it achieves the strength quickly. It sets quickly but does not harden quickly. In the manufacture of this cement, gypsum content is reduced to get the quick setting property. It is particularly used for underwater constructions. It sets very quickly so that the time available for mixing, transporting and placing the concrete is very short and its use in general works must be avoided.

## High Strength Cement:

It has very high strength as compared to ordinary portland cement and is used in special works such as prestressed concrete and precast concrete works. This cement must not be confused with rapid hardening cement.

## High Alumina Cement (IS : 6452 – 1989):

It is a non-portland cement. It is manufactured by melting mixture of aluminous and calcareous materials in suitable proportion and grinding the resulting clinker to fine powder which is black in colour. It hardens and develops strength very rapidly, giving out a great amount of heat. Its one day's strength is equal to 28 day's strength of ordinary cement. It is strongly resistant to chemical attack and is suitable to sea and underwater works. It is not recommended in tropical region.

## White Cement (IS : 8042 – 1989):

It is manufactured in the same way as portland cement. The grey colour of portland cement is due to the presence of iron oxide (about 4%). If the raw materials selected for manufacturing portland cement are such that they do not contain iron oxide, the resulting cement is white in colour. The raw materials are chosen to see that the maximum Iron oxide content is less than one%. White clay and China clay are used as raw materials in the manufacturing of this cement and coal firing is replaced by oil fuel firing. This results in white coloured cement. It is used for white concrete (as may be required architecturally) or for white finishing works.

## Coloured Cement:

These are manufactured by adding 5 to 10% of ground pigments to ordinary or white portland cement. The pigments are chemically inert and have fast colours. The proportion and type of pigments added vary according to the colour desired. Thus, iron oxide is added to give red and yellow cobalt to give blue colour and magnese dioxide to give black colour.

## Hydrophobic Cement (IS : 8043 – 1978):

It is manufactured by grinding ordinary portland cement clinker with 0.1 to 0.4 % of oleic acid, stearic acid. This addition forms water repellent film around each particle of cement and therefore transportation and storage of this cement is not affected by the moisture content of atmosphere. When concrete is prepared using this cement, the water repellent film breaks out which improves the workability of concrete. The storage of ordinary portland cement in humid places causes deterioration in the quality of cement. For such places this cement is useful.

### Masonry Cement (IS : 3466 – 1988):

It is specially manufactured for masonry works, plaster works etc. by intergrinding very finely ground portland cement, limestone and an air-entraining agent. It can also be manufactured by intergrinding portland cement and hydrated lime, granulated cement or crushed stone. Addition of these materials give good workability, reduces shrinkage and water retentivity. The cement mortar prepared from this cement is more plastic, cohesive and strong and yet workable, than that prepared from ordinary portland cement which produces a harsh mortar. When ordinary portland cement is used, due to its less water retentivity, the masonry absorbs water from the mortar resulting in a poor bond. This difficulty is overcome when masonry cement is used. However, the strength of mortar is reduced. This cement must not be used for concrete works.

### Expansive Cement:

It is used to neutralize the shrinkage of concrete to eliminate cracks. An ordinary portland cement shrinks while setting due to the loss of free water, whereas the volume of expanding cement increase on hardening. This does not mean that expanding cement produces a 'shrinkless' concrete but the magnitude of expansion can be adjusted in such a way that shrinkage and expansion of volume are numerically equal. A small percentage of this cement when added to the concrete, will eliminate cracks. This is specially used for hydraulic structures.

### Super-sulphate Cement:

This cement is made from well-granulated slag (80 to 85%) and calcium sulphate (10 to 15%) together with 1 to 2% of portland cement. Its specific surface is between 3500 and 5000 cm$^2$/g. It is free from false set having initial setting time between $2\frac{1}{2}$ to 4 hours and final setting between $4\frac{1}{2}$ and 7 hours.

Its total heat of hydration is very low, about 165 to 190 kJ/kg at 7 days and 190 to 210 kJ/kg at 28 days, which make it very suitable for mass concreting but requires great care while concreting in cold weather.

Concrete made from supersulphate cement may expand or contract slightly on setting according to conditions and hence should be properly cured.

Super-sulphate cement can be used for all purposes. Its setting action is different from other cements and admixtures should not be used with it. If used in R.C.C. work, a minimum cover of 35 mm is necessary. It must not be mixed with high alumina cement since the action will be different. It is highly resistant to chemical attack. If cured in air, the surface gets softened by atmospheric $CO_2$. Hence, water curing is always preferable.

In a normal 1 : 2 : 4 mix, with water-cement ratio 0.55, the strengths are 350 kg/cm² at 7 days; nearly 500 kg/cm² at 28 days and between 500 to 700 kg/cm² at 6 months.

This cement gives comparatively high resistance to chemical attack. Its rate of hardening increases with the temperature upto about 38°C but above that it decreases.

**Blended Cement:**

We are facing the problem of waste disposal due to industrialization. Many industries like iron and metal manufacturing industry, thermal power station produces extensively large amount of waste products such as blast furnace slag, fly ash respectively. So using waste materials such as blast furnace slag, fly ash as pozzolanic substitutes for portland cement can result in reduction of environmental pollution. The goal, then, is to specify blended cements.

Blended cement is the cement with a fixed percentage of pozzolana, replacing the portland cement clinker portion of the cement mix. The pozzolanic material should be mixed within the percentage given by ASTM. This percentage of substitution is generally 20 – 60% of total volume.

The pozzolanic materials which are mixed in the blended cement are: Fly ash, Ground granulated blast furnace slag, Rice husk, Silica fume etc.

Table 2.7 shows the allowable composition of blended cements:

**Table 2.7**

| Cement type | Component % | | |
|---|---|---|---|
| | Clinker | Fly ash | Slag |
| Portland flyash | 65 - 94 | 6 - 35 | Nil |
| Portland slag | 65 - 94 | Nil | 6 - 35 |
| Blast furnace | 20 - 64 | Nil | 35 - 80 |

On top of that, appropriate percentage of gypsum may be added.

Blended cement is more advantageous than other cements in the following respect:

1. Blended cement is more economical than other cements as it contains many industrial waste products.

2. Generation of green house gases can be minimised. As blended cement contains burnt material.

3. Less heat of hydration is produced in blended cement concrete.

4. Problem of waste disposal can be solved. As blended cement contains industrial waste.

5. Eco-friendly behaviour of concrete produced by blended cement.

6.  The use of blended cement is advantageous particularly when dealing with sulphate resistance, alkali-silica resistance or chloride induced corrosion resistance. Hence, it can be easily used in Marine construction.

7.  Concrete with blended cements require less amount of water for same workability level.

Blended cements are used in the following constructions:

(a)  Wall, floors and columns of building, bridges and industrial plants.

(b)  All types of foundations.

(c)  Concrete pipes, blocks; precast concrete elements.

(d)  Prestressed piles, concrete roads; soil stabilization.

(e)  Bridge in sea water environment; sewage systems etc.

**Examples: Portland pozzolana cement, blast furnace slag portland cement etc.**

**Portland Pozzolana Cement:**

This cement is manufactured by grinding portland cement clinker with pozzolana and required quantity of gypsum. The pozzolanas are materials which at ordinary temperatures, react with lime in presence of water, resulting in cementing materials. Fly ash, burnt clay and pumicite are used as pozzolana. Addition of pozzolana is 10 to 25% of the pozzolana cement by mass. The advantages of this cement are: reduced cost, increased impermeability, increased workability, less heat of hydration and if offers greater resistance to the attack of aggressive waters. However, the rate of hydration is low and gaining of strength is slower upto 14 days. If the concreting done by this cement is properly cured at 28 days, the strength of this cement is equal to that of ordinary portland cement.

**Blast Furnace Slag Portland Cement:**

It is manufactured by mixing portland cement clinker with granulated blast furnace slag (a waste product from blast furnace which contains oxide of lime, silica and alumina) and gypsum in suitable proportions and grinding the mixture to the required fineness. The slag proportion is limited to 65% of the mass of the mixture. According to IS : 455 - 1976, the slag content should not be less than 25% and not more than 65% of the total mass of the mixture. It has low heat of hydration, more durability and is better resistant to soil and water containing excessive amounts of sulphates; alkalies, metals as well as acidic waters. It is helpful for marine works.

## EXERCISE

1. Explain the terms :

   (i) Unit cell, (ii) Elements of symmetry, (iii) Anisotropic crystals.

2. State different laws of crystallography.

3. Define crystal lattice and describe different cubic lattices.

4. What are the elements of crystal symmetry ? Explain with reference to simple cubic structure.

5. Describe the method of determining the Miller's indices for a plane of cubic crystal.

6. Explain the terms : Weiss indices and Miller's indices. What is the law of rational indices ? Give its applications.

7. What are Miller's indices ? How are they superior to Weiss indices ? Explain with suitable examples.

8. Explain the terms :

   (i) Axis of symmetry, (ii) Plane of symmetry, (iii) Centre of symmetry.

9. What is meant by 'Space lattice' of a crystal ? Draw a unit cell for space lattices of the following types : (i) Simple cubic; (ii) Face-centered cubic, (iii) Body-centered cubic.

10. What is meant by co-ordination number in a crystal ?

11. What are the different types of defects in perfect crystal lattice ?

12. Write notes on Frenkel and Schottky defects.

13. Give an account of different types of line defects.

14. Describe the manufacture of Portland Cement. In what way does it differ from rapid hardening cement.

15. What is the influence of the tri and di calcium silicates and tri calcium aluminate on the properties of cement?

16. What is hydration? On which factors the rate of hydration depends?

17. What is the importance of testing fineness of cement? How is the surface area method more reliable than sieve test for testing fineness of cement?

18. (a)  Define consistency of standard cement paste.

    (b)  How is the initial setting time of cement determined? What is its significance?

19. (a) Differentiate between setting and hardening of cement. Is setting time of cement related with setting time of concrete?

    (b) How is the setting time of cement controlled?

    (c) Why are the excess quantities of magnesium oxide, free lime in cements considered undesirable?

20. (a) Explain the roles of $C_2S$, $C_3S$, $C_3A$ and $C_4AF$ in hydration of cement. State the role of gypsum in setting of cement.

    (b) State the important field test and their significance for OPC. State various grades of cements and their significance to construction engineer. State the limitations of initial and final setting time as per IS code.

## 3.1 INTRODUCTION

Any chemical process accompanied by the evolution of heat and light, commonly the union of substances with oxygen, is called as combustion. e.g. $C + O_2 \rightarrow CO_2$. It is a strongly exothermic reaction, hence carbon and its compounds have been used for many centuries as sources of heat energy.

**Definition of fuel :** "Any combustible substance, containing carbon as main constituent, which on proper burning, gives large amount of heat that can be used for domestic and industrial purposes is called as a fuel".

"Any combustible substance that combines with oxygen from the air with the evolution of large amount of heat capable of being applied or used economically for various purposes without the formation of excessively objectionable byproducts is called as a fuel."

Fuels undergo exothermic reaction with oxygen, during combustion.

$$\text{Fuel} + O_2 \xrightarrow{\text{Combustion}} \text{Products} + \text{Heat}$$

The primary sources of fuels, coal, petroleum oil, etc. are formed from the fossilized remains of plants and animals which are trapped and stored inside the earth's crust and are called 'fossil fuels'. The continual exploitation of these fossil fuels (coal, oil, gas etc.) may ultimately result in a fuel shortage because of the fossil fuels being used up much more rapidly than these are replenished by nature. Wood, coal, charcoal, kerosene oil, petrol, natural gas, etc. are some common examples of fuels.

Dry wood burns readily with bright and cheerful flame, whereas anthracite burns with a very small and feebly luminous flame. We are not concerned with the cheerfulness with which the fuel burns but we are concerned with : 'how much heat is given out in the process of combustion ?'

## 3.2 IMPORTANCE

Although many sources of power such as wind power, water power, etc. are available still then the chemical fuels constitute the most important source of heat and power for domestic as well as industrial purpose. Chemical fuels are primarily used for heating purposes but these have other functions too. For example, in internal combustion engine, petrol is not used for heating the engine but it is used for generating power. In metallurgy, coke used in blast furnace, acts as a reducing agent as well as provides heat. Whatever may be the manufactured product at some stage or the other of its manufacture, it is directly or indirectly dependent upon the fuel.

The primary sources of fuels (e.g. coal and petroleum oil) are dwindling day by day, therefore it is of utmost importance to utilize the natural fuels to the best of advantage.

## 3.3 CLASSIFICATION OF FUELS

The fuels can be classified according to their (1) Occurrence and preparation or (2) State of aggregation.

According to their occurrence and preparation, fuels are classified as :

**(a) Natural or Primary fuels :** These are found in nature as such e.g. wood, coal etc.

**(b) Prepared or Secondary fuels :** These are prepared from primary fuels e.g. charcoal, coke, kerosene oil, etc.

According to their state of aggregation, these are classified as :

(a) Solid fuels : Wood, coal, coke etc.

(b) Liquid fuels : Petroleum, diesel oil, fuel oil etc.

(c) Gaseous fuels : Natural gas, oil gas, bio-gas etc.

**According to occurrence**

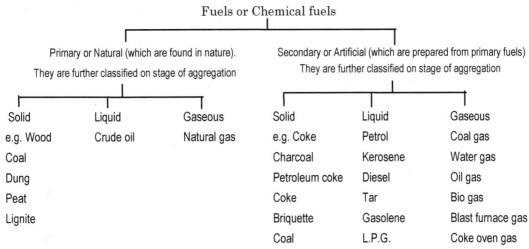

**According to state of aggregation**

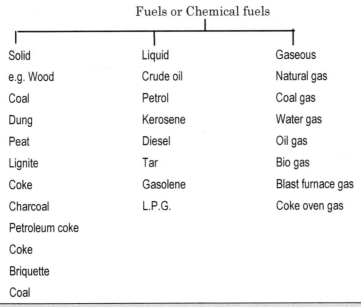

## 3.4 PROPERTIES OF FUELS

### (1) Ignition Temperature (Kindling Temperature) :

Fuels will exist in air practically indefinitely if not heated to a sufficiently high temperature to start active combustion. 'The minimum temperature required to ignite the substance and to continue its burning without further addition of heat is known as kindling or ignition temperature.'

This temperature is not definite as it is influenced by many factors such as fineness of subdivision or the extent of exposed surface if the combustion substance is in solid or liquid state. If it is gaseous then ignition temperature depends on (i) Pressure : ignition temperature usually decreases with increase in pressure. (ii) The ratio of combustible gas to air. (iii) The size and shape of the vessel. The ignition temperature increases as the ratio of surface to volume of the vessel increases. (iv) The presence of catalyst, which may lower the ignition temperature.

**(2) Calorific Value :**

Calorific value or capacity to supply heat is the most important property of a fuel. It is defined as, "Calorific value of a fuel is the total quantity of heat liberated by completely burning a unit mass (or volume) of it."

As the calorific value is measured in the quantity of heat produced, therefore, it is necessary to know the units of heat in various systems.

**Units of Heat :** The units for measuring the quantity of heat in different systems are as follows :

**M.K.S. system :** The unit is *kilocalorie* and is defined as 'the quantity of heat required to raise the temperature of one kilogram of water through one degree centigrade.'

**C.G.S. system :** The unit is *calorie* and is defined as, 'the amount of heat required to raise the temperature of one gram of water through one degree centigrade (from 15°C to 16°C).

Thus, 1 kilocalorie (kcal) = 1000 calorie (cal).

**British system (F.P.S.) :** The unit is British thermal unit (B.Th.U.) which is defined as, 'the quantity of heat required to raise the temperature of one pound of water through one degree Fahrenheit (from 60° F to 61°F).

$$1 \text{ B.Th.U.} = 252 \text{ cal} = 0.252 \text{ kcal}$$

$$1 \text{ kcal} = 3.961 \text{ B.Th.U.}$$

In the SI system, the unit of heat is joule (J).

$$1 \text{ kcal} = 4186.8 \text{ J or 1 cal at } 15°C = 4.18 \text{ J}$$

**(3) Higher or Gross Calorific Value :**

Usually all fuels contain hydrogen which is converted into steam during combustion. In the measurement of calorific value if the products of combustion are condensed to room temperature (say 15° C) then the latent heat of vaporization is also accounted for and the corresponding value is called as higher or gross calorific value. It is defined as, "Gross calorific value of a fuel is the total amount of heat produced by complete combustion of a unit mass of the fuel in air or oxygen and the products of combustion are cooled to room temperature (usually 15° C)". It is expressed in kilo-calories per kg.

**(4) Lower or Net Calorific Value :**

When the fuels are used in practice, water vapour and moisture etc. are not condensed but escape as such to the atmosphere alongwith the hot combustion gases. Therefore lesser quantity of heat is available. "The lower or net calorific value of a fuel is the net heat produced when unit mass or volume of a fuel is burnt completely allowing the gaseous products to escape."

Hence,

$$\text{Net calorific value } = \left\{ \begin{array}{c} \text{Gross calorific} \\ \text{value} \end{array} \right\} - \left\{ \begin{array}{c} \text{Latent heat of} \\ \text{water vapour} \\ \text{formed} \end{array} \right\}$$

$$= \left( \text{Gross C.V.} \right) - \left\{ \begin{array}{c} \text{Mass of hydrogen} \times \\ 9 \times \text{Latent} \\ \text{heat of steam} \end{array} \right\}$$

**Units of calorific value :**

In S.I. system the calorific value of a fuel is expressed in terms of joules per kilogram (J kg$^{-1}$) or joules per cubic metre (J m$^{-3}$) depending on whether the fuel is solid, liquid or gas. The calorific value of a gaseous fuel always refers to the value at one atmospheric pressure and 288°K (i.e. 15°C).

**For solid and liquid fuels :** Calorie per gram or kilocalorie per kilogram or British thermal unit per pound.

**For gaseous fuels :** Kilocalorie per cubic metre (kcal/m$^3$) or B.Th.U. per cubic feet (B.Th.U./ft$^3$). Hence

$$1 \text{ kcal/kg } = 1.8 \text{ B.Th.U./lb}$$
$$1 \text{ kcal/m}^3 = 0.1077 \text{ B.Th.U./ft}^3$$

**(5) Percentage of non-combustible matter :**

Any substance which does not burn and combine with oxygen is called as non-combustible matter. Therefore, it remains as ash or clinker. As it does not burn, therefore, it does not produce any heat. Thus the quantity of non-combustible matter will reduce the calorific value (heating value) of a fuel. Hence, the percentage of non-combustible matter should be as low as possible in any good fuel. More the percentage of non-combustible matter in a fuel, smaller will be its calorific value or heating capacity and vice versa.

## 3.5 ADVANTAGES AND DISADVANTAGES OF FUELS

**(a) Solid fuels :**

**Advantages :**

(i)     Solid fuels are easy to transport and can be conveniently stored without any risk of spontaneous combustion.

(ii)    Solid fuels have moderate ignition temperature and their cost of production is low.

**Disadvantages :**

(i)     Solid fuels have high ash content.

(ii)    The cost of handling of fuel and ash is high.

(iii)   The rate of combustion is difficult to control.

(iv)    Only few per cent of calorific value is actually utilized for useful work, because large portion of heat is wasted on account of lack of proper surface contact, by radiation and chimney losses,

(v)     A large amount of unburnt fuel is also wasted alongwith clinker, cinder etc.

## (b) Liquid fuels :

**Advantages :**

(i)     Liquid fuels possess higher calorific value per unit mass than solid fuels.

(ii)    They burn without ash, dust, clinker etc.

(iii)   Their firing is easy and the fire can be extinguished easily by stopping the fuel supply.

(iv)    They can be transported through pipes and stored indefinitely without any loss.

(v)     The flame produced by burning can be controlled by adjusting the fuel supply which is normally through pipe and one man can easily regulate large number of furnaces simultaneously.

(vi)    They are clean in use and economic in labour, therefore, heat loss to chimney is very low.

(vii)   They require less furnace space.

(viii)  There is no wear and tear of grate bars and cleaning of ash etc.

**Disadvantages :**

(i)     Liquid fuels are costlier as compared to solid fuels.

(ii)    Special storage tanks are necessary.

(iii)   In case of highly inflammable and volatile liquid fuels, there is a great risk of fire hazards.

(iv)    They give bad odour.

(v)     For efficient burning of liquid fuels, specially prepared burners and spraying apparatus are required.

### (c) Gaseous fuels :

#### Advantages :

(i)   They can be easily transported through pipelines, saving labour.

(ii)  They can develop higher temperatures because of high heat content.

(iii) Their combustion can be controlled according to the need e.g. oxidizing or reducing atmosphere, length of flame, temperature etc.

(iv)  They are clean, ashless, and burn without smoke.

(v)   Complete combustion without pollution is possible because of uniform mixing of air and fuel.

#### Disadvantages :

(i)   They need very large storage tanks.

(ii)  They are highly inflammable and therefore chances of fire hazards are high.

#### Table 3.1 : Comparison of solid, liquid and gaseous fuels

| | Property | Solid fuels | Liquid fuels | Gaseous fuels |
|---|---|---|---|---|
| 1. | Physical state | Solid | Liquid | Gas |
| 2. | Relative cost | Cheaper | Costly | More costly than other two |
| 3. | Calorific value | Low | Higher | Highest |
| 4. | Space of storage | Large | 50 % less than solid | Depends upon pressure |
| 5. | Specific gravity | Highest | Medium | Lowest |
| 6. | Products of combustion | Leaves much ash | Ashless, smokeless | Ashless, smokeless |
| 7. | Ignition point | High | Low | Lowest |
| 8. | Mode of supply | Cannot be piped | Can be piped | Can be piped |
| 9. | Thermal efficiency | Low | Good | Best |
| 10. | Care in storage and transportation | Less care is required | Care necessary if inflammable | Great care is necessary as highly inflammable |

## 3.6 MEASUREMENT OF CALORIFIC VALUE

The process of carbonisation is accompanied by a decrease of the amount of gaseous and volatile matter which the fuel can yield on being heated and this greatly affects the manner in which the different materials burn. For example, dry wood burns readily with bright and cheerful flame, whereas anthracite burns with a very small and not strongly luminous flame. Here we are not concerned with the cheerfulness with which the fuel burns but we are mainly concerned with how much heat is given out in the process of combustion. In other words, attention is to be focussed on calorific value of a fuel.

## 3.7 DETERMINATION OF CALORIFIC VALUE OF A FUEL (BOMB CALORIMETER METHOD)

**(For solid fuel and non-volatile liquid fuels)**

The calorific value of a solid fuel or non-volatile liquid fuel can be satisfactorily determined by using a high-pressure oxygen bomb calorimeter. (Fig. 3.1).

**Principle :** A known mass of a fuel is burnt completely in bomb calorimeter and quantity of heat produced is absorbed in water and measured accurately. Then the quantity of heat produced by burning a unit mass of the fuel is calculated.

**Construction :** The Bomb calorimeter consists of a strong stainless steel vessel which is corrosion resistant and is capable of withstanding a pressure of at least 50 atmospheres. The bomb is provided with a gas-tight screw-cap to which two stainless steel electrodes and a release valve are fitted. One of these electrodes is tubular which can therefore also act as an oxygen inlet. A small ring is attached to this electrode which acts as a support for the crucible.

The bomb is placed in a copper calorimeter, which is surrounded by an air-jacket which is further enclosed in water-jacket to prevent losses due to radiation. The calorimeter is provided with an electrically operated stirrer and Beckman's thermometer, which can read accurately temperature difference upto $1/100^{th}$ of a degree.

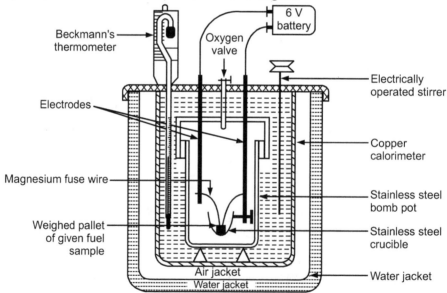

**Fig. 3.1 : Bomb calorimeter**

**Procedure :** About 0.5 to 1.0 g of a given fuel is accurately weighed into the crucible of the calorimeter.

A piece of fine platinum wire ($7.5 \times 10^{-3}$ cm thick) is made in the form of a loop and dipped in the fuel taken in the crucible and tightly stretched across the pole pieces of the bomb and the crucible is placed in position.

About 10 ml of distilled water are introduced into the bomb to absorb vapours of sulphuric acid and nitric acid formed during the combustion and the lid of the bomb is screwed. The bomb is then filled with oxygen upto 25 atmospheric pressure and the firing wires are attached to the terminals.

The copper calorimeter vessel is weighed with sufficient water to submerge the cover of the bomb. The copper calorimeter vessel is then kept in the outer jacket on the insulating feet provided. The bomb is then lowered in the copper calorimeter and the lid of the copper calorimeter vessel alongwith stirrer are placed in position. The Beckman thermometer is now adjusted and the stirrer is started. After 5 minutes the temperature of water is noted to the nearest $0.002°$ C and five more readings are taken at one minute intervals. At the end of the $5^{th}$ minute, the electrodes are connected to a 6 to 12 volt battery to ignite the charge and the readings are continued at one-minute intervals. After the maximum temperature is reached, readings are still continued until the rate of fall becomes uniform. Then the stirrer is stopped and the bomb is removed from the calorimeter. After about half an hour, when the acid mist in the bomb settles, the contents of the bomb are washed into a beaker and the amounts of $H_2SO_4$ and $HNO_3$ present in the solution are determined.

**Calculations :**

$X$ = Weight of fuel in gram

$W$ = Mass/weight of water in gram taken in copper calorimeter

$w$ = Water equivalence of calorimeter, stirrer, thermometer etc. (It is determined by using known weight of standard fuels)

$t_1$ = Temperature of water in copper calorimeter before combustion

$t_2$ = Temperature of water in copper calorimeter after complete combustion

$L$ = HCV and

$S$ = Specific heat of water (4.18 kJ/kg)

Heat liberated during the process of combustion = LX.

Heat absorbed by water and apparatus during process of combustion = $(W + w) (t_2 - t_1)$.

Heat liberated during the process of combustion = Heat absorbed by water and apparatus during the process of combustion

$$LX = (W + w) (t_2 - t_1)$$

Therefore,          $HCV = L = (W + w) (t_2 - t_1)/X$ in cal/g or kcal/kg and $\qquad$ HCV $= L = (W + w) (t_2 - t_1) S/X$ in joule or kJ

$\qquad$ LCV $=$ HCV $-$ ($9 \times$ % of hydrogen $\times$ latent heat of steam)

$\qquad$ $=$ HCV $-$ ($9 \times H \times 587/100$)

$\qquad$ $=$ HCV $-$ ($0.09 \times H \times 587$) in cal/g or kcal/kg

and $\qquad$ LCV $=$ Above answer $\times$ S in joule or kJ

(**Note :** To convert HCV and LCV from gm/cal or kg/kcal into joule or kJ, first find out answer of HCV and LCV in gm/cal or kg/kcal and then multiply both by specific heat value 4.18).

**Corrections :** For accurate and precise result, following corrections are needed.

**1. Fused wire correction ($F_c$) :** Heat liberated from fused wire is added in CV. It is subtracted.

**2. Acid correction ($A_c$) :** Fuel containing sulphur and nitrogen, on oxidation converted into $H_2SO_4$ and $HNO_3$ acids with liberation of heat, which is counted for CV. It is subtracted.

**3. Cooling correction ($C_c$) :** During estimation some amount of heat is lossed due to radiation. It is calculated in this way, time taken to cool the water from maximum to room temperature 't' and rate of cooling per minute 'dt'. Thus, cooling correction is t $\times$ dt. It is added.

Therefore, $\quad$ HCV $=$ $(W + w) (t_2 - t_1 + \text{cooling correction})$

$\qquad$ $-$ (Acid correction + Fused wire correction)/X in cal/g or kcal/kg

$\qquad$ HCV $=$ $(W + w) (t_2 - t_1 + C_c) - (A_c + F_c)/X$ in cal/g or kcal/kg

$\qquad$ HCV $=$ $(W + w) (t_2 - t_1 + C_c) - (A_c + F_c) \times S/X$ in joule or kJ

**Numerical problem :** A sample of coal containing 91% C, 5% H and 3% ash. When this coal was tested in laboratory for it's calorific value in bomb calorimeter, the following data were obtained.

Weight of coal burnt = 0.95 gm, Weight of water taken = 700 gm,

Water equivalent of apparatus = 2000 gm, Rise in temperature = 2.48°C,

Cooling correction = 0.020 C, Acid correction = 60 cal, Fused wire correction = 10 cal.

Calculate net and gross calorific value assuming latent heat of condensation of steam as 580 cal/gm.

Given : x = Weight of coal burnt = 0.95 gm, W = Weight of water taken = 700 gm,

w = Water equivalent of aparatus = 2000 gm, $t_2 - t_1$ = Rise in temperature = 2.48°C,

$C_c$ = Cooling correction = 0.020 C, $A_c$ = Acid correction = 60 cal,

$F_C$ = Fused wire correction = 10 cal and Latent heat of condensation of steam as 580 cal/gm.

$$HCV = (W + w)(t_2 - t_1 + \text{cooling correction})$$
$$- (\text{Acid correction} + \text{Fused wire correction})/X \text{ in cal/g or kcal/kg}$$
$$= (700 + 2000)(2.48 + 0.02) - (60 + 10)/0.95$$
$$= 7031.6 \text{ cal/g}$$
$$LCV = HCV - (0.09 \times H \times 580) \text{ in cal/g or kcal/kg}$$
$$= 7031.6 - (0.09 \times 5 \times 580) = 6770.6 \text{ cal/g or kcal kg}$$
$$HCV = 7031.6 \text{ cal/g or kcal/kg} = 7031.6 \times 4.18 = 29392 \text{ J or kJ}$$
$$LCV = 6770.6 \text{ cal/g or kcal/kg} = 6770.6 \times 4.18 = 28301.108 \text{ or kJ}$$

## 3.8 DETERMINATION OF CALORIFIC VALUE OF A FUEL (BOY'S CALORIMETER METHOD)

**For Gaseous Fuel and Volatile Liquid Fuels :**

The calorific value of gaseous fuels and volatile liquid fuels is measured by Boy's calorimeter.

**Principle :** The gaseous fuel is burnt at a known constant rate in a vessel under such conditions that the entire amount of heat produced is absorbed by water which is also flowing at a constant rate. From the volume of the gas burnt, volume of water collected and the mean rise of temperature of water, the calorific value of a gaseous fuel can be calculated.

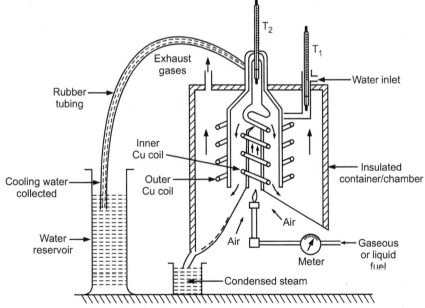

**Fig. 3.2 : Boy's calorimeter**

**Construction :** Boy's calorimeter consists of two flat flame burners situated in a chimney which forms the centre of combustion chamber or the annular vessel. The lower portion of vessel is provided with a trough where water condensed from the products of combustion gets collected which can be removed through the side tube for measuring the volume.

Around the combustion chamber or vessel has a copper tubing coiled inside as well as outside it, water at a constant rate passes through these coils. Water enters from the top of the outer coil moves to the bottom of chimney and then goes up through the inner coil to the exit at top. The thermometers $T_1$ and $T_2$ give the temperatures of incoming and outgoing water respectively. During the down and up movement through the coil, the water takes away practically all the heat of combustion of fuel and any steam formed during combustion is condensed back as water and collects in trough. The whole assembly is enclosed in an insulated chamber.

The products of combustion pass upto the chimney and are deflected downwards by the water cooled head over a spiral of copper tubing through which cold water flows. The gas is again deflected upwards by the insulating baffle over another spiral of similar copper tubing and finally passes out through a number of holes in the lid of the calorimeter.

The gas flows into the burner through an accurate gas - meter.

**Working :** Circulation of water and burning of gaseous fuel are continued at constant rate for about 15 minutes for initial worm up. The rate of fuel burning and water circulation is controlled so that the exit water leaves the apparatus nearly at atmospheric pressure. When steady conditions are established then readings are taken simultaneously of (i) the volume of gas burnt at given temperature and pressure in certain time 't', (ii) the quantity of water passing through the coil, during the same time 't', (iii) the steady rise in temperature $(T_2 - T_1)$ and (iv) mass of water condensed during same time 't'.

**Calculation :** V = Volume of gas burnt at STP in certain time 't', W = Mass of water in gram used in time 't', $T_1$ = Temperature of inlet water, $T_2$ = Temperature of outgoing water, m = Mass of steam condensed when V volume of gas burnt in time 't', L = HCV and S = Specific heat of water (4.18 kJ/kg).

Heat liberated during the process of combustion = LV.

Heat absorbed by circulating water during the process of combustion = $W(T_2 - T_1)$.

But heat liberated during the process of combustion = Heat absorbed by circulating water during the process of combustion

$$LV = W(T_2 - T_1)$$

Therefore,        $L = [W(T_2 - T_1)/V]$ in kcal/m³

$$HCV = L = [W(T_2 - T_1)/V] \times S \text{ in kJ}$$

Mass of water condensed from 1 m³ of gas = m/V

Therefore, latent heat of steam per m³ of gas = $m \times 587/V$

Therefore,     LCV $= [L - (m \times 587/V)]$ in kcal/m$^3$

LCV $= [L - (m \times 587/V)] \times S$ in kJ

**Numerical problem :** Following data were obtained in Boy's gas calorimeter.

Volume of gas used = 0.1 m$^3$ at STP, Weight of water used = 25 kg, Temperature of inlet water = 20°C, Temperature of outgoing water = 33°C, Weight of steam condensed = 0.025 kg. Calculate HCV and LCV. Take the heat liberated in condensing water vapour and cooling the condensate as 580 kcal/kg.

**Given :** V = Volume of gas used = 0.1 m$^3$ at STP, W = Weight of water used = 25 kg, $T_1$ = Temperature of inlet water = 20°C, $T_2$ = Temperature of outgoing water = 33°C, m = Weight of steam condensed = 0.025 kg. Take latent heat of condensation as 580 kcal/kg.

$$\text{HCV} = L = [W (T_2 - T_1)/V] \text{ in kcal/m}^3$$
$$= 25 (33 - 20)/0.1 = 3250 \text{ kcal/m}^3$$
$$= 3250 \times 4.18 = 13585 \text{ kJ}$$
$$\text{LCV} = [L - (m \times 580/V)] \text{ in kcal/m}^3$$
$$= [3250 - (0.025 \times 580/0.1)] = 3105 \text{ kcal/m}^3$$
$$= 3105 \times 4.18 = 12978.9 \text{ kJ}$$

# 3.9 SOLID FUELS

Solid fuels of practical importance are wood, peat and the different varieties of coal. All these materials are of common origin, wood or the woody fibres of plants.

**Wood :** It is obtained from forests. Freshly cut wood contains 25 to 50 % moisture. On air drying it is reduced to about 15 %. On dry moisture-free basis, the average composition of wood is : (1) C = 50 %, (2) O = 43 %, (3) H = 6 %, (4) Ash = 1 %.

The calorific value of air-dried wood is about 3500 - 4500 kcal/kg.

Wood burns readily producing non-smoky and long flame and it leaves behind a very little amount of ash. Wood is largely used as a domestic fuel. Its use as an engineering fuel is, however, restricted.

**Coal :** Coal is a highly carbonaceous matter which has been formed due to alteration of vegetable matter such as plants under certain favourable conditions.

It is mainly composed of C, H, N and O besides non-combustible matter of inorganic nature.

**Coalification :** Millions of years ago when the vegetation was quite thick, huge piles of wood might have got buried underground. Subsequently, under the combined effects of high temperature, excessive pressure, absence of oxygen, presence of bacteria and prolonged time, the cellulosic material of wood gradually underwent decomposition with simultaneous liberation of gases (such as $CO_2$, methane, etc.) and got converted into coal. This transformation of wood into coal is called as *coalification*. Variation in the proportion of various plant components and environmental conditions caused the different types of coal.

## 3.10 CLASSIFICATION OF COAL BY RANK (COALIFICATION)

The best established classification of coals is by ranks or degree of transformation or coalification from the parent material wood. It is based on proximate analysis. The progressive transformation or coalification of wood can be represented as below :

Wood → Peat → Lignite → Bituminous coal → Anthracite.

During this progressive coalification, (1) Carbon content, hardness and calorific value gradually increase while (2) oxygen content, moisture content and volatile matter decrease.

**1. Peat :** It is the first stage in the coalification of wood and is a brown fibrous jelley like mass. Its use as a fuel is not economical because it contains 80 – 90% of water but after 1 to 2 months of air drying, it burns freely. The average composition of air-dried sample of peat is C = 57%, H = 6%, O = 35% and ash content 2.5 to 6.0%. On dry-sample basis, its calorific value is 5400 kcal/kg. Though it is not an important fuel in India, it is used for power generation in countries like England, U.S.A. and Russia because of shortage of coal deposits. Peat is found in the Nilgirihills of South India.

**2. Lignite (Brown coal) :** It is soft, amorphous, brown coloured variety of coal. Though it contains more decomposed vegetable matter than peat still it is lowest rank coal. It is compact in texture contains 20 to 60% of moisture. It breaks up into small pieces on air-drying. Air-dried sample of lignite contains 60 to 70% of carbon, 20% of oxygen. 5% of hydrogen and remaining ash. It burns with long smoky flame. The calorific value on air-dry basis ranges from 5500 to 7000 kcal per kg. It is normally used in the form of small briquettes which are obtained by compressing the dried powder. Lignite briquettes are used as household fuel and for steam raising in boilers. Its most important use is in the manufacture of producer gas. Lignite deposits are found in Assam, Kashmir, Rajasthan (at Palana) and at Neyveli in Madras state.

**3. Bituminous Coals (Common coal) :** The colour of different grades of bituminous coals change from pitch black to dark grey and these usually soil hands. These possess laminated structure of alternate very bright and dull layers. The common bituminous coals are sub-classified on the basis of percentage of carbon as :

(a) Sub-bituminous coal,

(b) Bituminous coal and

(c) Semi-bituminous coal.

**(a) Sub-bituminous coals :** These are pitch black in colour. They are homogeneous and smooth in appearance. The moisture (11 to 16%) and volatile content (32 to 36%) are high. On exposure these crumble into small pieces. These are non-caking coals. The calorific value is about 7000 kcal per kg; the carbon content (including carbon present in volatile matter) varies from 75 to 78% and oxygen content from 10 to 15%.

**(b) Bituminous coals :** These possess a banded appearance. Their carbon content ranges from 78 to 90% and volatile matter from 20 to 40%. The calorific value on the ash free basis is about 8000-8500 kcal/kg. These possess the caking property and hence these are used in industries for making metallurgical coke, coal gas, for steam generation and domestic heating.

**(c) Semi-bituminous coals :** These have low volatile matter (9 to 13 %) and are rich in carbon (90 – 93 %). These also possess caking property and are therefore used for coke manufacture. Their calorific value is about 8500 to 8600 kcal/kg. Bituminous coals are found in Bihar, Bengal, Orissa and Madhya Pradesh, states of India.

**4.  Anthracite Coal :** It is a highest rank coal with carbon content 90 to 98% and very low in volatile matter (3 to 6%) and moisture content (2 to 3%). These are hardest of all kinds of coal and is supposed to be the final stage in coalification of wood. These are quite dense and lustrous in appearance. Because of low volatile matter, they ignite with difficulty, burn without smoke and produce intense local heating. They do not possess caking property. Their calorific value is about 8600 to 8700 kcal/kg and ash content is as low as 3%. These are used for household purposes, for steam raising, metallurgical processes where no smoke but high local heating is necessary.

Anthracite coal reserves are located in Kashmir and in Eastern Himalayas, of India.

## 3.11 SELECTION OF COAL

The following factors should be taken into consideration while selecting the coal for a particular use :

(1) *Calorific value should be high.* Higher is the calorific value, better is the coal. This will reduce the cost of storage and handling.

(2) *Moisture content* should be low as it reduces the heating value. Moisture also involves loss of money as it is paid at the same rate as the coal.

(3) *Ash content* should be *low*. Ash being non-combustible matter, reduces the heating value of coal. Moreover, it adds to the cost of storage, handling and disposal. Each percent of ash is equivalent to loss of 1.5% of heat. Composition of ash is important to metallurgists because the proper selection of flux for slag formation depends on it. When coal is used in boiler, fusion temperature of ash is of great importance. If the constituents of ash, fuse at temperature then lumps of ash (clinker) will be formed. This clinker formation results in loss of fuel. Moreover, low melting ash produces molten slag which has a tendency to damage the refractory lining of boiler. Therefore for common boilers, the fusion temperature of ash should be as high as 1430°C.

(4) *Calorific intensity* of coal should be high. It is the maximum temperature reached on complete combustion of coal in the theoretical amount of air and depends on quantity, nature and specific heat of the gaseous products formed. Theoretically, the

$$\text{Flame temperature} = \frac{\text{Heat of combustion + Sensible heat of air}}{\text{Total of (Combustion products} \times \text{Sp. heats)}}$$

(5) *Size* of coal should be uniform as smaller particles mixed with larger lumps interfere with the free movement of air and gases.

(6) *Coking quality* : Coal is called *caking* if on heating it softens, becomes plastic and particles of it fuse together giving large coherent masses impervious to air. Such coal is difficult to be oxidised. If the residue (i.e., coke) on heating is porous, hard and strong then the original coal is known as *coking coal* while if the residue swells excessively the original coal is called *non-coking coal.* Thus all coking coals are caking coals but all caking coals are not coking coals. Coking coals are required in metallurgical processes.

(7) Sulphur and phosphorus content for metallurgical purposes should be as low as possible. Impurities of coke are likely to be transferred to the metal because of direct contact between coke and metal. P and S badly affect the metal properties.

## 3.12 ANALYSIS OF COAL

In the preceding article the implications of different variable constituents on the quality of coal have been discussed. To ascertain the quality of coal, the percentage of these variable constituents should be known. For this purpose, the coal is subjected to analysis. The analysis is of two types : (1) Proximate analysis and (2) Ultimate analysis.

## 3.13 PROXIMATE ANALYSIS

In proximate analysis, percentages of (a) Moisture, (b) Volatile matter, (c) Ash, (d) Fixed carbon, present in the sample of coal are determined.

**(a) Moisture content :** An accurately weighed quantity of finely powdered coal sample is taken in a crucible with lid and heated in an electric hot air oven at a temperature of $105 \pm 3°C$ for one hour. Then the crucible alongwith its contents is cooled to room temperature in a dessicator and weighed again. The loss in weight of the coal and the percentage of moisture are calculated as below :

Let, (1) Mass of empty crucible with lid $\qquad = m_1$ gm

(2) Mass of (crucible with lid + sample) $\qquad = m_2$ gm

(3) Mass of (crucible with lid + anhydrous sample) $\quad = m_3$ gm

∴ Mass of coal sample $\qquad = (m_2 - m_1)$ gm

Mass of moisture $\qquad = (m_2 - m_3)$ gm

(i.e., loss in wt. of sample)

∴ Percentage of moisture $= \dfrac{\text{Mass of moisture}}{\text{Mass of coal sample}} \times 100$

$= \dfrac{(m_2 - m_3) \times 100}{(m_2 - m_1)}$

**(b) Percentage of volatile matter :** A known mass of the dried (moisture free) sample of coal in (a) is then heated in a silica crucible with lid at 950 ± 20° C in an electric furnace for exactly 7 minutes and the loss in mass is reported as volatile matter on percentage basis. The calculations are as below :

Let, (1) Mass of empty crucible with lid                  $= m_1$ gm

    (2) Mass of (crucible with lid + dried sample)         $= m_2$ gm

    (3) Mass of (crucible with lid + sample left over)     $= m_3$ gm

∴       Mass of dried sample taken                   $= (m_2 - m_1)$ gm

∴       Mass of volatile matter                      $= (m_2 - m_3)$ gm

$$\text{\% of volatile matter } = \left\{ \frac{\text{Mass of volatile matter removed}}{\text{Mass of dried sample}} \times 100 \right\}$$

$$= \frac{(m_2 - m_3) \times 100}{(m_2 - m_1)}$$

**(c) Ash content :** A known mass of the dried coal sample from (a) above is burnt in an open crucible (silica) in presence of air at 750-800°C in a muffle furnace till there are no black specks of carbon left behind. The silica crucible with residue is carefully cooled in dessicator and weighed. The process of heating, cooling, and weighing is repeated till constant mass of residue is obtained. The constant mass of residue is reported as ash on percentage basis as below.

Let, (1) Mass of empty crucible                            $= m_1$ gm

    (2) Mass of (crucible + coal sample)              $= m_2$ gm

    (3) Mass of (crucible + residue i.e., ash)        $= m_3$ gm

∴       Mass of coal sample taken                    $= (m_2 - m_1)$ gm

        Mass of ash formed                          $= (m_3 - m_1)$ gm

∴       $\text{\% of ash} = \dfrac{\text{Mass of ash} \times 100}{\text{Mass of coal sample}} = \dfrac{(m_3 - m_1) \times 100}{(m_2 - m_1)}$

**(d) % of fixed carbon :** It is ash free coke left after volatile matter has volatilised from coal. It is calculated by subtracting the percentage of moisture, ash and volatile matter from 100. Thus :

     % of fixed carbon = [100 – % of (Moisture + ash + volatile matter)]

**Importance of Proximate analysis :** By knowing the percentages of different constituents in a sample of coal, the probable effects of these on the quality of coal can be judged. This will facilitate the selection of a proper coal for the job in hand, for example :

The moisture content reduces the calorific value as well as excess moisture may quench the fire in the furnace, coal with high volatile matter burns with a long flame, high smoke and has low calorific value. It affects the furnace volume and arrangement of heating surfaces.

Ash is useless matter and it reduces the calorific value. Sometimes it causes trouble due to clinker formation which chokes the interspaces of grades on which coal is burnt, thereby making air supply irregular.

Higher the percentage of fixed carbon, greater will be the calorific value and hence better the quality of coal.

## 3.14 ULTIMATE ANALYSIS

In ultimate analysis, the percentages of the constituent elements are determined.

**(a) % of Carbon and Hydrogen :** Carbon and hydrogen are estimated together in a single experiment in which about 1 gm of the finely powdered coal sample (accurately weighed) is burnt in a stream of dry oxygen in a combustion apparatus. Carbon and hydrogen of the coal will be converted to $CO_2$ and $H_2O$ respectively. These gaseous products of combustion are passed through two 'U' tubes, one containing anhydrous calcium chloride ($CaCl_2$) and the other solution of KOH. Water vapour ($H_2O$) is absorbed by $CaCl_2$ while $CO_2$ is absorbed by KOH. By knowing the increase in mass of these tubes, the percentage of hydrogen and carbon are calculated as below :

The reactions are :

$$\text{Combustion}: \begin{bmatrix} C + O_2 \rightarrow CO_2 \\ 12 \qquad\qquad 44 \end{bmatrix}; \begin{bmatrix} 2H_2 + O_2 \rightarrow 2\,H_2O \\ 4 \qquad\qquad\quad 36 \end{bmatrix}$$

Absorption : $2KOH + CO_2 \rightarrow K_2CO_3 + H_2O$

$$CaCl_2 + 7H_2O \rightarrow CaCl_2 \cdot 7H_2O$$

Let,                         the mass of coal sample taken $= x$ gm

Increase in the mass of KOH tube $= y$ gm

Increase in the mass of $CaCl_2$ tube $= z$ gm

$\therefore$                    Amount of carbon in sample $= \dfrac{12 \times y}{44}$

$\therefore$          % of Carbon $= \dfrac{\text{Increase in mass of KOH tube} \times 12 \times 100}{\text{Mass of coal sample taken} \times 44}$

$$= \dfrac{y \times 12 \times 100}{x \times 44}$$

Amount of hydrogen in sample $= \dfrac{2 \times z}{18}$

$\therefore$          % of Hydrogen $= \dfrac{\text{Increase in mass of } CaCl_2 \text{ tube} \times 2 \times 100}{\text{Mass of coal sample taken} \times 18}$

$$= \dfrac{z \times 2 \times 100}{x \times 18}$$

**(b) % of Nitrogen :** Nitrogen is estimated by heating about 1 gm of accurately weighed finely divided coal with concentrated sulphuric acid alongwith $K_2SO_4$ as catalyst in a long necked flask called Kjeldahl's flask till the solution becomes clear (i.e., nitrogen present is quantitatively converted into ammonium sulphate). This clear solution of $(NH_4)_2SO_4$ is then boiled with a 50% solution of NaOH in excess. The liberated ammonia is distilled over and absorbed in a known excess volume of standard (say 0.1 N) sulphuric acid. The unused acid is then determined by back titration with standard (say 0.1 N) NaOH. Thus (Volume of 0.1 N $H_2SO_4$ taken) – (Volume of $H_2SO_4$ unused) = Volume of 0.1 N $H_2SO_4$ consumed for neutralisation of ammonia, (V ml). Knowing the volume of acid consumed by ammonia, the percentage of 'N' in coal sample is calculated as :

$$\text{% of Nitrogen } = \frac{\text{Volume of acid consumed} \times \text{Normality of acid} \times 1.4}{\text{Mass of coal sample taken}}$$

**(c) % of Sulphur :** When a known mass of a sample of coal is burnt in bomb calorimeter, the sulphur present is oxidised to sulphates. The washings of bomb calorimeter are treated with barium chloride solution when barium sulphate is precipitated. The precipitate is filtered, washed and heated to a constant mass. Knowing the mass of $BaSO_4$ formed, the percentage of sulphur is calculated as below :

(1) Mass of coal sample taken    = $m_1$ gm

(2) Mass of $BaSO_4$ formed    = $m_2$ gm

$$\text{Amount of sulphur in } BaSO_4 = \frac{32 \times m_2}{233}$$

$$\text{So % of Sulphur } = \frac{32 \times m_2 \times 100}{233 \times m_1}$$

**(d) % of Oxygen :** Oxygen content is determined by difference. The sum total of percentages of carbon, hydrogen, nitrogen, and sulphur when subtracted from 100, the percentage of oxygen is obtained.

$\therefore$         % of Oxygen  = 100 – (% of C + % of H + % of N + % of S)

**Importance of Ultimate analysis :** By knowing the percentage of the constituent elements in a sample of coal, their effects on the quality of coal can be ascertained. This facilitates the proper selection of coal for the required purpose. For example :

Greater the percentage of carbon, better is the coal quality. Higher percentage of carbon in coal reduces the size of combustion chamber required.

Hydrogen is mostly present as volatile matter which reduces the calorific value of fuel, hence percentage of hydrogen in coal should be as low as possible.

Presence of nitrogen in coal is undesirable as it is non-combustible, non-supporter of combustion and thus reduces the calorific value.

Though sulphur increases the heating value of coal, the products of combustion (i.e., $SO_2$ and $SO_3$) are harmful. These gases have corroding effect on equipments and also cause atmospheric pollution. Hence sulphur content should be as low as possible.

As the percentage of oxygen in coal increases, the capacity of the coal to hold the moisture also increases. This results in lowering of calorific value and decrease in the caking power of coal. Hence oxygen is undesirable in coal.

# 3.15 PULVERIZED COAL

The rate of combustion of solid fuels, like coal, is generally slow, because of the difficulty of thorough contact between the solid fuel and oxygen. The intimate contact between air and the fuel can be achieved by either (1) increasing the rate of oxygen supply, but this results in wastage of large amount of heat being carried away by air itself, or (2) by finely powdering (i.e. pulverizing) the coal so that its free surface area is increased resulting in large surface area of the fuel coming in intimate contact with air.

The process of pulverization (preparation of fine dust) of coal consists of crushing, drying and grinding to fine powdered (75 – 85% below 74 μm) form.

Combustion of fuel in the pulverized form offers the following advantages over the combustion of lumpy form.

**Advantages of Pulverization of Coal :**

1. Pulverized coal can be easily transported either by screw conveyors or by forcing a stream of air.

2. The rate of combustion of pulverized coal can be easily controlled, the heating can be started or stopped as and when needed. This avoids wastage of fuel.

3. The flame produced is large and temperature is more uniform because of uniform and complete combustion.

4. Low grade coals with high percentage of ash can be used efficiently by pulverizing them. This is particularly significant for the Indian coals as most of them have high ash content.

5. Both oxidizing and reducing atmosphere can be maintained in the furnace as required. This is important in metallurgical operations.

6. Pulverized coal responds well to automatic control.

7. Thermal efficiency is higher and higher temperatures can be obtained.

8. There is no formation of fuel bed as in the case of lumpy coal. Hence there is no clinker trouble as in the case of lumps of coal.

**Disadvantages :**

1. It requires extra cost for pulverization.

2. The ash produced by burning of pulverized coal being finely divided is carried over by flue gases and is discharged in the surrounding area, causing nuisance.

## 3.16 THEORETICAL CALCULATION OF CALORIFIC VALUE

**Dulong's formula for theoretical calculation of calorific value of solid fuel :**

Calorific values of fuel constituents are as follows :

Hydrogen = 34500 kcal/kg, Carbon = 8080 kcal/kg and Sulphur = 2240 kcal/kg. The oxygen if present in the fuel, is assumed to be present in combined form with hydrogen.

Therefore, amount of hydrogen available for combustion

= Total mass of hydrogen in fuel – Fixed hydrogen

= Total mass of hydrogen in fuel – (1/8) Mass of oxygen in the fuel

Dulong's formula for

HCV = 1/100 [8080 C + 34500 (H – O/8) + 2240 S] kcal/kg

HCV = 1/100 [8080 C + 34500 (H – O/8) + 2240 S] × Specific heat (4.18) kJ

where C, H, S and O are the % of carbon, hydrogen, sulphur and oxygen in the fuel respectively.

Therefore,    LCV = HCV – (0.09 × H × 587) in cal/g or kcal/kg

LCV = HCV – (0.09 × H × 587) × Specific heat (4.18)

**Numerical problem :** A coal has the following ultimate analysis, carbon 84%, sulphur 1.5%, nitrogen 0.6%, hydrogen 5.5% and oxygen 8.4%. Find out gross and net calorific value with the help of Dulong's formula.

**Given :** C = 84, H = 5.5, O = 8.4 and S = 1.5.

HCV = 1/100 [8080 C + 34500 (H – O/8) + 2240 S]

HCV = 1/100 [8080 × 84 + 34500 (5.5 – 8.4/8) + 2240 × 1.5] = 8356 kcal/kg

= 8356 × 4.18 = 34928.08 kJ

LCV = HCV – (0.09 × H × 587) = 8356 – (0.09 × 5.5 × 587)

= 8065.485 kcal/kg

= 8065.485 × 4.18 = 33713.72 kJ

## SOLVED PROBLEMS

**Problem 3.1 :**

A Bomb calorimeter experiment gave the following data :

(i)     Weight of coal sample = 1.1 g

(ii)    Water equivalent of calorimeter = 550 g

(iii)   Weight of water taken = 2.46 kg

(iv)   Observed rise of temperature = 2.51°C

(v)    Cooling correction = 0.043°C

(vi)   Correction due to acids = 60.0 cal

(vii)  Fuse wire correction = 4.0 cal

(viii) Specific heat of water = 4.18 kJ· kg$^{-1}$· °C$^{-1}$

Calculate the calorific value.

**Solution :**

$$\text{Gross C.V.} = \frac{(W + w) \cdot S \cdot (t_2 - t_1 + t_C) - (t_A + t_F)}{m}$$

**Given :** (1) W = 2.46 kg, (2) w = 550 = 0.55 kg, (3) S = 4.18 kJ$\cdot$ kg$^{-1}$°C$^{-1}$

(4) $t_2 - t_1$ = 2.51 °C, (5) $t_C$ = 0.043°C, (6) $t_A$ = 60 cal = 0.06 kcal = 0.06 × 4.18 = 0.2508 kJ

(7) $t_F$ = 4 cal = 0.004 × 4.18 = 0.01672 kJ, (8) m = 1.1 g = 0.0011 kg

$$\therefore \qquad \text{Gross C.V.} = \frac{(2.46 + 0.55) \times 4.18 \times (2.51 + 0.043) - (0.2508 + 0.01672)}{0.0011}$$

$$= \frac{(3.01 \times 4.18 \times 2.553) - (0.26752)}{0.0011}$$

$$= 28958.014 \text{ kJ}\cdot\text{kg}^{-1}$$

---

**Problem 3.2 :**

*Calculate the calorific value of a sample of coal from the following data :*

*(1) Mass of coal = 0.6 g,*

*(2) Water and water equivalent of calorimeter = 2.2 kg,*

*(3) Specific heat of water = 4.18 kJ$\cdot$ kg$^{-1}$ °C$^{-1}$,*

*(4) Rise in temperature = 6.52°C.*

*If the coal sample contains 5% hydrogen, calculate the gross and net calorific values of the coal sample. Take the latent heat of steam as 587 kcal/kg.*

**Solution :**

$$Q\text{ (Gross)} = \frac{W \times S \times (t_2 - t_1)}{m}$$

**Given :** (1) W = 2.2 kg, (2) S = 4.18 kJ$\cdot$ kg$^{-1}$°C$^{-1}$, (3) $(t_2 - t_1)$ = 6.52°C,

(4) m = 0.6 g = 0.6 × 10$^{-3}$ kg, (5) H = 5 %, (6) L = 587 × 4.18 kJ/kg

$$Q\text{ (Gross)} = \frac{2.2 \times 4.18 \times 6.52}{0.6 \times 10^{-3}} = 9.9929 \times 10^4 \text{ kJ}\cdot\text{kg}^{-1}$$

$$Q\text{ (Net)} = Q\text{ (Gross)} - 0.09 \times H \times 587 \times 4.18$$

$$= 99929 - 0.09 \times 5 \times 587 \times 4.18$$

$$= 99929 - 1104.147$$

$$= 98824.853 = 9.8824 \times 10^4 \text{ kJ}\cdot\text{kg}^{-1}$$

---

**Problem 3.3 :**

Calculate the calorific value of a gaseous fuel at STP from the following data :

(1) Volume of gas burnt = 0.02 m³,

(2) Temperature of gas = 293°K,

(3) Mass of water passing through calorimeter = 4.2 kg,

(4) Rise in temperature = 17.5°K,

(5) Absolute pressure of gas = 102 × 10³ Nm⁻²,

(6) Specific heat of water = 4.18 kJ· kg⁻¹ °C⁻¹

(7) Absolute standard atmospheric pressure = 101325 Nm⁻²

**Solution :**

(i) Heat absorbed by cold water

= Mass of water × Specific heat × Rise in temperature

= 4.2 × 4.18 × 17.5

= 307.23 kJ

(ii) Reduce the volume of gas at STP using gas equation

$$\frac{P_1 V_1}{T_1} = \frac{P_2 V_2}{T_2}$$

∴    $$\frac{102 \times 10^3 \times 0.02}{293} = \frac{101.325 \times 10^3 \times V}{273}$$

∴    $$V = \frac{102 \times 0.02 \times 273}{293 \times 101.325} = \frac{556.92}{29688.225} = 0.0187 \text{ m}^3$$

(iii)    Calorific value, $Q = \dfrac{\text{Heat absorbed by cold water}}{\text{Volume of gas}}$

$$= \frac{307.23}{0.0187} = 16429.4 \text{ kJ·m}^{-3}$$

**Problem 3.4 :**

The following observations were made in Boy's gas calorimeter experiment :

(1) Volume of gas burnt = 0.1 m³ at STP,

(2) Mass of water heated = 25 kg,

(3) Rise in temperature of water = 13°C,

(4) Weight of steam condensed = 0.025 kg,

(5) Latent heat of steam = (587 × 4.18) kJ/kg

Calculate the gross and net calorific values of the gas.

**Solution :**

Heat absorbed by cold water = Mass of water × Specific heat × Rise in temperature

$$= 25 \times 4.18 \times 13 = 1358.5$$

$$\therefore \qquad Q\ (Gross) \ = \ \frac{1358.5}{0.1} = 13585 \ kJ \cdot m^{-3}$$

$$Q\ (Net) \ = \ Q\ (Gross) - \left(\frac{mL}{V}\right)$$

$$= \ 13585 - \frac{0.025 \times 587 \times 4.18}{0.1}$$

$$= \ 13585 - 613.415$$

$$= \ 12971.585 \ kJ \cdot m^{-3}$$

### Problem 3.5 :

*A sample of a certain variety of coal contains 60 % carbon, 33 % oxygen, 6 % hydrogen, 0.5 % sulphur, 0.2 % nitrogen and 0.3 % ash. Calculate the gross and net calorific values of a coal sample.*

**Solution :**

Since nitrogen and ash do not produce any heat on combining with oxygen, therefore they are not accounted for.

$$Gross\ C.V. \ = \ \frac{1}{100}\left[8080\ C + 34500 \left(H - \frac{O}{8}\right) + 2240\ S\right]$$

$$Gross\ C.V. \ = \ \frac{1}{100}\left[8080 \times 60 + 34500 \left(6 - \frac{33}{8}\right) + 2240 \times 0.5\right]$$

$$= \ \frac{1}{100}\left[484800 + 34500\ (6 - 4.125) + 1120\right]$$

$$= \ 5506.07 \ kcal/kg$$

$$= \ 5506.07 \times 4.18 = 23015.37 \ kJ \cdot kg^{-1}$$

$$Net\ C.V. \ = \ Gross\ C.V. - 0.09 \times 6 \times 587 \times 4.18$$

$$= \ 23015.37 - 1324.97 = 21690.4 \ kJ \cdot kg^{-1}$$

### Problem 3.6 :

*0.25 gm of coal sample on burning in combustion chamber in the current of dry oxygen, was found to increase the weight of 'U' tube with anhydrous $CaCl_2$, by 0.075 gm and KOH tube by 0.52 gm. Find out % of carbon and hydrogen in coal.*

*Given : Weight of coal sample = 0.25 gm, Increase in the weight of 'U' tube containing anhydrous $CaCl_2$ tube is 0.075 gm and KOH tube is 0.52 gm.*

**Solution :**

Therefore,

$$\% \text{ of carbon} = \frac{(\text{Increase in weight of KOH tube} \times 12 \times 100)}{(\text{Weight of coal sample taken} \times 44)}$$

$$= \frac{(0.52 \times 12 \times 100)}{(0.25 \times 44)} = 56.72\%$$

and    $$\% \text{ of hydrogen} = \frac{(\text{Increase in weight of CaCl}_2 \text{ tube} \times 2 \times 100)}{(\text{Weight of coal sample taken} \times 18)}$$

$$= \frac{(0.075 \times 2 \times 100)}{(0.25 \times 18)} = 3.33\%$$

### Problem 3.7 :

0.75 gm of coal is combusted in Bomb calorimeter. The solution from the bottom of bomb put on treatment with $BaCl_2$ solution forms 0.0465 gm $BaSO_4$. Calculate the % of sulphur in coal.

Given : Weight of coal sample = 0.75 gm, Weight of $BaSO_4$ = 0.0465 gm.

**Solution :**

$$\text{Therefore, } \% \text{ of sulphur} = \frac{(\text{Weight of BaSO}_4 \text{ obtained} \times 32 \times 100)}{(\text{Weight of coal sample taken in bomb} \times 233)}$$

$$= \frac{(0.0465 \times 32 \times 100)}{(0.75 \times 233)} = 0.85\%$$

### Problem 3.8 :

$NH_3$ gas is liberated on heating the content of Kjeldahl's flask. It neutralizes 7.15 ml of 0.12 N HCl solution. Find out the % of nitrogen, if weight of coal taken for experiment was 0.45 gm.

Given : Weight of coal taken = 0.45 gm, Normality of HCl = 0.12 N, Volume of HCl consumed = 7.15 ml.

**Solution :**

$$\text{Therefore, } \% \text{ of nitrogen} = \frac{(\text{Volume of acid used} \times \text{Normality} \times 1.4)}{(\text{Weight of coal sample taken})}$$

$$= \frac{(7.15 \times 0.12 \times 32 \times 100)}{(0.45)} = 2.67\%$$

### Problem 3.9 :

2.5 gm of coal sample was placed in silica crucible and heated at 1100°C for one hour in electric furnace. The residue 2.015 gm on heating in crucible with lid at 950°C left 1.528 gm after 7 minutes. This residue on burning produces a constant mass of 0.245 gm ash. Calculate the proximate analysis of coal.

Given : Weight of coal = 2.5 gm, Weight of moisture = 2.5 – 2.015 = 0.487 gm,

Weight of volatile matter = 2.015 – 1.528 = 0.487 gm, Weight of ash = 0.245 gm.

**Solution :**   % of moisture $= \dfrac{\text{Loss in weight}}{\text{Weight of coal taken}} \times 100$

$$= \dfrac{0.485}{2.5} \times 100 = 19.4\%$$

% of volatile matter $= \dfrac{\text{Loss in weight due to removal of volatile matter}}{\text{Weight of coal sample taken (initial)}} \times 100$

$$= \dfrac{0.487}{2.5} \times 100 = 19.5\ \%$$

% of ash $= \dfrac{\text{Weight of ash left}}{\text{Weight of coal taken}} \times 100$

$$= \dfrac{0.245}{2.5} \times 100 = 9.8\%$$

% of fixed carbon $=$ 100 – (% of moisture + volatile matter + ash)

$$= 100 - (\% \text{ of } 19.4 + 19.5 + 9.8) = 51.3\ \%$$

## 3.17 LIQUID FUELS

They are very important as almost all internal combustion engines run on them. They are also used in heat generation in oven and furnaces.

## 3.17.1 Origin of Petroleum/Crude Oil

## (Theories underlying petroleum formation)

**(1) Inorganic Theory (Mendeleef's theory) :**

The theory was put forth by Berthelot. Acetylene is considered as basic material for oil formation and large quantities of acetylene were assumed to have been produced by reaction of water with carbides which in turn were formed by the action of alkali metals on carbonates. The acetylene was converted to petroleum at high temperature and pressure.

$$CaCO_3 \xrightarrow{\text{alkali metal}} CaC_2 \xrightarrow{H_2O} HC \equiv CH \longrightarrow \text{Petroleum}$$

Calcium carbonate        Calcium carbide  Acetylene

The another theory put forth by Mendeleeff says that the action of dilute acids or hot water on mixed iron and manganese carbides produced a mixture of hydrocarbons from which petroleum is evolved.

$$Fe_3C \ + \ Mn_3C \xrightarrow{H^{\oplus}/H_2O} \text{Hydrocarbons} \to \text{Petroleum}$$

Iron carbide    Manganese carbide

## (2) Organic Theory (Engler's theory) :

It is most widely accepted theory, some of the evidences which suggest that oil has organic origin are :

(1) High molecular weight compounds (as $C_{30}$ and above) are common in living organisms and petroleum.

(2) The petroleum contains porphyrins and nitrogen substances which are commonly found in living matter.

(3) Petroleum has presence of organic remains such as spores and pollens.

(4) Petroleum rotates the plane of plane polarised light like plant sugar solution.

(5) Nearly 98 % oil is derived from sedimentary environment and sedimentary rock.

The existence of petroleum source rocks is outcome of formation, accumulation and preservation of undegraded organic matter both of vegetable and animal origin in a sedimentary basin, in marine environment. The biomass involved was originally composed of proteins, carbohydrates, lipids which cover fat substances such as animal fat, vegetable oil and waxes. Lignins present in plant tissue are high molecular weight polyphenols. Tannins contain both phenolic and carboxyl group on their aromatic structure.

For formation of sedimentary rock, preservation of dead organic matter is essential. For this absence of molecular oxygen, matter is essential. [If there is enough supply of molecular oxygen, the organic matter will be destroyed due to oxidation]. The non-lipid fraction of biomass is soluble in water and gets adsorbed on fine clay sized mineral particles. Water insoluble lipid fraction is in particle form. Both, the adsorbed material on fine clay sized minerals and particulate organic materials, are of low density and are carried to calm water where they get deposited. This deposition of fine grained particles limits the access of dissolved molecular oxygen and enhances the chance of preservation. Initially, bacteria must have degraded this organic matter. At surface the aerobic bacteria and at depth anaerobic bacteria were responsible for transformation, which degraded this material to get their food and oxygen for their survival. The residue of unused organic material was further converted to petroleum as a result of temperature, pressure and time. Methane was main byproduct of the transformation.

However, mixed theory came to the force following inability of both theories to explain organic and inorganic (both) nature of petroleum.

# EXERCISE

1. Define net calorific value of a fuel.
2. Define the term calorific value of a fuel. What do you understand by gross and net calorific value of a fuel ? State any two advantages and two disadvantages of gaseous fuels over solid fuels.
3. What is meant by calorific value of a fuel ? How calorific value of solid fuel is determined ?
4. Draw a neat diagram and explain the working of a Bomb calorimeter.
5. How are fuels classified ? What is meant by lower calorific value of a fuel ?
6. How the calorific value of a gaseous fuel is determined ?
7. (a) How is calorific value of a non-volatile liquid determined by Bomb calorimeter ?
   (b) The following data is obtained in a bomb calorimeter experiment :
      (i) Mass of fuel = 0.85 g,
      (ii) Mass of water taken in the calorimeter = 2000 g,
      (iii) Water equivalent of the calorimeter = 540 g,
      (iv) Difference in final and initial temperature = 1.9°C,
      (v) Cooling correction = 0.041°C,
      (vi) Fuse wire correction = 3.8 calories,
      (vii) Acid correction = 48.8 calories.
   Calculate the net calorific value of the fuel if it contains 3.6 % of hydrogen and 1.2 % oxygen.
8. Calculate the approximate calorific value (by Dulong formula) of a coal sample having the following composition : C = 80 %; H = 3.5 %; S = 2.8 %; O = 5.0 %; N = 1.5 %; and ash = 7.2 %.
9. Composition of a coal sample by weight is : C = 81%; H = 5.0%; O = 8.5 %; S = 1.0 %; N = 1.5 % and ash = 3 %. Calculate the gross and net calorific values of the coal sample.
10. During the determination of calorific value of a volatile fuel by Boy's calorimeter, the following observations are recorded :
   (i) Volume of the gaseous fuel burnt at NTP = 0.093 $m^3$;
   (ii) Weight of water used for cooling the combustion products = 30.5 kg;
   (iii) Weight of steam condensed = 0.031 kg;
   (iv) Temperature of inlet water = 26.1 °C;
   (v) Temperature of outlet water = 36.5 °C.
      Determine the net calorific value of the volatile fuel per cubic metre at NTP, provided that the heat liberated in condensation of water vapour and cooling the condensate is 587 kcal/kg.
11. State and explain the criteria of selecting a proper fuel for a particular purpose.
12. Compare and contrast the solid, liquid and gaseous fuels.

13. Draw a neat sketch of Bomb calorimeter and explain how the water equivalent of Bomb calorimeter is determined.
14. Draw a neat sketch of Boy's calorimeter and explain its principle.
15. Define and explain the following terms in relation to fuels : (a) Kindling temperature, (b) Calorific value, (c) Higher calorific value, (d) Lower calorific value.
16. 1.05 gram of a fuel on complete combustion in excess of oxygen increased the temperature of water in the calorimeter by 3.8 $^\circ$C. The water in the calorimeter was 1650 gram. Determine the water equivalent of calorimeter, if calorific value of fuel is 6300 cal/gm.
17. Explain in brief the significance of various corrections that are made in determining the calorific value of a fuel by Bomb calorimeter.
18. Explain how the different factors are determined in proximate analysis of coal.
19. What are the characteristics of a good fuel ?
20. Give the significance of ultimate analysis of fuel. How is the percentage of carbon and hydrogen determined in this analysis ?
21. How would you assess the good quality of coal on the basis of proximate analysis ?
22. Name the elements which affect the calorific value of a coal and state their effect.
23. Why should coal of good quality contain low percentage of moisture and high percentage of carbon ?
24. Why should a good fuel have high calorific value but low content of non-combustible matter ?
25. What are the types of coal based on the degree of transformation ? Give the carbon content and use of each type of coal.
26. Define fuel. How the fuels are classified ?
27. Explain the importance of ultimate analysis of coal.
28. Name the highest rank of coal obtained from coalification of wood. Give its composition, properties and uses.
29. (a) What is a fuel ?
    (b) How are fuels classified ?
    (c) What do you understand by gross and net calorific value of fuel ?
30. What is a coal ? Name the different varieties of coal and give the percentage of carbon and calorific value of each variety.
31. (a) What do you understand by the term 'calorific value' of a fuel ?
    (b) What are its units in different systems of measurement ?
    (c) What is the criterion for selecting fuel for industrial purpose ?
32. How is the calorific value of a solid fuel determined ?
33. Calculate the gross and net calorific value of a coal sample having the following composition :
    C = 80%, H = 7%, O = 3%, S = 3.5%, N = 2.1% and ash = 4.4%.

34. Write notes on :
    (a) Bomb calorimeter
    (b) Boy's calorimeter
35. Explain the origin, composition and refining of petroleum.
36. Explain the octane number of petrol.
37. What is knocking ? Explain it.
38. Explain the cetane number or rating of diesel oil.
39. Give merits and demerits of power alcohol or gasohol.
40. Explain preparation and properties of biodiesel.
41. Explain composition, properties and applications of natural gas.
42. What is cracking ? Give its advantages.
43. Explain the preparation of synthetic petrol.
44. Explain refining of gasoline.
45. What is reforming ? Explain any one method.
46. Explain the preparation of oil gas.
47. Explain the analysis of flue gas.

# CORROSION AND ITS PREVENTION

## 4.1 DEFINITION

Corrosion is a slow and continuous phenomenon. Corrosion costs enormous money each year in replacement, maintenance and repair of machine parts. Corrosion is the degradation of a material over a long period due to environmental effect.

**Corrosion can be defined as the destruction of a solid body through chemical** (e.g. dry gases) **or electrochemical action** (e.g. acids, alkalies and salts) **starting at its surface.** It is invariantly used to denote destruction of metals.

**Causes of Corrosion :**

Most metals exist in nature as oxides, carbonates, sulphides, sulphates and silicates etc. They are extracted from their corresponding ores by reduction process which requires considerable amount of energy. So isolated metals are in higher energy state or less stable state than in their corresponding ores (less energy or more stable state).

It is the natural tendency of isolated metals to return to their lower energy state i.e. oxides, sulphides, carbonates etc. Thus, the corrosion of metals can be regarded as reverse process of reduction of metals from their ores (Metallurgical process) and it is a spontaneous process. Only in inert atmospheres and vacuums, metals are free from corrosion.

## 4.2 TYPES OF CORROSION

The corrosion of metals is a result of chemical reaction between metal surface and the environment. Depending on types of attack on metal, corrosion is classified as

**(A) Direct chemical or Dry corrosion :** The corrosion caused by chemical reaction of gases such as oxygen, halogens, hydrogen, nitrogen and sulphur dioxide with metal or alloy surface is called dry corrosion.

**(B) Electrochemical or Wet corrosion :** Corrosion phenomena are electrochemical in nature and involve the presence of an electrolyte in contact with metal. Electrolyte is an aqueous solution of salt, acid or alkali. This type of corrosion of metals occurring as a result of electrochemical reaction between metal surface and electrolyte is called wet corrosion.

But there is no sharp dividing line between these two general types of attack on metals.

## 4.2.1 Dry or Atmospheric or Direct Chemical Corrosion

The extent of corrosion due to attack of atmospheric gases depends on the chemical affinity between gas and metal as well as on the ability of metal to form a protective film.

**(i) Corrosion Due to Oxygen or Oxidative Corrosion :**

Surfaces of many metals, oxidise very rapidly when they are exposed to air.

$$2\,M + O_2 \longrightarrow 2\,MO$$

Formation of oxide film and their growth is a stepwise process. At the initial stage, oxygen gas is adsorbed on the metal surface - Van der Waal's forces are responsible for this adsorption. Oxidation by gaseous oxygen is an electrochemical process, it is not simply combination of metal with oxygen. After adsorption, oxygen molecules dissociate into atoms or ions. These oxygen ions combine with metal by electron transfer or electron sharing between oxygen and metal atoms. The mechanism of oxidative corrosion is diffusion.

$$M \longrightarrow M^{n+} + ne^- \text{ (oxidation)}$$

$$O_2 + ne^- \longrightarrow 2O^{n-} \text{ (reduction)}$$

i.e. $$M^{n+} + 2O^{n-} \longrightarrow MO_2$$

where, n is an oxidation state of metal and it can be +1, +2, +3 ……

This type of adsorption is called **chemisorption**, it continues till unimolecular oxide layer covers the metal surface.

All metal oxides conduct both ions and electrons to some extent. The oxide layer serves as (1) an ionic conductor (electrolyte), (2) an electronic conductor, (3) an electrode at which oxygen is reduced, and (4) diffusion barrier through which ions and electrons migrate.

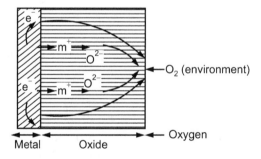

**Fig. 4.1 : Electrochemical process of oxidation**

Once the oxide films are formed, the oxidation reaction slows down. Oxide films formed at room temperature are thin or dense, porous or non-porous. The oxide films formed by alkali metals (Li, Na, K, Rb) and alkaline earth metals (Ca, Sr, Ba, Mg) are porous. Other metals form dense non-porous oxide films. Metals like gold, silver do not oxidise even at elevated temperature. While metals like molybdenum form volatile oxide, $MoO_3$, when heated in air. Many metals on prolonged heating at higher temperature form thick oxide layers called **scales**. Scales may or may not protect metals.

Further growth of oxide layer will depend upon the diffusion of metal ions and oxygen ions and flow of electrons through the oxide layer. If oxide layer is porous and if metal ions are smaller than oxide ions, outward diffusion of metal ions through oxide layer will take place and layer grows at scale-gas interface. That is why alkali and alkaline earth metals corrode more in air. If oxide layers are non-porous and uniform, outward diffusion of metal ions through them will not take place. The oxide layer film will protect the metal from further oxidation. The oxide films formed by metals like chromium, aluminium are more protective than iron, because they are thin and non-porous.

Protective value or protectivity of films can be decided from Pilling Bedworth ratio.

$$\text{Pilling Bedworth ratio (P.B. ratio)} = \frac{\text{Volume of oxide formed}}{\text{Volume of equivalent amount of metal consumed to form oxide}}$$

If P.B. ratio > 1, coating will be non-porous and protective. e.g. Cr, Ni, W, Al etc.

If P.B. ratio < 1, coating will be porous and non-protective. e.g. Alkali and alkaline earth metals.

Metals on prolonged heating at higher temperature form thick oxide layers called 'scales.' They may or may not protect metal from further corrosion.

**Mechanism of Atmospheric Corrosion :**

The mechanism of the growth of oxide film or scale can be expressed in terms of four growth laws.

**1.    Parabolic law :** The contact between metal and air in oxide films is maintained by diffusion of either metal ions outward or oxygen ions inward, to the film-metal interface. The increase in the rate of thickness Y with time t is inversely proportional to the thickness of the film Y and proportional to k.

$$\frac{dY}{dt} = \frac{k}{Y}$$

where k is characteristic constant for each metal.

On integration, parabolic equation is obtained, so it is called parabolic law.

Copper, iron, cobalt and nickel form oxide films of parabolic type.

**2.  Linear law :** When oxidation is constant at a given temperature, the growth of film obeys linear law. If outer oxide layer breaks, it is renewed very fast. It is given by the equation :

$$Y = k_1 t$$

where,    Y is the film thickness

   $k_1$ is constant characteristic for each metal.

Group I metals (sodium, potassium ... etc.) forming porous films obey this growth law.

**3.  Logarithmic law :** The oxide lattice of metals contain excess metal occupying interstitial position. So film ceases to grow after certain thickness is obtained to the film. Oxide layer is protective.

Aluminium, chromium, beryllium follow the logarithmic law which is given by the equation :

$$Y = k_1 \log (at + 1)$$

where,    $k_1$ and a are constants.

**4.  Cubic law :** The cubic law for growth of oxide film is given by the equation,

$$Y^3 = k_3 t$$

The metals obeying this law and logarithmic law are suitable for service at elevated temperature because rate of growth of scale is smallest in them.

## Effect of Temperature :

According to Arrhenius, rate of oxidation increases with temperature, which is given by

$$k = A e^{-E/RT}$$

where,                 k  → Rate of oxidation

                 E  → Energy of activation (Constant for a particular metal)

                 R  → Gas constant

                 A  → Frequency factor

Arrhenius equation can be checked by determining k at different temperatures. Plot of log k versus 1/T will be a straight line. Rate of scale growth can be studied from such graph. Growth of oxide film and its protective nature in all metals will not be depending on temperatures, the metals obey different growth laws at lower temperature and higher temperature.

In case of magnesium above 500ºC, oxide layer (scales) forms cracks, but in case of titanium even above 800ºC coherent oxide film is maintained, which protects the metal.

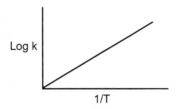

**Fig. 4.2 : Graph**

In some cases, scales formed are complex oxides. Oxides formed on copper and iron, contain less metal than expected from their formula FeO or $Cu_2O$. On copper metal, film formed is of cuprous oxide, CuO, but on further oxidation, black cupric oxide begins to coat cuprous oxide film till continuous layer is formed. This complex film is protective.

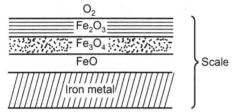

**Fig. 4.3 : High temperature scales on iron**

In case of iron, depending on service temperature, different scales are formed. Above 575°C, three distinct layers are formed - FeO, $Fe_3O_4$ and outer $Fe_2O_3$. While below 575°C, lower layer of FeO is not stable. On decreasing temperature, only single layer of $Fe_2O_3$ is observed. Homogeneous coating of one layer should be more protective than three layered complex coating; but $Fe_2O_3$ itself is not protective oxide layer, so metal corrodes.

**(ii) Corrosion Due to Other Gases :**

Gases like carbon dioxide, sulphur dioxide, nitrogen oxides, chlorine, fluorine under dry conditions corrode metals. The degree of corrosion due to other gases depend upon chemical affinity of metal and above gases, as well as on the protective nature of the films formed on the surface of metal. In case of silver, due to action of chlorine, silver chloride film is formed. It protects the metal from further corrosion.

But chlorine when attacks tin, stannic chloride being volatile, easily escapes as soon as it is formed leaving metal for further exposure. Thus, more and more metal gets corroded due to chlorine attack.

$$2\,Ag + Cl_2 \longrightarrow 2\,AgCl$$
$$Sn + 2\,Cl_2 \longrightarrow SnCl_4$$

In an industrial atmosphere, all types of contaminants of sulphur in the form of sulphur dioxide and hydrogen sulphide are corrosive. In petroleum industry, hydrogen sulphide at high temperature corrodes steel.

$$H_2S + Fe \longrightarrow FeS + H_2 \uparrow$$

Scale

---

The burning of fossil fuels generate large amount of sulphur dioxide. Primary cause of atmospheric corrosion is the dry deposition of sulphur dioxide on metallic surface.

$$S + O_2 \longrightarrow SO_2;$$

$$SO_2 + H_2O \longrightarrow H_2SO_3$$

(Sulfurous acid)

$$SO_2 + H_2O + \frac{1}{2} O_2 \longrightarrow H_2SO_4$$

In presence of oxygen and moisture, sulphur dioxide is oxidised to sulphuric and sulphurous acid, which are highly corrosive to metallic equipments. Oxides of nitrogen emitted in combustion process cause atmospheric corrosion.

The basic reaction is

$$N_2 + O_2 \xrightarrow[\text{1700°C}]{\text{12010 to}} 2\,NO$$

Nitric oxide

$$2\,NO + O_2 \xrightarrow{\text{1100°C}} 2\,NO_2$$

Nitrogen dioxide

They react with ozone from atmosphere.

$$NO_2 + O_3 \longrightarrow NO_3 + O_2$$

$$NO_2 + NO_3 \longrightarrow N_2O_5$$

$$N_2O_5 + H_2O \longrightarrow 2\,HNO_3$$

**(iii) Corrosion Due to Hydrogen :**

Attack of hydrogen on metals is of two types. This is also studied under wet corrosion as hydrogen damage.

**(a) Hydrogen embrittlement :** Action of hydrogen on metals at low temperature is called hydrogen embrittlement. Under specific environment, as a result of chemical or electrochemical action of metal surface, atomic hydrogen is formed. For example, aqueous solution of hydrogen sulphide reacts with iron surface and evolves atomic hydrogen. This atomic hydrogen diffuses into a metal and collects in voids. There it combines to form molecular hydrogen.

$$Fe + H_2S \longrightarrow FeS + 2\,H$$

Atomic or Nascent hydrogen

$$2\,H \longrightarrow H_2 \uparrow$$

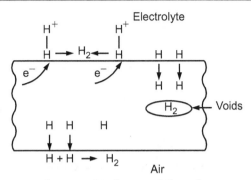

**Fig. 4.4 : Hydrogen blistering**

If this process continues, large amount of molecular hydrogen gets accumulated in voids. Some amount tries to escape over the surface which causes blistering in metal fissure formation. Penetration of hydrogen into metal decreases ductility and tensile strength in metals which is called hydrogen embrittlement.

**(b) Hydrogen attack at higher temperature :** At higher temperature, molecular hydrogen dissociates into atomic hydrogen.

$$H_2 \uparrow \xrightarrow[\text{Dissociation}]{\text{Thermal}} \underset{\text{Atomic hydrogen}}{2H}$$

At high temperature, atomic hydrogen is chemically very active. It combines with carbon, sulphur, oxygen or nitrogen which are present in metals to small extent.

$$\underset{\text{From steel}}{C} + \underset{\substack{\text{Atomic} \\ \text{hydrogen}}}{4H} \longrightarrow \underset{\text{Methane gas}}{CH_4 \uparrow}$$

At high temperature, atomic hydrogen reacts with carbon from steel and forms high pressure methane which causes intergranular cracking, fissuring and blistering. This reduces strength of steel. i.e. the atomic hydrogen eats away C, S, N etc. from around the area where it gets.

# 4.2.2 Wet or Electrochemical or Immersion Corrosion

**Electrochemical corrosion can be defined as the corrosion caused by exposure of a metal or two dissimilar metals to be in electrical contact, to an electrolytic solution (acid, base or salt). Formation of an electrochemical or galvanic cell governs electrochemical corrosion. Electrochemical cell is set up due to difference in electrode potential between two separate areas out of which one is anodic and other one cathodic.**

Anodic area dissolves, corrodes or oxidizes leading to formation of metallic ions or cations and electrons are set free by the reaction

$$M \longrightarrow M^{n+} + n\,e^- \qquad \qquad \text{... Oxidation}$$

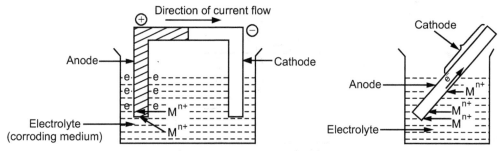

**Fig. 4.5 : Electrochemical corrosion**

At cathodic area, on the other hand, reduction reaction takes place to discharge anions (e.g. $O^{2-}$, $OH^-$ etc.) depending upon the nature of conducting or corroding medium (electrolyte).

e.g. $\qquad 2\,ne^- + n\,H_2O + \dfrac{n}{2}\,O_2 \longrightarrow 2\,n\,OH^-$ $\qquad\qquad\qquad$ ... Reduction

The rate of electrochemical corrosion in general depends upon :

1. Solubility of corrosion product
2. Location of corrosion product

**Solubility of corrosion product :** Corrosion products (metal oxides) are formed by cations generated at anodic area and anions generated at cathodic area. This process takes place due to diffusion of ions through wet medium. If the corrosion product is soluble in the corroding medium, rate of corrosion at anode is comparatively faster.

(i) Either in the vicinity of anode or cathode then the corrosion product forms a protective barrier either around anode or cathode and thus corrosion rate is affected substantially.

(ii) In between anode and cathode or away from either of them, corrosion rate is not much affected.

Further, electrochemical corrosion is also influenced by the following two factors namely, polarisation of electrodes and hydrogen overvoltage.

### (i) Polarisation of Electrodes :

In every reversible cell, an oxidation occurs at anode ($M \rightarrow M^{n+} + n\,e^-$) and reduction occurs at cathode ($M^{n+} + n\,e^- \rightarrow M$). When external circuit is completed, electrons flow from anode to cathode, while in the cell the positive current flows from anode to cathode. The electromotive force of such a cell formed by combining two normal electrodes is as shown below.

$$E = E_c - E_a$$

where, $\qquad E_c \longrightarrow$ Electrode potential of cathode

$\qquad\qquad\quad E_a \longrightarrow$ Electrode potential of anode

When current is drawn from such cells, certain irreversible effect occurs adjacent to electrodes that tend to oppose the direction of current flow. It is called polarisation of electrodes. Because of this, potential of anode becomes more cathodic while potential of cathode becomes more anodic. This decreases potential difference between electrodes and amount of current in the closed circuit leading to reduction in corrosion current and thus corrosion rate too.

**(ii) Hydrogen Overvoltage or Over Potential :**

All metals above hydrogen in the electrochemical series liberate hydrogen when they are immersed in an acid solution. But some metals even standing above hydrogen in the electrochemical series, do not liberate hydrogen from dilute hydrochloric acid solution. For example, pure tin and lead in absence of air do not get attacked by dilute hydrochloric acid solution. Pure zinc with high negative value is attacked by acid very slowly first. These observations are because of hydrogen overpotentials of metals.

**Table 4.1**

| Metal | Electrode potential (volts) | Hydrogen overvoltage (volts) |
|---|---|---|
| Platinum | 1.20 | 0.12 |
| Silver | 0.797 | 0.29 |
| Copper | 0.337 | 0.25 |
| Hydrogen | 0.00 | – |
| Lead | – 0.13 | 0.60 |
| Tin | – 0.14 | 0.50 |
| Nickel | – 0.23 | 0.25 |
| Iron | – 0.44 | 0.27 |
| Zinc | – 0.761 | 0.70 |

**Overpotential of hydrogen is the difference between the potential of the electrode at which evolution of hydrogen gas is observed and the theoretical value of potential at which hydrogen gas evolution takes place.** The hydrogen overvoltage is inversely related to corrosive tendency of metals.

The overpotential of tin and lead are 0.5 and 0.6 volts respectively, while their electrode potentials are – 0.14 and – 0.13 volts respectively. So evolution of hydrogen in normal acid solution will not take place as net potential of tin and lead has become 0.5 – 0.14 = 0.36 volts and 0.6 – 0.13 = 0.47 volts. In case of zinc, electrode potential is slightly higher than its hydrogen overvoltage, so evolution of hydrogen is slow at the beginning. More is hydrogen overvoltage, less is corrosion tendency of metals and less is hydrogen overvoltage, more is the corrosion tendency of metals.

## 4.2.3 Galvanic Corrosion

It is wet corrosion. When two dissimilar metals are in electrical contact with each other and are exposed to an electrolyte, a potential difference is created between two dissimilar metals. This potential difference produces electron flow between them. The less noble metal will dissolve and act as anode while more noble metal will act as the cathode. This type of corrosion of metal is called as galvanic corrosion.

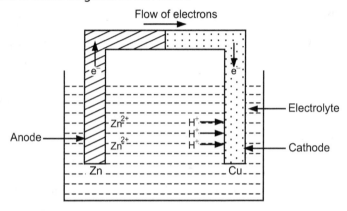

**Fig. 4.6 : Galvanic corrosion**

In Fig. 4.6, zinc and copper plates are in electrical contact with each other and are immersed into a solution of an electrolyte. As zinc has more negative potential than copper, it acts as anode while copper acts as cathode.

The reaction at the anode will be,

$$Zn \longrightarrow Zn^{2+} + 2\,e^-$$

The electronic current flows from anode to cathode through metal and corrosion current flows from anode to cathode with dissolution of anode metal. While cathodic reaction is accompanied by evolution of hydrogen or absorption of oxygen in acidic or alkaline medium.

In the galvanic corrosion, cathodic metal is always protected from the corrosion attack. The extent of corrosion depends on corrosive environment as well as the difference in the electrode potential of two contacting metals i.e. their position in the galvanic series.
Further apart the metals from each other, more is the intensity of corrosion. Galvanic corrosion depends upon relative areas of anode and cathode.

For example :

(1)   Steel screws corrode in contact with brass in marine environment.

(2)   Steel pipes corrode preferentially connected to copper plumbing corrode.

**Mechanism of Wet Corrosion :**

Wet corrosion of metal occurs by electrochemical mechanism. It is associated with flow of electric current between anodic and cathodic areas. At anode, metal dissolves forming corresponding positive ions and electrons.

$$M \longrightarrow M^{n+} + n\, e^-$$

While depending upon the nature of the corrosive environment, cathodic reactions will be of two types :

(1)  Hydrogen evolution mechanism

(2)  Oxygen absorption mechanism

**(1)  Hydrogen evolution mechanism :** Hydrogen evolution type of corrosion of metals occurs when metals are exposed to acidic environment. It is nothing but displacement of hydrogen ions from the solution by metal ions which can be written as

$$M \rightleftharpoons M^{2+} + 2\, e^- \qquad \text{at anode}$$

$$Acid \rightleftharpoons H^+$$

$$2\, H^+ + 2\, e^- \longrightarrow H_2 \uparrow \qquad\qquad \text{at cathode}$$

The cathodic reaction consists of evolution of hydrogen gas.

All metals above hydrogen in the electrochemical series will dissolve in acid solution with the evolution of hydrogen gas.

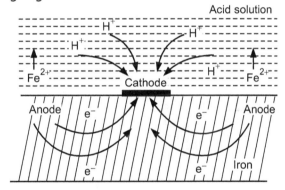

**Fig. 4.7 : Mechanism of corrosion - hydrogen evolution**

Consider iron plate in acidic solution (See Fig. 4.7). Certain part of metal becomes anodic while certain parts become cathodic (small area). From iron (anode), electrons flow through a metal to the small cathodic area. Iron will pass into solution in the form of $Fe^{2+}$ and $Fe^{3+}$. Hydrogen ions from acid are getting reduced at cathode, they accept electrons from cathode and evolution of hydrogen gas takes place at cathode. In this type of corrosion, cathodes are small points while anodes are of large area.

$$Fe \longrightarrow Fe^{2+} + 2\, e^-$$

$$2\, H^+ + 2\, e^- \longrightarrow H_2 \uparrow$$

This type of corrosion occurs when industrial waste of acidic nature or small copper scrap is stored in steel tank. Copper scrap or industrial waste becomes cathodic while steel becomes anodic and in presence of acid electrolyte, a galvanic cell is formed. Steel corrodes by passing iron ions in solution as above.

In galvanic corrosion i.e. when two dissimilar metals are in electrical contact with each other and are exposed to acidic environment, cathodic reaction will be hydrogen evolution process. In this case, corrosion is more of a uniform type.

**(2) Oxygen absorption mechanism :** Rusting of iron in water containing dissolved oxygen occurs by oxygen absorption mechanism. At anodic area, iron will dissolve by oxidation.

$$Fe \rightleftharpoons Fe^{2+} + 2\,e^-$$

The electrons will flow to cathodic area through iron and will be accepted by oxygen.

$$2\,e^- + H_2O + \frac{1}{2}\,O_2 \rightleftharpoons 2\,OH^-$$

$$Fe^{2+} + 2\,OH^- \longrightarrow Fe\,(OH)_2 \downarrow$$

$$2\,Fe\,(OH)_2 + \frac{1}{2}\,O_2 + H_2O \longrightarrow 2\,Fe\,(OH)_3 \downarrow$$

rust

In this case, anodic areas on the surface of iron are due to presence of cracks in the oxide coating of the metal. The cathodic areas will be the surface of coated metal i.e. cathode will be large while anode will be small area. This results in localised corrosion attack on the exposed iron surface.

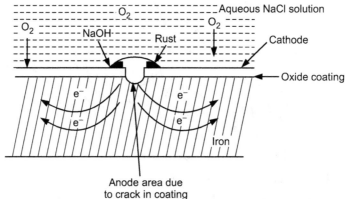

**Fig. 4.8 : Mechanism of corrosion - oxygen absorption**

If environment is neutral aqueous solution of an electrolyte (NaCl) containing dissolved oxygen

As                                  $NaCl \xrightarrow{H_2O} Na^+ + Cl^-$

At cathode ............    $Na^+ + OH^- \longrightarrow NaOH$, sodium hydroxide is formed.

At anode ...............    $Fe^{2+} + 2\,Cl^- \longrightarrow FeCl_2$, ferrous chloride is formed.

As cathodic product NaOH and anodic product FeCl$_2$ are soluble in water, when they meet, ferrous hydroxide precipitates and in enough oxygen it oxidises to ferric hydroxide.

$$Na^+ + OH^- + Fe^{2+} + Cl^- \longrightarrow Fe\,(OH)_2$$

$$2\,Fe\,(OH)_2 + \frac{1}{2}\,O_2 + H_2O \longrightarrow Fe\,(OH)_3 \downarrow$$

Ferric hydroxide

Thus, ferrous iron formed is removed as precipitate of ferric hydroxide, the corrosion proceeds till fresh oxygen is available. Oxygen absorption type corrosion is more in strongly aerated solutions. Here corrosion product is formed in the vicinity of cathode although corrosion takes place at anode.

## 2.2.4 Concentration Cell Corrosion

**The corrosion of metal due to electrochemical attack on the metal surface exposed to an electrolyte of varying concentration or of varying aeration is called as concentration cell corrosion.** It is wet corrosion. The difference in concentration of metal ions may be due to difference in temperature or inadequate agitation of solution of metal ions.

**Forms of Concentration Cell Corrosion :**

**(a) Differential aeration :** When one part of metal is exposed to a different air concentration from the other part, it causes a difference in potential between differently aerated areas.

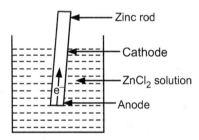

**Fig. 4.9 : Differential aeration**

The areas on the metal surface where oxygen concentration is low are anodic and the areas where the oxygen concentration is high are cathodic. This creates small difference of potential thus setting up differential aeration or oxygen concentration cell and causes flow of current between them. Metal dissolves at the anodic area. (Fig. 4.9)

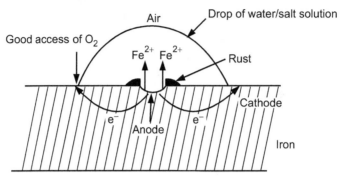

**Fig. 4.10 : Differential aeration**

If piece of zinc metal is partially immersed in a solution of its salt and the solution is not agitated, the parts adjacent to water line are strongly aerated, thus become cathodic. The part immersed at depth shows smaller concentration of oxygen and becomes anodic. This creates a difference of potential and causes a flow of current between two differentially aerated areas of zinc. As an anodic reaction, zinc will dissolve by forming electrons, which will be taken by oxygen at cathodic area to form hydroxyl ions. Circuit gets completed by flow of $OH^-$ ions through electrolyte and flow of electrons from anode to cathode through metal.

$$Zn \longrightarrow Zn^{2+} + 2\,e^- \qquad\qquad \text{Anodic reaction}$$

$$\frac{1}{2}\,O_2 + 2\,e^- + H_2O \longrightarrow 2\,OH^- \qquad\qquad \text{Cathodic reaction}$$

Iron corrodes under drop of water or drop of salt solution in the similar way. Area of metal covered by droplet, have less access of oxygen, so becomes anodic with respect to other areas exposed to air. (See Fig. 4.10)

Thus, a difference of potential is created which causes a current to flow between differentially aerated areas of the metal.

**Crevice Corrosion :**

Intense localized corrosion frequently occurring within crevices and other shielded areas on metal surfaces exposed to corrosives like dirt, sand particles and other solids is called crevice corrosion. Contact between metallic and non-metallic surfaces can cause crevice corrosions as in the case of gasket.

e.g. A riverted plate section of metal - iron or steel - immersed in aerated sea water. Mechanism of crevice corrosion is oxygen absorption type.

$$M \longrightarrow M^{2+} + 2\,e^- \qquad\qquad \text{Oxidation}$$

$$2\,H_2O + O_2 + 4\,e^- \longrightarrow 4\,OH^- \qquad\qquad \text{Reduction}$$

$$M^{2+} + 2\,OH^- \longrightarrow M\,(OH)_2 \downarrow$$

$$\text{Insoluble hydroxide}$$

Crevice corrosion is intense in medium containing chloride ions. When oxygen is depleted, no further oxygen reduction occurs.

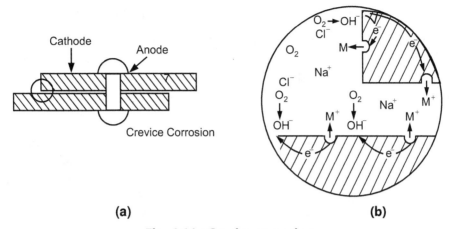

(a)                                                                (b)

**Fig. 4.11 : Crevice corrosion**

As dissolution of metal continues, excess positive charge is produced in solution. Chloride ions migrate and form metal chloride in crevices. Aqueous solution of metal chloride in crevices dissociate into insoluble hydroxide and free acid.

$$M^{2+} + 2\,Cl^- + H_2O \longrightarrow M\,(OH)_2 \downarrow + H^+ + Cl^-$$

Both chloride ions and hydrogen ions accelerate the dissolution rate of metal.

**Pitting :**

Pitting corrosion is extremely localised attack resulting in the formation of cavities or holes in the metal around which the metal is relatively unattacked. Pitting may penetrate deep into the metal, it is very destructive and can ruin the metal. Pits usually grow in the direction of gravity i.e. they grow downward from horizontal surfaces.

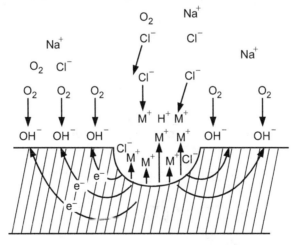

**Fig. 4.12 : Autocatalytic processes occurring in corrosion pits**

e.g. Corrosion of stainless steel by sulphuric acid containing ferric chloride.

Pitting is the result of the breakdown or cracking of the protective film on a metal at specific points. Breakdown of films may be because of mechanical factors like surface roughness, scratches, cut edges, sliding under load or because of particular type of chemical attack. Cracking of protective films form small anodic and big cathodic areas which in corrosive environment give rise to corrosion current.

A corrosion pit is a type of autocatalytic process. That is the corrosion processes within a pit produce conditions which are stimulating and necessary for the continuing activity of the pit (See Fig. 4.12). Here metal is pitted by aerated sodium chloride solution. Rapid dissolution of metal takes place within the pit and oxygen reduction takes place on adjacent surfaces. This process is self-stimulating and self-propagating. Rapid dissolution of metal within the pit produces more positive charge in the pits, chloride ions migrate into pits resulting deposition of metal chloride. Corrosion is furthered because the corrosion product is accumulated in the close proximity of anodic area making oxygen more and more inaccessible to it resulting in self-accelerated and localized attack. This undergoes hydrolysis as

$$M^+ + Cl^- + H_2O \longrightarrow MOH \downarrow + H^+ + Cl^-$$

Both hydrogen and chloride ions stimulate dissolution of metal or alloy, thus process is accelerated. Since solubility of oxygen is zero in concentrated solution, no oxygen reduction occurs in pits. The oxygen reduction on surfaces adjacent to pits suppress corrosion cathodically protecting the metal surface.

## 4.3 FORMS OF CORROSION

It is convenient to classify corrosion according to the appearance of the corroded metal. The basic mechanism involved in such corrosion forms are same as those previously discussed. These are classified into the following eight forms.

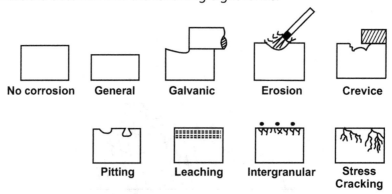

Fig. 4.13 : Forms of corrosion

### (A) Uniform Corrosion :

Uniform attack is the most common form of corrosion. The corrosion attack may start at certain specific areas, it proceeds by chemical or electrochemical reaction uniformly over the entire exposed surface. As a result, the whole surface is uniformly corroded.

e.g. A piece of steel or zinc immersed in dilute sulphuric acid will dissolve at uniform rate over its entire surface.

### (B) Galvanic Corrosion :

Already discussed.

### (C) Intergranular Corrosion :

This type of corrosion occurs along grain boundaries. Under certain conditions, grain interfaces are very reactive and intergranular corrosion results. Grain boundaries contain material which shows a solution potential more anodic than that of the grain center in particular corrosive medium. The material - impurity at the grain boundaries are enriched or depleted in one of the alloying elements.

e.g. (1) Depletion of chromium in the grain boundary regions result in intergranular corrosion of stainless steel. (See Fig. 4.14). Addition of chromium to ordinary steels imparts corrosion resistance to the steel in many environments. But more than 10% chromium is needed to make corrosion resistance steel. If per cent of chromium is effectively lowered, intergranular corrosion results.

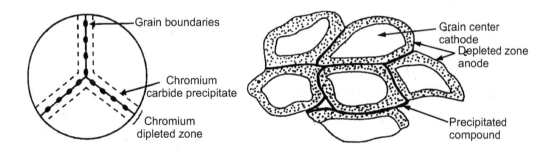

**Fig. 4.14 : Intergranular corrosion**

(2) In Al - Cu alloy, the precipitation of the compound $CuAl_2$ is richer in copper in the area adjacent to grains than alloy at the interior of the grains. So zone adjacent to it is depleted in copper and is more anodic with respect to grains.

### (D) Erosion Corrosion :

It is the attack on metal, because of relative movement between corrosive fluid and the metal surface. It is combined effect of corrosion and wear. Erosion corrosion is characterised by appearance of grooves, waves, rounded holes and valleys and usually exhibits a directional pattern. Erosion corrosion is caused by the breakdown of protective film at the spot and its inability to repair itself under existing conditions. In erosion corrosion, metal is removed from the surface as dissolved ions or solid corrosion product, which are mechanically swept from the metals. Corrosive mediums like gases, aqueous solutions, organic systems could cause erosion corrosion.

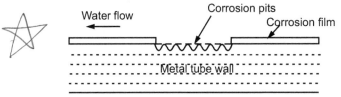

**Fig. 4.15 : Erosion corrosion of condenser tube wall**

e.g. Corrosion of heat exchanger tubes (handling water), condenser tubes, piping, agitators etc.

**(E) Stress Corrosion :**

Stress corrosion cracking refers to cracking caused by simultaneous presence of tensile stress and corrosive environment on a metal. Most commercial alloys are susceptible to stress corrosion cracking while pure metals are relatively immune to stress corrosion cracking. During stress corrosion cracking, the metal or alloy is unattacked over most of the surface while fine cracks progress through it.

For example :

(1) Alpha brasses when highly stressed undergrow cracking in the atmosphere containing traces of ammonia, it is known as season cracking of brass.

(2) Caustic embrittlement is also a stress corrosion occurring on mild steel exposed to alkaline solution at high temperature and stresses.

(3) Mild steel cracking in hot concentrated nitrate solution is an example of intergranular cracking.

**(H) Corrosion Fatigue :**

Fatigue corrosion is described as reduction in fatigue strength by corrosive environment. **It is defined as the tendency of a metal to fracture under repeated cyclic stresses.** Protective films on the metal also break repeatedly under action of cyclic stresses, anodes are formed, attack will be localised and then spreads through cracks forming pits. Corrosion products block the pits, so oxygen will not be available for repair of primary film. Thus as a combined action of the corrosive environment and alternating stresses, fatigue strength of materials decreases and failure of material takes place.

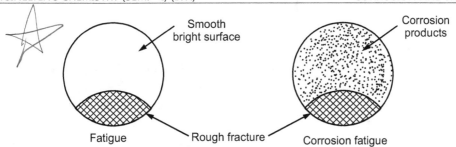

**Fig. 4.16 : Corrosion fatigue failure**

## 4.4 PASSIVITY OR PASSIVATION

**It is defined as a phenomenon in which metal or alloy exhibits outstanding higher corrosion resistance than its position in the electrochemical or galvanic series.** Passivity is the result of formation of highly protective but very thin invisible film on the surface of metal or an alloy, which makes the metal more noble. Metals become passive because of this unimolecular adsorbed film of oxide which is self repairing on the metal surface.

Titanium, aluminium, chromium and stainless-steel alloys containing chromium are passive in oxidising environment. But they become chemically active in reducing environment.

Austenitic stainless steel has corrosion resistance in aerated dilute sulphuric acid but gets corroded in air free acid. The protective oxide film gets repaired in presence of oxygen, while in absence of oxygen the passive metal becomes chemically active and corrodes. This shows 'passivation' applies only to certain environmental conditions which can maintain the protective oxide film on the metallic surface. Thus, passivation is not a static state but dynamic one which keeps on changing with nature of environment.

By physical isolation of the metal from the corroding environment, pseudopassivity can be achieved which is useful in reducing corrosion. This is due to the deposition of thick protective reaction product films on metal. e.g. Film of lead sulphate on lead in sulphuric acid. Use of inhibitors, anodic polarisation, etc. are different ways of achieving pseudopassivity in metals.

Active metals like Al, Fe when treated with concentrated nitric acid produce protective oxide film. This reduces anodic corrosion making metal passive. But in dilute nitric acid rapid corrosion of metal (i.e. iron) occurs without evolution of hydrogen, as dilute nitric acid stimulates cathodic reaction.

## 4.5 FACTORS INFLUENCING CORROSION

Corrosion is destruction of metal through electrochemical action with its environment. So it depends on nature of metal as well as nature of environment.

### (A) Nature of Metal :

**(a) Position of metal in galvanic series :** According to Nernst, all metals have a tendency to pass into solution in the form of ions. But all metals will not corrode at same rate under similar conditions of environment, corrosion of metals depend upon its position in the electrochemical series and galvanic series. More the negative value of the standard electrode potential, more the metal corrodes. e.g. If zinc, sodium and copper electrodes are dipped in the solution of electrolyte, having same concentration, for some period, it is found sodium corrodes more, than zinc corrodes, copper is noble compared to them as former figures higher in position in galvanic series (having more negative potential) than latter.

**(b) Hydrogen overvoltage or overpotential :** Overpotential of hydrogen plays very important role in corrosion process. Overpotential of hydrogen makes the metal more noble or cathodic with respect to hydrogen evolution than they really are. If overpotential of hydrogen is high, rate of corrosion will be less.

e.g. Pure zinc, though it has high negative value will not liberate hydrogen gas in acid solution in the beginning because of hydrogen overvoltage. If drop of copper sulphate is added to acidic solution, hydrogen overvoltage is lowered, evolution of hydrogen gas is accelerated. This results increase in corrosion. Hydrogen overvoltage varies from metal to metal.

**(c) Relative areas of cathode and anode :** The important factor in galvanic corrosion is the area effect, ratio of cathodic to anodic areas. When cathode and anode areas are equal, cathodic and anodic current densities are equal. Corrosion phenomenon will not get accelerated. If cathode area is much larger than anode area, anodic current density will be greater, as a result corrosion of anode metal will be more.

In more easier way we can say that if the areas of cathode and anode are different, the intensity of corrosion of anode is directly proportional to the area of cathode. Thus, the corrosion is more if the area of cathode is larger than the area of anode. This is because if cathode area is larger than anode, the demand of electrons is more for reduction reaction to take place and thus more dissolution of metal at anode takes place.

e.g. Steel rivets in copper plate get completely corroded in corrosive environment because of unfavourable area ratio. (Copper is noble which acts as a cathode).

**(d) Nature of protective films :** Many metals are susceptible to oxidation when exposed to air and they get covered with oxide films. Depending upon protective nature of film, corrosion continues or stops. If films are porous, metal or oxygen will diffuse, thus furthers corrosion. If films are non-porous, they protect metal from further attack.

Lead forms lead sulphate surface coatings with strong sulphuric acid which protects lead for long time in sulphuric acid environment. Titanium is reactive metal but is resistant to erosion corrosion in many environments because of stability of the $TiO_2$ film formed.

**(e) Purity of metals :** The corrosion resistance of pure metal is usually better than that of one containing small amounts of impurities. Presence of impurities accumulated on certain areas of metal are the sources of the potential difference on the metal. In corrosive environment, minute galvanic cell will form and anodic metal will corrode.

e.g. Pure aluminium (99.5% plus) has good corrosion resistance. But minute amount of impurities even 0.02% iron and 0.05% nickel present in aluminium will decrease its corrosion resistance.

But pure metals are expensive (except aluminium), soft and weak, so they have less structural applications.

**(B) Nature of Environment :**

**(a) Temperature :** As rates of all chemical reactions increase with temperature, corrosion increases with temperature. Increase in temperature increases ionisation and mobility of all reacting ions and molecules, it also increases diffusion rate. e.g. Intergranular corrosion like caustic embrittlement takes place at high temperature in high pressure boilers. Rate of corrosion of copper and monel metal is less in boiling sulphuric acid while steel corrodes more in boiling sulphuric acid. Dissolved oxygen is absent in boiling sulphuric acid. For corrosion of copper, oxygen is necessary. In absence of oxygen, corrosion of copper is less. But in case of steel, oxygen is necessary to keep steel in passive condition, steel corrodes in absence of oxygen.

**(b) Presence of moisture :** Atmospheric corrosion of few metals is slow in dry air but it increases rapidly in the presence of moisture. Moisture provides solvent for oxygen or other gases and furnishes electrolyte for setting corrosion cell. In some cases, moisture reacts with metal and oxides.

Corrosion of iron is more in moisture than that in presence of dry air. In moisture primary product of rusting is ferrous hydroxide which oxidises to ferric hydroxide. If moisture contains enough oxygen, ferric hydroxide will oxidise to ferric oxide. If supply of oxygen is limited, corrosion product is magnetite. Rain provides moisture for electrochemical attack. If corrosion products are adherent, they form film. If they are not adherent, rain washes them away exposing new more surface for corrosion attack.

$$Fe^{2+} + 2\,OH^- \longrightarrow Fe\,(OH)_2 \quad \text{Ferrous hydroxide}$$

$$Fe\,(OH)_2 \longrightarrow Fe\,(OH)_3 \quad \text{Ferric hydroxide}$$

$$Fe\,(OH)_2 \xrightarrow[\;O_2\;]{\text{enough}} Fe_2O_3 \cdot 2\,H_2O \quad \text{Ferric oxide}$$

$$Fe\,(OH)_2 \xrightarrow[\;O_2\;]{\text{limited}} Fe_3O_4 \quad \text{Magnetite}$$

e.g. $Fe_2O_3$ is not adherent to iron surface, so corrosion of iron is more in rain. Metals like chromium, stainless steels, aluminium and nickel show good resistance to atmosphere as well as rain.

**(c) Effect of pH :** Acidic environment is more corrosive than alkaline or neutral environment. Zinc rapidly corrodes in weakly acidic solution but suffers less corrosion in solution having pH 10 to 11. Many metals are readily attacked by acid but are resistance to alkali. By altering the chemical character of corroding medium i.e. pH, corrosion rate of a given metal can be controlled.

**Pourbaix diagram :** Redox potentials are useful in predicting corrosion behaviour of metals. Corrosion will not occur till spontaneous direction of the reaction indicates metal oxidation. The applications of thermodynamics or more specifically, half cell potential to corrosion phenomena can be understood by means of potential-pH plots. These plots are known as Pourbaix diagrams, after scientist Pourbaix. He first suggested the use of above plots. The diagram for iron is given in Fig. 4.17.

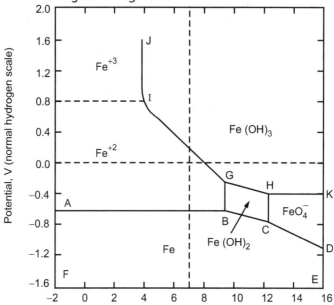

**Fig. 4.17 : Potential-pH diagram for Fe-H₂O system given by M. Pourbaix**

The electrode potential of a system in which the reactants are not at unit activity, can be calculated using Nernst equation

$$E \ = \ E^\circ + 2.303 \ \frac{RT}{nF} \ \log \frac{[\text{Oxidised species}]}{[\text{Reduced species}]}$$

where    E -  Half cell potential of an electrode

E° - The standard half cell potential of an electrode

F -  Faraday's constant

n -  Number of electrons transferred.

Pourbaix diagrams can be constructed using above calculations. In the above diagram, iron, iron hydroxide, ferrous ions etc. are thermodynamically stable in particular areas. They are in their states of lowest free energies.

---

**Uses of these diagrams are :**

1.  We can predict spontaneous direction of a reaction.

2.  Composition of corrosion product can be estimated.

3.  The environmental changes which will prevent or reduce corrosion attack also can be predicted.

In the above diagram, the area ABCDEF, indicates that iron is inert under these conditions of potential and pH.

**(d) Conductance of medium :** Stray current is that direct current which has leaked from an electric power circuit and flows through metallic structures in earth. The points at which stray current leaves the metallic structure, become anode where metal dissolves. In stray current corrosion, cathodes and anodes are remote from each other. If soil contents moisture and soluble salts, it will increase conductivity of soil. Increase in conductivity will increase stray current corrosion. Moisture present in soil also increases conductance of medium, which increases underground soil corrosion of metals.

**(e)  Nature of electrolyte :** The electrolyte itself is a source of potential difference. The solution potential of metal depends on type of ions and their concentration in the solution. So change in concentration of an electrolyte will change electrode potential and in turn will affect corrosion of metal. Crevice corrosion is intense in medium containing chloride ions. Stray current corrosion is more in soil containing soluble salts.

## 4.6 METHODS OF CONTROLLING CORROSION

There are many methods to control and prevent corrosion of metals. The choice of method depends on the environment to which a metal is exposed. Control over metallic corrosion can be achieved by proper design of structure, by controlling corrosion mechanism or by application of protective coatings on metal. The available methods are discussed here.

**(A) Proper Selection and Design of Material :**

The selection of the proper metal or alloy for a particular corrosive environment and sound engineering design are the best means of controlling and preventing corrosion.

The criterias in the design selection are :

1.  Noble metals should be used in surgical instruments, ornaments as they are most immune to corrosion.

2.  The use of two dissimilar metal contacts should be avoided.

3.  If two dissimilar metals have to be used, they should be as close as possible in the galvanic series.

4. Weld rather than rivet tanks and other containers.

5. The anodic metal should have as large area as possible while cathodic material should have much smaller area (nuts, bolts..... etc.).

6. An insulating material should be applied to prevent access of an electrolyte to the junction, but it should not be porous, as porous materials absorb and hold liquids.

7. Avoid electrical contact between two dissimilar metals to prevent galvanic corrosion.

8. Design tanks and other containers such that it provides for easy draining and easy cleaning.

9. Sharp corners and recesses should be avoided because they favour accumulation of solids.

10. During designing, presence of crevices between adjacent parts of structure should be avoided.

11. The corrosion resistance of pure metal is usually better than that of one containing small amounts of other elements. So pure metals should be used. But pure metals are expensive and are soft and weak, so can be used in few cases. Exception is aluminium metal, it is not expensive and can be used in fairly pure state, 99.5 % plus purity.

### (B) Modifying the Environment :

Altering the environment helps in reducing corrosion. The environment can be made less corrosive either by adding some chemical which will neutralize the effect of corrosive material or by removing harmful constituent.

**Deaeration :** Lowering temperature decreases corrosion rate. But under some conditions, increasing temperature decreases corrosion attack. Boiling sea water or boiling fresh water is less corrosive than hot sea water because of decrease in oxygen content of boiling sea or fresh water. Thus, by decreasing oxygen content of aqueous solutions, corrosion of metals can be reduced. This can be done by deaeration. Carbon dioxide content is also reduced by deaeration.

**Deactivation :** Sodium sulphite ($Na_2SO_3$) or hydrazine hydrate ($N_2H_4 \cdot H_2O$) are used to remove oxygen from corrosive environment.

**Alkali neutralisation :** Alkaline neutralisers like ammonia, sodium hydroxide, lime, sodium salts of petroleum, phenols reduce corrosive rates of an acidic environment.

### (C) Use of Inhibitors :

A corrosion inhibitor is a substance which when added in small concentrations to an corrosive environment, decreases the corrosion rate. They are divided into cathodic and anodic inhibitors on the basis of whether they inhibit anodic or cathodic reaction.

**(a) Anodic and Cathodic inhibitors :** As corrosion is electrochemical in nature, the inhibitive action of any substance is the result of control of anodic and cathodic reactions. Anodic inhibitors form soluble compounds with dissolved metal ions, which deposit on metal surface to form protective film, which reduces corrosion of anode. They are oxidising agents like chromates, nitrates and ferric salts.

In acidic environment, evolution of hydrogen gas takes place at cathode. Corrosion can be reduced by slowing diffusion of hydrated hydrogen ions to the cathode or by increasing the overpotential of hydrogen evolution. Antimony and arsenic ions deposit metallic film on cathode and retard hydrogen-evolution reaction. In neutral environment, cathodic reaction is the result of oxygen absorption and formation of hydroxyl ions. Sodium sulphite or hydrazine are used to remove oxygen from solution.

$$2\ Na_2\ S_2\ O_3 + O_2 \ \longrightarrow 2\ Na_2SO_4$$
$$N_2H_4 + O_2 \ \longrightarrow N_2 \uparrow + 2\ H_2O$$

Cathodic inorganic inhibitors like magnesium, zinc or nickel salts are effective in neutral and alkaline environment. They react with hydroxyl ions at cathode and form insoluble hydroxides. These get deposited on the cathode. Above inhibitors also can be classified as :

**(b) Inorganic inhibitors and organic inhibitors :** In neutral and alkaline solutions, chromates and nitrites act as anodic inhibitors. They are most efficient inhibitors for controlling corrosion of iron and steel in neutral and alkaline waters. Alkali inhibitors like sodium hydroxide, sodium carbonates and bicarbonates form metal hydroxides which serve as protective deposits. They are anodic inhibitors. Inorganic inhibitors do not give any protection in presence of acids and reducing conditions. For such conditions, polar organic compounds and colloidal organic materials are used as inhibitors. Their inhibitive action is because of physical and chemical adsorption of molecules on metal surface. They act as anodic, cathodic or mixed inhibitors. Because of physical adsorption of inhibitor, resistance to current flow at cathodic area increases. Because of chemisorption, co-ordinate covalent bond is formed between inhibitor and metal, so anodic polarisation takes place. Amines, heterocyclic nitrogen compounds, substituted urea and thiourea and metal soaps are used as organic inhibitors.

Vapour phase inhibitors are used to inhibit atmospheric corrosion of metals without placing in direct contact of metal's surface. They possess high vapour pressure and are effective if used in close spaces like inside of packages. Some heterocyclic nitro-compounds, esters of carboxylic acid can be used as vapour-phase inhibitors.

## (D) Use of Pure Metals :

Pure metals exhibit higher corrosion resistance than the impure ones. Even minute impurities form galvanic cells and corrosion of metal takes place. But in many cases, it is practically not possible to produce metal of high purity. Very pure metals have inadequate mechanical properties as they are weak and soft. Further getting metals in pure form is expensive and purpose of obtaining it in pure form is served provided we know nature of environment.

**Use of Metal Alloys :**

Corrosion resistance and strength of most commercial metal is best secured by alloying them with suitable constituents. Homogeneous alloys have maximum corrosion resistance. Aluminium, magnesium and lead have more corrosion resistance than their alloys have because they form heterogeneous alloys with other elements. Their corrosion resistance can be increased by purification. Variety of stainless steels, i.e. alloys containing 11.5 to 30% chromium and 0 to 22% nickel together in iron, have good corrosion resistance in most corrosives. They have less corrosion resistance in chloride containing medium and stressed structures than ordinary structural steels. Commercial use of alloy for particular environment depends on the achievement of passivity for their corrosion resistance.

**(E) Cathodic and Anodic Protection :**

**(a) Cathodic Protection :** Cathodic protection is a method of preventing metal corrosion in an electrolyte solution by supplying external current. The metal to be protected is made cathode. It can be explained by considering the corrosion of metal M in acid environment. Electrochemical reactions occurring are dissolution of metal and the evolution of hydrogen gas. Cathodic protection is achieved by supplying electrons to the metal structure to be protected. Addition of electrons to metal structure will suppress metal dissolution and increase the rate of hydrogen evolution.

$$M \longrightarrow M^{n+} + n\,e^-$$

$$2\,H^+ + 2\,e^- \longrightarrow H_2 \uparrow$$

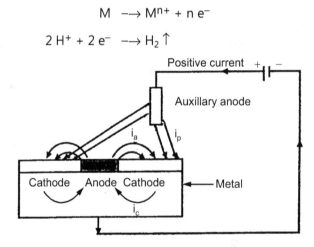

**Fig. 4.18 : Cathodic protection**

Suppose a piece of corroding metal is to be protected cathodically by an applied current from an auxiliary anode. The battery shown in the circuit produces protective current. The negative end of the battery is connected to the metal to be protected while positive end is connected to auxiliary anode i.e. anode placed in corrosive environment. Current from the anode passes to the protected metal through an electrolyte making it cathodic. From the anodic area on the metal surface, local corrosion current flows to cathode.

To prevent corrosion of metal an impressed current is applied from auxiliary anode to nullify the corrosion current. This stops corrosion of metal by making it cathodic. Cathodic protection is the most effective method of corrosion control, in fact prevention of corrosion.

There are two ways to protect a structure cathodically : (1) By an external power supply and (2) By appropriate galvanic coupling.

**(1) Cathodic protection by external power supply** (Cathodic protection by impressed current) : Underground metallic structure can be protected by this method. Here external D.C. power supply is connected to underground metallic tank or pipe line to be protected. Negative terminal of the current source is connected to the tank and positive end to an inert anode like graphite, immersed in corroding medium. Anode is surrounded by backfill consisting of gypsum or bentonite to improve contact between anode and surrounding soil. Current from the anode passes to metallic structure through an electrolyte and corrosion of cathode is suppressed. This cathodic protection by impressed current is economical where electric power supply is cheap.

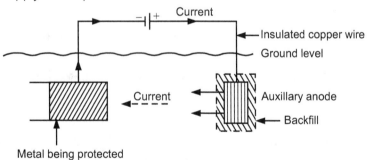

**Fig. 4.19 : Impressed current protection of underground tank**

**(2) Cathodic protection by galvanic coupling :** In this method, the metallic structure to be protected is connected by wire to metal which has more negative potential i.e. anodic with respect to metal to be protected. The anodic metal gets corroded while cathodic metal is protected.

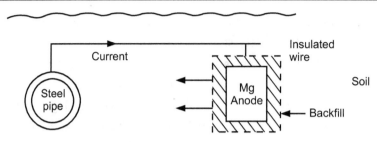

**Fig. 4.20 : Cathodic protection by galvanic coupling**

Magnesium is anodic with respect to steel and corrodes preferentially when galvanically coupled with steel. The anode in this case is called **sacrificial anode**, since it is consumed during protection of steel structure. Cathodic protection using sacrificial anodes can be used to protect buried pipelines as shown in Fig. 4.21. Anode selection for cathodic protection is based on engineering and economic considerations. Among several sacrificial anodes (steels, graphite, silicon, iron, magnesium), magnesium is widely used.

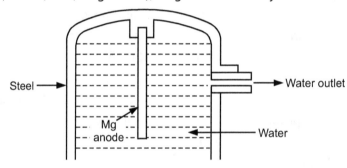

**Fig. 4.21 : Cathodic protection of domestic hot water tank using sacrificial anode**

**(b) Anodic Protection :** Anodic protection is based on the formation of a protective film on metals by externally applied anodic currents. i.e. by passivating the metal. Actually, the application of anodic current to a structure increases dissolution rate of metal. This type of behaviour occurs except for metals exhibiting active-passive transitions. Anodic protection can be applied for metals like nickel, chromium, titanium and their alloys as they exhibit active - passive transitions. If carefully controlled anodic currents are applied to above metals, they are passivated and the rate of metal dissolution is decreased.

To protect structure anodically, an electronic device potentiostat is used. Potentiostat maintains a metal at constant potential with respect to reference electrode. Out of three terminals of potentiostat, one is connected to the metal i.e. tank to be protected, another to an auxiliary cathode (platinum) and third to reference electrode. (Calomel electrode). Potentiostat maintains a constant potential between tank and reference electrode.

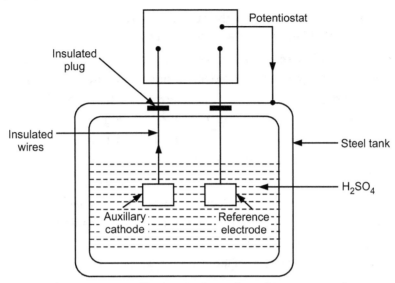

**Fig. 4.22 : Anodic protection of steel storage tank**

Anodic protection is limited to passive metals and alloys, it requires low current and is applicable in extremely corrosive environment. Cathodic protection is applicable in moderately corrosive conditions and current requirement for this is high. Installation cost for cathodic protection is less while for that of anodic protection is high.

**(F) Protective Coatings :**

The surface of engineering material can be protected from corrosion by covering it with metallic, inorganic or organic materials.

**Properties of good protective coatings :**

1.   They provide satisfactory barrier between metal and its environment.

2.   These coatings impart mechanical properties, thermal insulating properties, electrical properties and oxidation resistance to the protected surface. Coatings are used for decoration also.

3.   The effectiveness of these coatings depend on their thickness, type of environment and required degree of protection.

**Surface Preparation or Surface Treatment Methods :**

To obtain excellent surface adhesion and service behaviour, surface treatment is a must.

For application of any type of coating, the surface to be coated must be free from dirt and other corrosion products and it must be properly prepared. Cleaning and preparation of metal surface for coating is done in steps.

**(a) Removal of greases and other impurities :** Oils, greases and fatty substances present on metal surface are removed by using organic solvents like naphtha, xylene, toluene, acetone, etc. Then surface is cleaned with steam and hot water containing wetting agents like alkalies. After alkali cleaning, the surface is washed with water followed by water containing 1 % chromic acid to remove last traces of alkali.

**(b) Removal of oxides, scales and corrosion product :** Mechanical cleaning is done by bristle brush and detergent, knife scrapers, grinder and cutters followed by hot water. This removes dirt and scales. Loose scale is removed by flame heating and mechanical brushing while oxide scale is removed by sand blasting. Sand blasting consists of introducing sand into an air stream under pressure. The blast impacts on the surface to be cleaned and removes scales present on the surface.

For complete removal of scales, metals are immersed in various pickling solutions. Acid pickling is more convenient method of scale removal than mechanical cleaning and sand blasting. Temperature of bath, time of immersion and composition of pickling solution depend on type of scale to be removed.

Plane carbon steels are pickled in dilute warm sulphuric acid, then cold hydrochloric acid with inhibitor and finally with alkaline solution of soda ash or lime.

## 4.6.1 Metallic and Other Inorganic Coatings

Metal coatings are applied by electrodeposition, flame spraying, cladding, hot dipping or vapour deposition. Inorganic coatings are formed by spraying, diffusion or chemical conversion. Spraying is followed by baking or firing at elevated temperature. In both cases, complete barrier must be provided. Porosity or defect in coating results in accelerated localized attack on metal. Metal to be protected is called base metal while the metal used for protection is called coating metal.

**Methods of Applying Metallic Coatings on Base Metal :**

**(1) Electroplating :** It is one of the most important methods for the application of metallic coatings on the metals. In this method, coating metal is deposited on the base metal by immersing base metal in a solution of coating metal and passing direct current between base metal and another electrode.

Electroplating consists of immersing a part to be coated in a solution of salt of coating metal and passing a direct current between the part and another electrode. The base metal is made cathode of an electrolytic cell and anode is of coating metal. The metal to be plated electrolytically is cleaned and surface is made proper. Then it is made cathode of an electrolytic cell. The electrolytic solution is of soluble salt of metal to be coated. Direct current is passed after immersing cathode and anode in electroplating tank. Metal at anode dissolves and ions migrate to cathode and get deposited on base metal. Thus, a thin coating layer is formed on base metal. Properties of coating depend on the concentration of plating solution, agitation, temperature of solution and its pH.

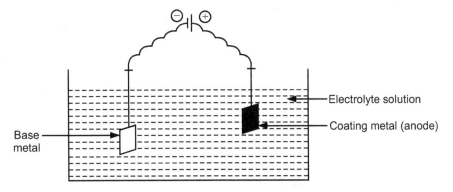

**Fig. 4.23 : Electroplating bath**

Electroplating is one of the most important methods for commercial production of metallic coatings. Zinc, lead, nickel, iron, tin, chromium and copper are frequently used for metallic coating. Precious metals like gold, silver, platinum are used for plating to smaller extent. Recently certain alloys like lead - tin, tin - copper, tin - zinc are used in electroplating.

**Types of Metallic Coating :**

Depending upon position of coating metal in the electrochemical series with respect to base metal, the coatings are called cathodic coatings or anodic coatings.

**Anodic coating :** In anodic coating, coatings are produced from metals which are anodic to base metal. Aluminium, zinc, cadmium have their solution potentials greater than that of steel. So they are used to coat steel anodically. If any scratch is developed on zinc coated steel, a galvanic cell is formed between zinc and exposed iron. Zinc being anodic to steel, it will dissolve protecting steel or iron. Thus, iron is protected cathodically by sacrificial zinc. No attack on iron or steel occurs till all zinc gets corroded almost practically.

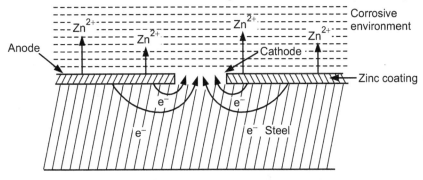

**Fig. 4.24 : Anodic coating**

**Cathodic coating :** Cathodic coatings can be obtained by application of more noble metal than base metal, for coating of base metal. They protect base metal because they have more corrosion resistance than base metal. Gold, copper, platinum, nickel, silver and chromium are the metals which can be used for cathodic coatings. Only continuous and pore free coating gives protection to the base metal. If pores are present on the cathodically coated iron, iron being anodic to coating, intensive localized attack at the pores will take place. This will result severe pitting.

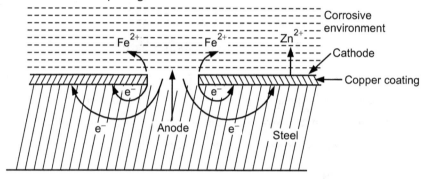

**Fig. 4.25 : Cathodic coating**

**(2) Immersion :** In this process, coating is produced by immersing base metal in an electrolyte solution containing a salt of coating metal. For this process, current is not required, the deposition occurs by simple displacement. The base metal should be anodic to coating metal. Ions of nobler metal are displaced from salt solution by ions of active metal. Immersion coatings are uniform but thin. By controlling composition of bath, temperature of bath and pH, uniform coatings can be produced by this method. These coatings are used as a base for other metallic coatings. Coating of zinc on aluminium and magnesium is used as a base for nickel plating on aluminium and magnesium. Nickel, gold, silver and tin platings can be produced by this method.

**(3) Hot dipping :** Hot dip coatings are applied on base metal by immersing them in molten metal bath covered by molten flux layer of $ZnCl_2 \cdot 3\ NH_4Cl$. This method is useful for producing coatings of metals having low melting points, on the metals having high melting points. Zinc, tin and lead are used to coat steel, iron and copper. Hot dipping coatings are of two layers, first layer is alloying layer adhering directly to metal while second layer is of pure coating metal. For proper adhesion, base metal surface must be cleaned properly.

For coating lead on iron, first iron is coated with thin coating of tin by immersion method and then by hot dipping lead is applied on it to form second layer.

Galvanized steel is a popular example of steel sheets having thin coat of zinc. Zinc prevents steel from corrosion due to atmosphere. But galvanized iron has poor acid resistance. Galvanized wares cannot be used for preserving food-stuffs as zinc will form toxic compounds with food preservatives.

Tin is applied on iron in a similar way as zinc is applied on iron. But tin cannot protect iron like galvanized iron, as tin coating cannot cover the iron surface completely. When coated surface is exposed to air, iron being anodic to tin, rapid corrosion of iron takes place (See Fig. 4.26). Tin can be used for coating over mild steel. Tin-coated containers can be used for storing and preserving food-stuffs because tin has corrosion resistance to dilute acids and water and it is non-toxic.

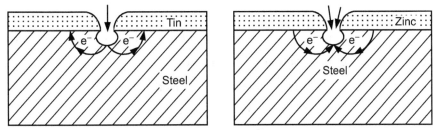

**Fig. 4.26 : Galvanic corrosion in tin and zinc coated steel**

**Arrows indicated corrosive attack**

By hot dipping method, thickness of the coating produced on base metal is more. Afterwards the coated part is heat treated to form an alloy bond between coating and base metal.

**(4) Metal spraying or flame spraying :** Metallized coatings are obtained by spraying heated metal particles on the roughened surface of base metal. This can be achieved by using spraying guns or by powder method. When the molten metal particles strike the metal surface, they flatten and fill up the surface irregularities. Finely divided molten metal particles are obtained by feeding metal wire through a melting flame. Oxyacetylene flame is commonly used for melting the metal. The atomized metal is then blown out into a fine spray with the help of compressed air. Thus, the sprayed metal adheres to the surface of base metal. This method is limited to low melting metals like zinc, lead, tin as coating metals.

Coatings produced by spraying are uniform but porous, so they are less protective under severe corrosion attack. Sprayed metal provides a good base for paint.

**(5) Metal cladding :** It is the process by which dense homogeneous layer of metal is bonded firmly and permanently to the base metal on one side or both sides. The protecting layer of the covering metal is called the cladding metal. Thin sheets of base metal and coating metal are passed through roller under pressure and high temperature. The two metals form a composite material. The choice of cladding metal depends upon environment in which it is to be used. Mild steel clad by stainless steels, nickel, nickel alloys, copper, copper alloys, platinum is used in many environments. Sandwich rolling, hot pressing, fusion welding are the different ways of metal cladding.

**(6) Diffusion coating :** Diffusion coating involves heat treatment to cause alloy formation by diffusion of one metal into other. It is also called as surface alloying. Metal part to be coated is heated with powdered coating metal to a high temperature to allow for diffusion of fine particles into it. Small articles like bolt, screws, valves etc. can be coated-alloyed-with metals like zinc, chromium and aluminium.

If zinc coating is done by diffusion method, it is called sherardizing. In this method, small article to be coated is cleaned and then packed with zinc dust in metal drum. Drum is sealed and slowly rotated and heated to 350 – 400°C in an inert atmosphere for 3 - 12 hours. During heating zinc diffuses into base metal forming alloy layer adjacent to it.

In chromising base metal is heated in powdered mixture of 55% chromium and 45% alumina at 1350 - 1400°C for 3 - 4 hours.

## 4.6.2 Surface Conversion Coatings or Inorganic Barriers

**Inorganic Coatings :**

They are produced by 'corroding' the metal surface to form an adherent and protective corrosion product. They are also called chemical conversion coatings because metallic surface is converted into some other chemical form by a chemical reaction. They are used as primary coatings.

**(a) Anodizing :** Anodizing consists of anodic oxidation in an acid bath to build up an oxide layer. Anodized coatings can be produced on aluminium, magnesium and their alloys by electrolysis in acid like sulphuric acid, chromic acid or phosphoric acid at moderate temperature and current densities. Initially, the oxide film formed as a result of anodic oxidation is thin, it grows in thickness as oxidation proceeds. The surface layers - coatings - are porous, so are used as adherent layer for paints. Minute pores can be sealed by exposing the coat to boiling water or sealed with oils, waxes, chromates and various resins.

**(b) Phosphate coatings :** A process of producing phosphate coatings on a base metal by reaction between aqueous solution of phosphate and phosphoric acid with the base metal is called phosphatizing. Automobile bodies are examples of phosphatizing, it provides good base for paints. Phosphate coatings are applied on iron, steel, zinc by using phosphates of iron, manganese and zinc and various accelerators. These coatings can be produced by spraying, brushing or by immersion.

**(c) Chromate coatings :** These conversion coatings are applied by immersion of base metal into solution of hexavalent chromium ion and mineral acid. They are used for protection of zinc, aluminium and magnesium. Chromate coatings have more corrosion resistance than that of phosphate coating. They can be applied in various colours and shades.

**(d) Oxide coatings :** These are produced by treating base metal with alkaline oxidising solution. This increases thickness of original oxide film. They have less protective value and mostly used for decorative purpose.

## 4.6.3 Organic Coatings or Organic Barriers

These involve thin barrier between substrate material and environment. They are applied for corrosion protection and decoration. Paints, varnishes, enamels and lacquers are types of organic coatings applied on metallic surfaces. Protective value of organic coatings always depends on the film formed and to what extent they prevent the penetration of water, oxygen and ions.

**(a) Paints :** Paint is a dispersion of one or more pigments in a vehicle consisting essentially of drying oil and solvent thinner. Drying oils contain triglycerides consisting of unsaturated long-chain molecule and ester group. Linseed oil, tung oil, soyabean oil, and synthetic fatty oils produced from petroleum are widely used drying oils. When paint is applied to metal surface, thinner evaporates and drying oil oxidises to form dry pigment film. Pigments are finely powdered materials, insoluble in organic binders, solvents and film forming resins. They provide colour and opacity to the coating. Certain pigments work as inhibitors by controlling electrochemical reactions at the metal surface. To accelerate drying, small amounts of catalysts (driers) like metallic soaps of cobalt, iron, lead or calcium with monobasic acids are added to vehicle (mixture of binder with thinner). For maximum protection, paint should be applied at minimum of three coats.

**(b) Varnishes, enamels and lacquers :** Varnish consists of drying oil, natural thermosetting synthetic resin and solvent thinner. When varnish is applied to a metal surface, thinner evaporates. The oil resin mixture on oxidation and polymerisation forms clear dry film.

An enamel is an intimate dispersion of pigments in a varnish or resin vehicle. It also forms film like varnish when applied on metal surface.

A lacquer is a solvent solution of resins and plasticizers with or without pigment dispersed throughout, they dry through evaporation of solvent.

These all organic coatings are applied on metals by brushing or spraying.

**(c) Dispersions, emulsions and latex coatings :** Dispersion coatings consist of finely divided insoluble resins dispersed in organic media. When it is applied on metal surface, the resin particles coagulate, organic thinner evaporates and film of resin particles is formed. Emulsion coatings are suspension of oil phase (drying oil, varnish and resin) in water. When emulsion is applied on metal, coagulation of dispersed particles take place, water separates and film of resin or varnish is formed.

Latex coatings are dispersions of resinous solids in water.

# EXERCISE

1.  What is corrosion ? Discuss the corrosion caused due to combination of metals of different electrode potentials.
2.  What is corrosion ? How do metals undergo corrosion ?
3.  Define corrosion. Explain with suitable example dry corrosion theory.
4.  Why steel pipe connected to the copper plumbing gets corroded ? Name and explain the type of corrosion.
5.  Explain galvanic corrosion with the help of galvanic series.
6.  Define the term corrosion. Explain electrochemical theory of corrosion.
7.  Explain rusting of iron with suitable diagram and chemical reaction.
8.  Explain hydrogen evolution and oxygen absorption mechanism of electrochemical corrosion.

9. What happens when metals like gold, aluminium and iron are exposed to moist atmosphere ?

10. Discuss atmospheric corrosion in case of silver, molybdenum, sodium and aluminium.

11. Define the term corrosion. What are the consequences of corrosion ?

12. Define the terms uniform corrosion and localised corrosion. Explain with a suitable example why is latter more severe than the former ?

13. What is the principle underlying differential aeration corrosion ? Explain the various forms of corrosion coming within the purview of it ?

14. State the principle underlying electrochemical or wet corrosion. Under what conditions does it occur ?

15. What is the relation between hydrogen overvoltage and corrosion rate ? Explain.

16. "Passivity is not a static but a dynamic phenomenon." Comment.

17. "Anodic metallic coatings provide better protection to metals than cathodic ones". Comment.

18. What are preventive measures for corrosion ? Explain.

19. What kind of corrosion occur if metal is exposed to -

    (i)   Acidic environment

    (ii)  Slightly alkaline or aqueous salt solution (aerated) ?

    Explain with a suitable diagram and example.

20. Distinguish between hydrogen evolution and oxygen absorption mechanisms for corrosion.

21. What are the key factors influencing dry and wet corrosion ?

22. Distinguish between cathodic and anodic protection methods for controlling corrosion.

23. Distinguish between anodic and cathodic metallic coatings. Which is more preferred one ? Why ?

24. What are the merits and demerits of organic and inorganic coatings ?

25. Give an account of non-metallic coatings for protection against corrosion.

26. How do inhibitors inhibit corrosion ? Explain.

27. When is the cathodic protection method used for controlling corrosion ? What are the modes for employing it ?

28. What are the precautions to be taken in the choice of suitable metal and proper design selection in checking corrosion ?

29. What are the merits and limitations of use of pure metal and metal alloys methods ?

30. Which method would you choose under the following circumstances for controlling corrosion :

    (a)   Modification of the environment is not possible.

    (b)   Chances of electrochemical corrosion to occur are more.

    (c)   The metal surface is to be coated with a primer coat.

    (d)   When the metal is to be made to behave as passive.

    (e)   When modification in the corrosive environment is possible.

31. What are the characteristic features of a good protective coating ? How is it superior to other methods for corrosion control ?

# ELECTROCHEMISTRY

## 5.1 INTRODUCTION

In chemical reactions, the electrons travel through only interatomic distances; while in electrochemical reactions, the electrons taking part travel distances greater than interatomic distances. For example, when zinc oxide dissolves in sulphuric acid to generate zinc sulphate, it is a chemical reaction, whereas when technical grade zinc metal dissolves in sulphuric acid, it is electrochemical reaction. This can be represented by two partial reactions :

$$Zn \rightarrow Zn^{++} + 2e^- \qquad \text{... (oxidation)} \qquad \text{... (1)}$$

$$2H^+ + 2e^- \rightarrow H_2 \qquad \text{... (reduction)} \qquad \text{... (2)}$$

If one of the above two partial reactions is prevented, the reaction will stop. If super purity stress-free zinc metal is used, the evolution of hydrogen can be suppressed and hence dissolution of zinc metal. Fig. 5.1 illustrates the dissolution of zinc metal.

The main points of this reaction are (i) loss of electrons (oxidation), (ii) gain of electrons (reduction), (iii) movement of ions within the solution and electrons outside it.

In the above example, the sites of oxidations and reductions are inherently short-circuited; whereas most electrochemical processes are carried out such that oxidations and reductions take place at considerable distances.

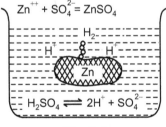

**Fig. 5.1**

On the basis of the free energy of total reaction, the various electrochemical reactions are classified as :

(a)  Energy producers such as dry cell, charged lead accumulator.

(b)  Energy consumers such as electroplating, refining etc.

(c)  Energy wasters such as corrosion of metals.

Thus, electrochemistry is that branch of chemistry which deals mainly with a systematic study of (i) production of electricity by chemical reactions and (ii) chemical changes induced by the passage of electric current i.e. electrolysis.

## 5.2 CONDUCTION OF ELECTRICITY

An electric current is a flow of electrons (electric charge) through a conductor just as flow of water molecules through a pipe.

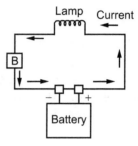

**Fig. 5.2 : Electric current**

Fig. 5.2 shows an electric circuit in which the battery functions as a pump and pushes electrons into the metal wire, which contains free electrons. The electrons pass through the lamp and come back to the battery. If in the circuit a block 'B' is introduced, which does not allow the electrons to flow through it, then no current can pass and the lamp will not glow.

Different substances behave differently when electricity is passed through them. Some of them allow the electricity to pass through them while others do not.

## 5.3 CONDUCTORS AND NON-CONDUCTORS

Substances are divided into two categories as : **conductors and non-conductors or insulators.**

"Conductor is a substance which allows the electric current to pass through it." e.g. all metals, many sulphides such as pyrites, galena, etc.; aqueous solution of bases, acids and salts, fused salts and impure water.

"Non-conductors or insulators are those substances which do not allow the electric current to pass through them." e.g. pure water, glass, mica, rubber, organic compounds such as urea, sugar, etc.

Conductors are further sub-divided as **metallic conductors** and **electrolytic conductors** or **electrolytes.**

**"Those conductors through which electricity flows without producing chemical changes are called metallic conductors."** In this case, conduction takes place by the movement of electrons under an action of applied potential e.g. all metals, graphite, etc. The flow of an electric current through a copper wire is an example of metallic conduction.

**"Those substances which in the fused state or in the state of solution conduct electric current and at the same time undergo chemical decomposition are called electrolytes or electrolytic conductors."**

**Explanation :** As shown in Fig. 5.3, $CuSO_4$ solution in the circuit conducts electric current (i.e. the lamp glows) and gets decomposed as a result of passage of electric current. The solution of $CuSO_4$ is therefore an electrolyte.

In this case, conduction takes place by the movement of ions. Examples are solutions of salts, acids and bases. Electrolytes also conduct electricity in the fused state and undergo decomposition by the passage of electric current.

**"The substances which in the fused state or in the state of solution do not conduct electric current are called non-electrolytes."**

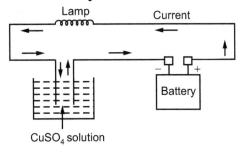

**Fig. 5.3 : Conduction through electrolyte**

**Examples :** Solutions of cane sugar, alcohol, glycerine, glucose, urea etc. are non-electrolytes.

In the above explanation (Fig. 5.3) for electrolytes, if $CuSO_4$ solution is replaced by sugar solution or urea solution or pure water, the electric current does not flow and the lamp will not glow, showing that sugar solution or urea solution are non-electrolytes.

**Distinction between Metallic and Electrolytic Conduction :**

| Metallic conduction | Electrolytic conduction |
|---|---|
| 1. Electricity is conducted by movement of *electrons.* | 1. Electricity is conducted by movement of *ions.* |
| 2. *Electrons* flow from negative end to positive end of battery. | 2. *Ions* move towards oppositely charged *electrodes.* |
| 3. There are *no chemical reactions* and hence no change in the composition of the conductor (metal). | 3. *Chemical reactions* do take place at the electrodes with the decomposition of conductor (electrolyte). |
| 4. No transfer of matter takes place. | 4. *Transfer of matter* does take place (ions). |
| 5. With *increase in temperature, resistance* to the flow of current also *increases* thereby *decreasing conduction.* | 5. With *increase in temperature, resistance* to the flow of current *decreases* thereby *increasing conduction.* |

# 5.4 ARRHENIUS THEORY OR THEORY OF IONISATION

To explain the anomalous behaviour of electrolytes, a Swedish chemist, Svante Arrhenius proposed the theory of ionisation in the year 1887. In spite of the fact that this theory has undergone some changes after it was first proposed, still the basic ideas in the theory are accepted, even in today's time. The main postulates of the **'theory of electrolytic dissociation'** or **'theory of ionisation'** are :

1.    The molecules of an electrolyte (e.g. acids, bases and salts) when dissolved in water yield two kinds of charged particles, one carrying a positive charge and the other carrying equal but negative charge. These charged particles are called **ions** and the process is known as **ionisation** or **electrolytic dissociation.** [The term ion had been used by Faraday in 1834. It was in reference to discharge of electricity through gases. The term is derived from the Greek word 'ion' meaning 'wanderer' or 'traveller'.

The positively charged ions are called **cations** and the negatively charged ions are called **anions.** [The prefixes 'cata' and 'ana' mean down and up respectively. Anion is the ion which moves up the potential gradient i.e. towards positively charged electrode.

The total charge on cations present is equal but opposite to that of anions present so that the solution is electrically neutral.

The solid electrolyte is a combination of charged ions which are held together by the electrostatic forces. When fused or dissolved in water, these electrostatic forces of attraction between the ions are cut-off and the ions move out freely.

$$A^+B^- \rightleftharpoons A^+ + B^-$$

2.    Cations are generally metallic radicals obtained by loss of electrons from the metallic atoms, while anions are non-metallic radicals by gain of electrons by non-metallic atoms or group of atoms.

$$M \longrightarrow M^{+n} + ne^-$$
$$\text{(metal)} \qquad \text{(cation)}$$

$$A + me^- \longrightarrow A^{-m}$$
$$\text{(non-metal)} \qquad \text{(anion)}$$

3.    The properties of electrolytes in the solution are the properties of the ions produced.

4.    The electrolytes may not be completely ionised. Only a fraction of the total number of molecules is ionised. This fraction is called **degree of ionisation.**

5.    Molecules of the solute are constantly splitting up into ions and the ions are constantly reuniting to give original molecules. Thus, a state of dynamic equilibrium between ionised and unionised molecules exists, e.g. in sodium chloride solution in water, the following equilibrium is set up :

$$NaCl \rightleftharpoons Na^+ + Cl^-$$

6.    Conductivity of a solution is due to the presence of ions in the solution. The number of ions depend on the degree of ionisation. Greater the degree of ionisation, larger is the number of ions.

7.    The ions are free to move and are in random motion. Under the influence of electric current these are directed towards oppositely charged electrodes. Electric current does not produce ions, but it only has a directive effect.

## 5.5 ELECTROLYSIS AND RELATED TERMINOLOGIES

1.   **Electrolytic cell or voltameter :** Electrolytic cell (i.e. an apparatus of convenient shape, size and material) is a device in which an external source of voltage (i.e. electrical energy) is used to bring about a chemical change.

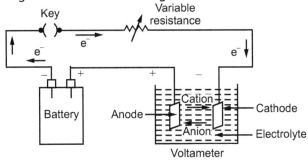

**Fig. 5.4**

2.   **Electric current :** A battery which is the source of electric current has two poles, called +ve and –ve terminals. The +ve terminal is short of electrons and thus acquires +ve charge. The negative terminal has excess of electrons and thus acquires –ve charge. Thus, a potential difference exists between the two poles.

As shown in Fig. 5.4 when the two poles of the battery are connected with metal wire through a key, electrons start moving from the –ve terminal of the battery to the positive terminal. The terminal of the battery through which electrons are sent out in the external circuit is called **negative pole of the battery** and the terminal at which electrons after moving through the circuit enter the battery is called **positive pole of the battery**. The direction of the conventional electric current is taken as opposite to the actual flow of electrons through the circuit.

3.   **Electrodes :** In order to conduct electric current through electrolyte, some metal conductors have to be dipped in the solution. Such metal conductors are known as electrodes. "The rods, plates or foils through which electric current enters or leaves the electrolyte are called electrodes."

Electrodes are electron carriers. They carry the electrons into and out of the solution in voltameter. Those electrodes which take part in chemical reactions in addition to acting as electron carriers are called 'Active electrodes' (e.g. copper, silver, etc.), while those electrodes which act as only electron carriers are called 'Inert electrodes' (e.g. platinum, graphite, etc.).

As shown in Fig. 5.4, one plate is connected to the +ve terminal of the battery and current enters the electrolyte through this plate and another plate is connected to the –ve terminal of the battery and the current leaves the electrolyte through this plate. These plates are known as anode and cathode respectively.

**Anode :** The electrode, which is connected to the +ve terminal of the battery, is called **anode** or **positive electrode.** It is this rod, plate or foil through which the current enters the electrolyte.

**Cathode :** The electrode which is connected to the –ve terminal of the battery is called **cathode** or **negative electrode.** It is this rod, plate or foil through which current leaves the electrolyte.

4.  **Current density :** It is the current strength (measured in amperes) per unit area (usually expressed in square decimeter i.e. 100 sq. cm.) of the surface of electrode.

$$\therefore \qquad \text{Current density} \ = \ \frac{\text{Current}}{\text{Area}} = \frac{\text{Amperes}}{\text{Sq. decimeter}} \text{ i.e. amp/sq.dm.}$$

Current density has great significance in the extraction of metals and electroplating.

5.  **Strong and weak electrolytes :** On the basis of extent of ionisation, electrolytes are called strong and weak electrolytes. *Those electrolytes which are highly ionised in the solution and hence have a high degree of ionisation are called strong electrolytes.* Examples are strong acids like $HCl$, $H_2SO_4$, $HNO_3$, strong bases like $NaOH$, $KOH$ and almost all salts. *Those electrolytes which are only feebly ionised in the solution and hence have a low degree of ionisation are called weak electrolytes.* Examples are $H_2CO_3$, $Al(OH)_3$, $CH_3COOH$, $NH_4OH$, $H_3BO_3$, etc.

**Distinction Between Strong and Weak Electrolytes :**

| Strong electrolyte | Weak electrolyte |
| --- | --- |
| 1. Almost completely dissociated. | 1. Dissociated to very small extent. |
| 2. Law of mass action can not be applicable. | 2. Law of mass action can be applicable. |
| 3. Possess high conductivity values. | 3. Possess low conductivity values. |
| 4. Strong acids, strong bases and salts are examples e.g. HCl, KOH, NaCl. | 4. All weak acids and weak bases are examples e.g. $CH_3COOH$, $NH_2OH$. |

# 5.6 ELECTROLYSIS

"The process of chemical decomposition of an electrolyte by the passage of electric current is called **electrolysis**."

**Mechanism of electrolysis :** Consider a glass vessel (voltameter) containing NaCl in the fused state (electrolyte) and two platinum plates (electrodes) dipped in it as shown in Fig. 5.5. NaCl molecules split up into $Na^+$ and $Cl^-$ ions i.e. ionisation of NaCl takes place and the ions wander about so long as the key is open.

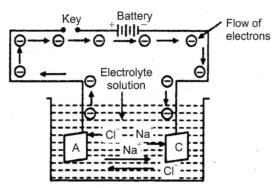

**Fig. 5.5 : Mechanism of electrolysis**

When the key is closed, these ions under the influence of electric current travel towards the oppositely charged electrodes. Those ions travelling towards the cathode are called 'cations' (positive ions or cathode seeking ions) while those moving towards the anode are called anions (negative ions or anode seeking ions).

The ions on reaching the respective electrodes lose their charge (i.e. get discharged) and become neutral atoms or group of atoms. The following primary reactions occur around the two electrodes.

**At cathode :** When the cation reaches the cathode, it acquires electrons from the cathode, thereby its charge is neutralised. (Reduction or electronation).

$$Na^+ + e^- \longrightarrow Na$$
(Neutral sodium atom)

Thus, a reduction process takes place around the cathode (cations reduced).

**At anode :** When the anion reaches the anode, the electrons from anion are given or removed, leaving behind the discharged neutral atom or group of atoms. (Oxidation or de-electronation).

$$Cl^- \longrightarrow Cl + e^-$$
(Neutral chlorine atom)

Thus, an oxidation process occurs around the anode (Anions oxidised).

This process goes on and more and more of the electrolyte molecules are decomposed and the cations and the anions continue to get discharged at the respective electrodes. Thus, the electric current only directs the ions to the respective electrodes and the process of electrolysis continues. When the current is stopped, however, the process of electrolysis also stops.

From the above discussion, it can be concluded that :

(i)   The phenomenon of electrolysis (i.e. conversion of electrical energy into chemical energy) takes place only at the electrodes.

(ii)  The electrolyte as a whole remains neutral during the process as equal number of charges are neutralised at the electrodes.

(iii) The deposition of different ions at the electrodes takes place only till the time the electricity is passed and stops as soon as the electric current is switched off.

The electrolysis takes place in two stages.

1. **Primary stage of electrolysis or primary reaction** is a first stage of electrolysis in which the electrons are either accepted or lost by the ions forming neutral particles.

2. **Secondary stage of electrolysis or secondary reaction** is a reaction in which the neutral particles combine to form a stable end-product at the two electrodes.

**Reactions at Cathode :**

During primary reaction, electrons are removed from cathode and these electrons are gained or accepted by cations (+ve ions) forming neutral atoms or group of atoms. Hence, there is reduction of cation or electronation takes place.

**For example :**

$$K^+ + e^- \longrightarrow K \text{ (Neutral potassium atom)}$$

$$NH_4^+ + e^- \longrightarrow NH_4 \text{ (Neutral ammonium group)}$$

$$H^+ + e^- \longrightarrow H \text{ (Neutral hydrogen atom)}$$

$$Cu^{++} + 2e^- \longrightarrow Cu \text{ (Neutral copper atom)}$$

During secondary stage, if the neutral particles formed in primary stage are of gaseous elements such as hydrogen, then they combine to form molecules (stable end-product) and these are evolved at cathode as bubbles.

e.g.            $H + H \longrightarrow H_2 \uparrow$

**Reactions at anode :**

During primary reaction at anode the anions give up or release the electrons and become neutral particles. These released electrons are taken away by the anode. Thus, there is oxidation of anion or de-electronation takes place.

**For example :**

$$Cl^- \longrightarrow Cl \text{ (Neutral chlorine atom)} + e^-$$

$$OH^- \longrightarrow OH \text{ (Neutral hydroxyl group)} + e^-$$

During secondary stage, if the neutral particles formed in primary stage are of gaseous elements, they combine to form stable molecules.

e.g.            $Cl + Cl \longrightarrow Cl_2 \uparrow$

While in the primary stage neutral particle is a group of atoms which cannot be liberated as such because it does not exist in free state, will combine together to form stable end product.

e.g.            $4(OH) \longrightarrow 2H_2O + O_2 \uparrow$

The above mentioned reactions at cathode and anode take place when only one type of cation and one type of anion is present in the vicinity of electrodes.

If two or more different types of ions are present in the vicinity of electrodes then preferential discharge theory is to be applied.

**Activity of Ions and Preferential Discharge :**

Usually there are several different kinds of ions around each electrode competing for an opportunity for giving up electrons (i.e. de-electronation) to the anode and competing for receiving electrons (i.e. electronation) from the cathode. It is found experimentally that if a mixture of ions is electrolysed, certain ions are liberated (i.e. get neutralised) at the electrodes in preference to others. This is explained by the *preferential discharge theory which states that if more than one type of ions are attracted to a given electrode, then the one liberated is that ion which requires least energy for getting neutralised.*

A measure of energy required to liberate the ions is provided by the potential difference which must be applied between the electrodes to effect electrolysis. This potential is termed as *discharge potential* or *deposition potential*. '*The minimum voltage required to discharge a given ion is called discharge or deposition potential*'.

The same results are obtained from the chemical activity series considerations. On this basis let us consider the reactions at the two electrodes.

**Reaction at cathode :** Higher the activity of the metal, lesser will be the tendency to accept electrons. Thus such metals will have more tendency to form ions (i.e. cations) rather than their ions undergoing a reaction of electronation. Therefore, such ions will difficulty get discharged at cathode. In the activity series (Table 5.1), the cations are so arranged that the cation occurring earlier (more at the top) will accept electrons less readily than the cation occurring latter (towards bottom). For example, if a solution contains $Ag^+$, $H^+$ and $Na^+$ ions then $Ag^+$ ions will be preferentially discharged and silver metal will get deposited on cathode. When all silver ions in the solution get discharged, then only and at a slightly higher voltage, the hydrogen ions can get discharged at cathode, evolving hydrogen gas at it.

Similarly, if an electrolytic solution contains $K^+$, $Zn^{++}$ and $Cu^{++}$ ions, then $Cu^{++}$ ions will be selectively discharged and deposited as copper metal at the cathode. If the process is continued until all the $Cu^{++}$ have been removed then $Zn^{++}$ ions will start discharging at the cathode but at a slightly higher voltage and more active $K^+$ ions still remain in the solution.

According to Magnus rule, "*When a solution containing different salts is electrolysed, then at a certain voltage, ions of one and only one of the metals are discharged and deposited at cathode, leaving all other ions in the solution.*"

Just as activity of the element has a deciding effect so also the concentration of different ions and nature of the electrode material used, plays a part. Hence, the factors deciding the preference of cation are (i) position of the element in the activity series, (ii) the concentration of ions and (iii) nature of the cathode.

e.g. In the electrolysis of sodium chloride solution in water, hydrogen gas evolves at cathode if platinum electrodes are used while sodium metal is obtained at cathode if mercury is used as cathode.

**Table 5.1 : Activity series**

| Cation | Anion |
|---|---|
| $K^+$ | $SO_4^{--}$ |
| $Na^+$ | $NO_3^-$ |
| $Ca^{++}$ | $OH^-$ |
| $Mg^{++}$ | $Cl^-$ |
| $Al^{+++}$ | $Br^-$ |
| $Zn^{++}$ | $S^{--}$ |
| $Cr^{+++}$ | $I^-$ |
| $Fe^{++}$ | |
| $Cd^{++}$ | |
| $H^+$ | |
| $Cu^{++}$ | |
| $Ag^+$ | |
| $Au^+$ | |

**Reaction at anode :** If two or more anions are present, then the ion having higher tendency to lose electrons will be discharged in preference to other. The anion activity series (Table 5.1) gives the relative ease with which the anions will lose the electrons. The anions more towards bottom of the series are discharged more readily than those above them.

Apart from the position in the activity series, the discharge of anions also depends upon concentration of different anions in the solution and the nature of the electrode material, e.g. in the electrolysis of aqueous solution of copper sulphate, oxygen gas is evolved at anode if platinum electrodes are used and copper metal if used as electrodes then copper from anode dissolves in preference to other processes.

## 5.7 ELECTROCHEMICAL CELL

**Electrochemical cell** is a set up or device involved in the inter-conversion of electrical energy and chemical energy.

Hence there are two types of cells.

1.  A device where electrical energy is converted into chemical energy is called **electrolytic cell.**

2.  A device where chemical energy is converted into electrical energy is called **galvanic cell.**

**Electrolytic Cells :**

*Electrolytic cell is a device or set up in which an external source of voltage i.e. electrical energy is used to bring about a chemical change.*

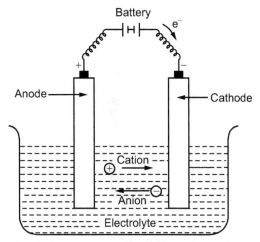

**Fig. 5.6 : Electrolytic cell for electrolysis**

These cells are mainly used for metal plating; in the extraction of metals and in many engineering and military appliances.

**Galvanic Cells :**

*Galvanic cell is a set up or device which is used to convert chemical energy into electrical energy.* The electrical energy set free in certain chemical reactions can be used in the form of electricity for various purposes. The amount and force with which this energy is available will depend on the intensity of chemical reaction taking place inside the cell. The *process going on in a galvanic cell is exactly the reverse of that in the electrolytic cell.*

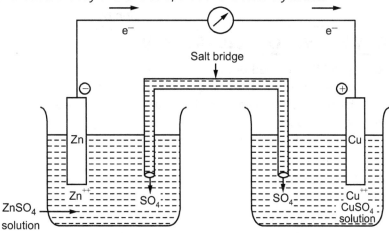

**Fig. 5.7 : Galvanic cell using salt bridge**

Daniel cell and dry cell are galvanic cells which are the combination of two half cells connected internally by salt bridge and externally by metal conductors forming an electrochemical cell.

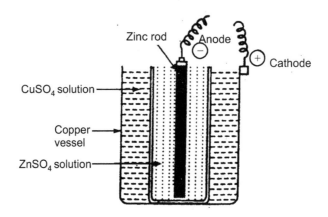

**Fig. 5.8 : Daniel cell**

**Distinction between Electrolytic and Galvanic Cell :**

| Electrolytic cell | Galvanic cell |
|---|---|
| 1. It converts electrical energy to chemical energy. | 1. It converts chemical energy to electrical energy. |
| 2. It is used to bring about electrolysis (non-spontaneous chemical reaction). | 2. It is used to produce electricity (spontaneous chemical reaction). |
| 3. Used in electroplating, extraction of metals, refining of metals, etc. | 3. Used in calculators, torches, transistors, etc. Protection of metals (ships) from corrosion by sea water. |

# 5.8 FARADAY'S LAWS OF ELECTROLYSIS

Michael Faraday in 1834, carried out a series of experiments in which he passed known currents through different electrolytes and actually weighed the substances that are liberated at the electrodes. On generalising the results of these experiments with different electrolytes, he stated the conclusions in the form of two relations. As these relations govern the decomposition of an electrolyte with the passage of electric current, therefore, these are known as *laws of electrolysis*.

To understand the significance of these laws clearly, the knowledge of the following terminologies is essential.

**(a) Coulomb :** It is defined as the quantity of electricity that pass through a circuit when a current of one ampere strength is passed through the circuit for one second.

Thus,             1 coulomb  =  1 ampere × 1 second

It can also be defined as the *quantity of electricity which deposit 0.001118 g of silver on a silver cathode from a 15% silver nitrate solution.*

**(b) Ampere :** It measures the strength of an electric current. When a coulomb of electricity passed through a point in a conductor in one second, the quantity of electric current is one ampere.

*"A current of one ampere corresponds to a flow of 6.3 $\times 10^{18}$ electrons per second through any cross-section of a conductor."*

"Ampere is a unit of current which when passing through a circuit for one second liberates 0.001118 g of silver or 0.0000104 g of hydrogen."

**(c) Faraday :** *It is the quantity of electricity required to liberate or deposit one gram equivalent of a substance from its solution.*

It is a bigger unit than coulomb.

$$1 \text{ faraday (F)} = 96,500 \text{ coulombs}$$

## 5.9 FARADAY'S FIRST LAW OF ELECTROLYSIS

It states that *the amount of any substance that is liberated or deposited at an electrode during electrolysis is directly proportional to the quantity of electricity passed through the electrolyte.*

**Mathematical Expression :**

If W is the weight of a substance deposited or liberated at the electrode during electrolysis and Q is the quantity of electricity passed through the electrolyte, then,

$$W \propto Q$$

But the quantity of electricity Q is measured in coulombs and is equal to the product of the current strength in ampere (I) and the time in seconds (t) for which it is passed.

i.e.                          $Q$ = Current strength $\times$ Time

$\therefore$                          $Q = I \times t$

Therefore,          $W \propto I \times t$

$\therefore$                          $W = Z \times I \times t$

where Z is a constant known as **electrochemical equivalent.**

When I = 1 ampere and   t = 1 second, then W = Z

Thus, electrochemical equivalent of a substance is defined as the weight of a substance deposited or dissolved by 1 ampere current passing for 1 second i.e. by the passage of 1 coulomb of electricity.

The electrochemical equivalents (e.c.e.) of some elements are given in Table 5.2.

**Table 5.2 : E.C.E. of some elements**

| Element | | Mass | | E.C.E. |
| --- | --- | --- | --- | --- |
| Name | Symbol | Number | Valency | (gm per coulomb) |
| Hydrogen | H | 1.008 | 1 | 0.0000104 |
| Oxygen | O | 16.0 | 2 | 0.0000829 |
| Aluminium | Al | 27.0 | 3 | 0.0000932 |
| Nickel | Ni | 59.0 | 2 | 0.0003044 |
| Copper | Cu | 63.56 | 2 | 0.000329 |
| Zinc | Zn | 65.0 | 2 | 0.0003337 |
| Silver | Ag | 108.0 | 1 | 0.001118 |
| Gold | Au | 197.0 | 1 | 0.00204 |

## 5.10 FARADAY'S SECOND LAW OF ELECTROLYSIS

The law states that *when the same quantity of electricity is passed through different electrolytes arranged in series, the amounts of different substances liberated at the electrodes are directly proportional to their chemical equivalents i.e. equivalent weights (eq. wts.).*

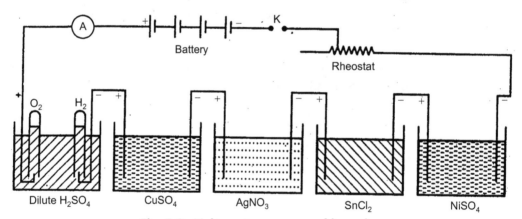

**Fig. 5.9 : Voltameters arranged in series**

**Explanation and Mathematical Expression :**

If the same current is passed through a number of voltameters arranged in series (Fig. 5.9) then the weights of hydrogen, copper, silver, tin and nickel deposited on respective cathodes will be in the ratio of their chemical equivalents (i.e. eq. wts.).

Wt. of Cu deposited $\propto$ Eq. wt. of Cu

Wt. of Ag deposited $\propto$ Eq. wt. of Ag

$\vdots$ $\qquad\qquad$ $\vdots$

$\qquad$ and so on $\qquad$ and so on

i.e. $\qquad$ $\dfrac{\text{Wt. of deposited Cu}}{\text{Eq. wt. of Cu}} = \dfrac{\text{Wt. of deposited Ag}}{\text{Eq. wt. of Ag}}$ = and so on

If $W_1$, $W_2$ etc. are the weights of the elements deposited by passing a certain quantity of electricity through their salt solutions and $E_1$, $E_2$ etc. are their respective equivalent weights, then,

$$\frac{W_1}{E_1} = \frac{W_2}{E_2} = \text{and so on}$$

If $W_1$ and $W_2$ are the weights of copper and silver deposited, and $E_1$ and $E_2$ are their equivalent weights, then,

$$\frac{\text{Weight of copper deposited}}{\text{Weight of silver deposited}} = \frac{\text{Eq. wt. of copper}}{\text{Eq. wt. of silver}}$$

$\therefore$ $$\frac{W_1}{W_2} = \frac{E_1}{E_2}$$

## Relation between Coulomb and Faraday

We know that $Ag^+$ ion takes up one electron from the cathode and gets converted into Ag atom.

$$Ag^+ + e^- \rightarrow Ag$$

The equivalent weight of silver (Ag) is equal to its atomic weight (107.88). There are $6.023 \times 10^{23}$ (Avogadro's number) atoms in one atomic weight or one mole. Thus, one mole of silver will be deposited when 1 mole of $Ag^+$ ion takes up one mole of electrons. The charge on each electron is $1.603 \times 10^{-19}$ coulombs. The total charge of 1 mole of electrons is therefore $1.603 \times 10^{-19} \times 6.023 \times 10^{23} = 96500$ coulombs. Hence 96500 coulombs of electricity is required to deposit one gm equivalent weight of silver. Thus, 96500 coulombs of electricity is called one Faraday.

Faraday (F) is also the quantity of charge carried by one mole by electrons, as

$$F = e \times N = 1.603 \times 10^{-19} \times 6.023 \times 10^{23} = 96500 \text{ coulombs}$$

## Relation between Chemical Equivalent and Electrochemical Equivalent

Let $Z_A$ and $Z_B$ be the electrochemical equivalents of the two elements, then according to Faraday's first law (W – $Z \times I \times t$),

$\therefore$ $\qquad\qquad\qquad W_A = Z_A \times I \times t$

and $\qquad\qquad\qquad W_B = Z_B \times I \times t$

According to the second law, we have,

$$\frac{W_A}{W_B} = \frac{E_A}{E_B}$$

where $W_A$, $W_B$ are weights deposited and $E_A$, $E_B$ are the corresponding chemical equivalents of the two elements.

Therefore, putting the values of $W_A$ and $W_B$, we get,

$$\frac{Z_A \times I \times t}{Z_B \times I \times t} = \frac{E_A}{E_B}$$

$$\therefore \qquad \frac{Z_A}{Z_B} = \frac{E_A}{E_B}$$

Thus, the electrochemical equivalent (Z) of an element is directly proportional to its equivalent weight (i.e. chemical equivalent).

i.e. $\qquad\qquad Z \propto E$

$$\therefore \qquad Z = \frac{1}{Constant} \times E$$

$$\therefore \qquad Z = \frac{1}{F} \times E$$

where constant of proportionality is denoted by F and is equal to 96500 coulombs.

Thus, $\qquad\qquad E = F \times Z$

$$= 96500 \times Z$$

or $\qquad\qquad Z = \frac{E}{96500}$

$\therefore \qquad$ Chemical equivalent $= 96500 \times$ Electrochemical equivalent

## Determination of Equivalent Weight of an Element

For determining the equivalent weight of an element (say A), its salt solution is taken as an electrolyte. The other electrolyte is of the element (say B) whose equivalent weight is known. These two electrolytes are placed in two different voltameters connected in series (so that same quantity of electricity pass through both) and the known current is passed for some time. Then the masses of the two elements liberated at the respective electrodes are determined.

**Difference of final weight and initial weight of the respective electrode :**

The equivalent weight of the experimental element can be found out by the following equation :

$$\frac{\text{Mass of element (A) deposited}}{\text{Mass of element (B) deposited}} = \frac{\text{Equivalent wt. of (A)}}{\text{Equivalent wt. of (B)}}$$

$$\therefore \qquad \text{Equivalent wt. of (A)} = \left[ \frac{\text{Mass deposited of (A)}}{\text{Mass deposited of (B)}} \times \text{Eq. wt. of (B)} \right]$$

The quantities on the right hand side being known now, by substituting their values in the above relation, the equivalent weight of (A) can be calculated.

## SOLVED PROBLEMS ON FARADAY'S LAWS

**Problem 5.1 :**

*A given quantity of electricity is passed through two voltameters, containing a salt solution of a metal M and a solution of ZnSO$_4$ arranged in series. If 0.348 gm of M and 1.264 gm of Zn are deposited, calculate the equivalent weight of metal M.*

*(Given : Eq. wt. of Zn = 32.7)*

**Solution :**

$$\frac{\text{Eq. wt. of M}}{\text{Eq. wt. of Zn}} = \frac{\text{Wt. of M}}{\text{Wt. of Zn}}$$

$$\therefore \qquad \text{Eq. wt. of M} = \frac{0.348 \times 32.7}{1.264} = 8.999$$

So the equivalent weight of metal M is 9.

**Problem 5.2 :**

*What is the quantity of electricity necessary to deposit 216 mg of silver from its solution ?*

*(Given : At. wt. of Ag = 108)*

**Solution :**

$$\text{Eq. wt. of Ag} = \frac{\text{At. wt.}}{\text{Valency}} = \frac{108}{1} = 108 = E$$

$$\text{Wt. of deposit} = 216 \text{ mg} = 0.216 \text{ gm} = m$$

$$\therefore \qquad E = 96540 \times Z = 96540 \times \frac{m}{Q} \text{ since } Z = \frac{m}{Q} \text{ from first law.}$$

$$\therefore \qquad Q = \frac{96540 \times m}{E} = \frac{96540 \times 0.216}{108}$$

$$= 96540 \times 0.002 = 193.08 \text{ coulombs}$$

**Problem 5.3 :**

A spoon having an area 20 sq. cm. is to be coated with silver to a thickness of 0.1 mm. If a current of 1.5 A is used, calculate the time required for completing the process.

(Given : e.c.e. of Ag = 0.001118 gm/C and density of silver = 10.5 gm/ml)

**Solution :**

$$\text{Volume of Ag deposited} = \text{Area} \times \text{Thickness}$$
$$= 20 \times (0.1 \times 10^{-1})$$
$$= 2 \times 10^{-1} \text{ cm}^3$$

$\therefore$ $$\text{Mass of Ag deposited} = \text{Volume} \times \text{Density}$$
$$= 2 \times 10^{-1} \times 10.5 = 21 \times 10^{-1} \text{ gm}$$

From Faraday's first law, $\quad m = Z I t$

$\therefore$ $$t = \frac{m}{ZI} = \frac{21 \times 10^{-1}}{0.001118 \times 1.5}$$

$$= \frac{21 \times 10^{-1}}{1118 \times 10^{-6} \times 15 \times 10^{-1}}$$

$$= \frac{21 \times 10^6}{1118 \times 15} = 1252 \text{ seconds i.e. } 20 \text{ min } 52 \text{ sec}$$

**Problem 5.4 :**

By the passage of electric current through solutions of copper sulphate and silver cyanide connected in series, if in a given time, 0.35 gm of copper is deposited, what will be the weight of silver deposited ?

(Given : Eq. wt. of Cu = 31.5 and Eq. wt. of Ag = 108)

**Solution :**

$$\frac{\text{Wt. of copper deposited}}{\text{Wt. of silver deposited}} = \frac{\text{Eq. wt. of copper}}{\text{Eq. wt. of silver}}$$

$\therefore$ $$\frac{0.35}{x} = \frac{31.5}{108}$$

$\therefore$ $$x = \frac{0.35 \times 108}{31.5} = 1.2$$

So the weight of silver deposited is 1.2 gm.

**Problem 5.5 :**

A current of 3 ampere passing through silver nitrate solution for 20 minutes deposits 4 gm of silver. What is the electrochemical equivalent of silver ?

**Solution :**

By Faraday's first law, m = ZIt

Given : I = 3 amp, t = 20 × 60 = 1200 seconds and m = 4 gm

$$\therefore \qquad Z = \frac{m}{It} = \frac{4}{3 \times 1200} = \frac{1}{3 \times 300} = 0.001111$$

So the e.c.e. of silver is 0.001111 gm/coulomb.

**Problem 5.6 :**

*An electric current of 0.65 ampere was passed through a solution of silver nitrate for 1 hour and 5 gm of silver nitrate was decomposed. Calculate the current efficiency.*

**Solution :**

As per Faraday's first law, m = ZIt

Given : I = 0.65 amp, t = 60 × 60 = 3600 seconds

$$\text{and} \qquad Z = \frac{\text{Eq. wt.}}{96540} = \frac{108}{96540}$$

$$\therefore \qquad m = \frac{108 \times 0.65 \times 3600}{96540} = 2.617 \text{ gm (practical value)}$$

Theoretically, $AgNO_3$ decomposes to give Ag.

$$108 + 14 + 48 = 170 \text{ gm}$$

170 gm decomposes to give 108 gm

$$\therefore \quad 5 \text{ gm of } AgNO_3 \text{ will give } \frac{5 \times 108}{170} = \frac{540}{170} = \frac{54}{17} = 3.177 \text{ gm (theoretical value)}$$

$$\text{Current efficiency} = \frac{\text{Practical value}}{\text{Theoretical value}} \times 100$$

$$= \frac{2.617 \times 100}{3.177} = 82.4$$

So current efficiency is 82.4%.

**Problem 5.7 :**

*A solution of a salt of a metal of atomic weight 24 was electrolysed for one hour with a current of 0.25 amp. The weight of the metal deposited was 0.112 gm. Find the valency of the metal in the salt.*

**Solution :**

$$m = ZIt$$

**Given :** I = 0.25 amp, t = 60 × 60 = 3600 seconds, $Z = \dfrac{\text{Eq. wt.}}{96540}$ and m = 0.112 gm

$$\therefore \qquad 0.112 = \frac{\text{Eq. wt.}}{96540} \times 0.25 \times 3600$$

$$\therefore \qquad \text{Eq. wt.} = \frac{0.112 \times 96540}{0.25 \times 3600} = 12.01$$

$$\text{Valency} = \frac{\text{Atomic weight}}{\text{Equivalent weight}} = \frac{24}{12.01} = 1.998 \text{ i.e. } 2$$

So the valency of the element is 2.

### Problem 5.8 :

An electric current is passed through a solution of zinc sulphate and copper sulphate connected in series. If in a given time 0.716 gm of zinc is deposited, what would be the weight of copper that would deposit in the same time ?

(Given : At. wt. of Cu = 63.5 and At. wt. of Zn = 65)

**Solution :**

According to second law of Faraday,

$$\frac{W_1}{E_1} = \frac{W_2}{E_2}$$

where
$$W_1 = \text{Wt. of copper deposited}$$
$$W_2 = \text{Wt. of zinc deposited}$$
$$E_1 = \text{Eq. wt. of copper}$$
$$E_2 = \text{Eq. wt. of zinc}$$

Both copper and zinc are bivalent i.e. their valency is 2.

So $\qquad$ Eq. wt. of Cu $= \dfrac{63.5}{2} = 31.75$

and $\qquad$ Eq. wt. of Zn $= \dfrac{65}{2} = 32.5$

So $\qquad W_1 = \dfrac{W_2 \times E_1}{E_2} = \dfrac{0.716 \times 31.75}{32.5} = 0.6994$

The weight of copper that would deposit is 0.6994 gm.

### Problem 5.9 :

What quantity of electricity is necessary to deposit 216 milligrams of silver from its solution ?

(Given : At. wt. of Ag = 108)

**Solution :**

$$\text{At. wt.} = \text{Eq. wt.} \times \text{Valency}$$

Valency of Ag is one. So At. wt. of Ag = Eq. wt. of Ag

$$E = 96500 \times Z$$

$$\therefore \qquad Z = \frac{E}{96500} = \frac{108}{96500} = 1.119 \times 10^{-3}$$

From Faraday's first law,

$$W = ZIt = Z \times Q$$

Given :      $W = 216$ mg $= 216 \times 10^{-3}$ g

$\therefore$      $Q = \dfrac{W}{Z} = \dfrac{216 \times 10^{-3}}{1.119 \times 10^{-3}} = 193.029$

$\therefore$   The quantity of electricity necessary is 193 coulombs.

### Problem 5.10 :

A solution of a salt of a metal was electrolysed for 150 minutes with a current of 0.15 ampere. The weight of the metal deposited was 0.783 gm. Find the equivalent weight and valency of the metal in the salt. Atomic weight of the metal is 112.

### Solution :

From Faraday's first law,

$$W = Z \times I \times t$$

Given : $W = 0.783$ gm, $I = 0.15$ amp, $t = 150$ min $= 150 \times 60$ sec

$\therefore$      $Z = \dfrac{W}{I \times t} = \dfrac{0.783}{0.15 \times 150 \times 60}$

$= 5.8 \times 10^{-4}$

Eq. wt. $= 96500 \times Z$

$= 96500 \times 5.8 \times 10^{-4}$

$= 55.97$

Now,      At. wt. $=$ Eq. wt. $\times$ Valency

$\therefore$      Valency $= \dfrac{\text{At. wt.}}{\text{Eq. wt.}} = \dfrac{112}{55.97} = 2$

$\therefore$   Equivalent weight is 55.97 and valency is 2.

### Problem 5.11 :

Calculate the time in seconds in which 0.3 gm of copper is liberated from copper sulphate solution when a current of 0.5 amperes is passed.

(Given : Eq. wt. of copper = 31.6)

### Solution :

From Faraday's first law,

$$W = Z \times I \times t$$

Also,      $E = 96500 \times Z$  $\therefore Z = \dfrac{E}{96500}$

Given : $W = 0.3$ gm, $E = 31.6$, $I = 0.5$ amp

$$\therefore \quad W = \frac{E \times I \times t}{96500}$$

$$\therefore \quad t = \frac{W \times 96500}{E \times I}$$

$$= \frac{0.3 \times 96500}{31.6 \times 0.5} = 1832.278 \text{ i.e. } 1833$$

$\therefore$    The time in seconds is 1833 seconds.

### Problem 5.12 :

When the same amount of current is passed through the solutions of $CuSO_4$ and $ZnSO_4$ then 0.7 and 0.7164 gm of Cu and Zn get deposited on respective electrodes. Calculate equivalent weight of Zn.

(Given : At. wt. of Cu = 63.5)

### Solution :

Copper is bivalent i.e. its valency is 2.

$$\therefore \quad \text{Eq. wt. of copper} = \frac{\text{At. wt.}}{\text{Valency}} = \frac{63.5}{2} = 31.75$$

From Faraday's second law,

$$\frac{\text{Wt. of Cu deposited}}{\text{Wt. of Zn deposited}} = \frac{\text{Eq. wt. of copper}}{\text{Eq. wt. of zinc}}$$

$$\therefore \quad \text{Eq. wt. of Zn} = \frac{\text{Eq. wt. of Cu} \times \text{Wt. of Zn deposited}}{\text{Wt. of Cu deposited}}$$

$$= \frac{31.75 \times 0.7164}{0.7} = 32.49$$

$\therefore$    The equivalent weight of zinc is 32.49.

### Problem 5.13 :

Same quantity of current was passed through solutions of copper sulphate and silver nitrate. If the amount of copper liberated in this process is 3.177 gm, calculate the weight of silver deposited on cathode in silver nitrate solution.

### Solution :

$$\text{Eq. wt. of Cu} = \frac{\text{At. wt.}}{\text{Valency}} = \frac{63.54}{2} = 31.77$$

$$\text{Eq. wt. of Ag} = \frac{\text{At. wt.}}{\text{Valency}} = \frac{108}{1} = 108$$

From Faraday's second law,

$$\frac{\text{Wt. of copper deposited}}{\text{Wt. of silver deposited}} = \frac{\text{Eq. wt. of copper}}{\text{Eq. wt. of silver}}$$

$\therefore$    Wt. of silver deposited $= \dfrac{\text{Wt. of copper deposited} \times \text{Eq. wt. of silver}}{\text{Eq. wt. of copper}}$

$$= \frac{3.177 \times 108}{31.77}$$

$$= 10.8$$

$\therefore$    The weight of silver deposited is 10.8 gm.

## 5.11 KOHLRAUSCH'S LAW OF INDEPENDENT MIGRATION OF IONS

Kohlrausch's law states that, the equivalent conductance of an electrolyte at infinite dilution is equal to the sum of the equivalent conductances of the component ions.

The law may be expressed mathematically as,

$$\Lambda_o = \Lambda_o^+ + \Lambda_o^-$$

where $\Lambda_o^-$ is the equivalent conductance of the anion and $\Lambda_o^+$ that of the cation.

For example, the equivalent conductance of NaCl at infinite dilution at 25°C is found to be 126.45. The equivalent conductance of $Na^+$ and $Cl^-$ ions is 50.11 ohm$^{-1}$ and 76.34 ohm$^{-1}$ respectively.

Thus,        $(\Lambda_o)_{NaCl} = (\Lambda_o^+)_{Na^+} + (\Lambda_o^-)_{Cl^-}$

or            $126.45 = 50.11 + 76.34$

This is in confirmity with the Kohlrausch's law.

Table 5.3 gives the equivalent conductances at infinite dilution of different electrolytes. The independent contribution of the ions is seen from the observation of $\Lambda_o$ values of electrolytes containing common ion. The difference between such electrolytes should be constant and must be equal to the difference in equivalent conductance of ion not in common. For example, the difference between $\Lambda_o$ of $K^+$ and $Na^+$ ions is 21.1 and that of $K^+$ and $Li^+$ ions is 34.9. Same is true for anions. Difference between $\Lambda_o$ of $F^-$ and $Cl^-$ is 18.8 and that of $Cl^-$ and $NO_3^-$ is 4.9.

### Table 5.3 : Equivalent conductances of electrolytes at 298 K

| Electrolyte | $\Lambda_o$ | Difference | Electrolyte | $\Lambda_o$ | Difference |
|---|---|---|---|---|---|
| KF | 211.2 | 21.1 | NaF | 90.1 | 18.8 |
| NaF | 90.1 | | NaCl | 108.9 | |
| $KIO_3$ | 98.5 | 21.1 | KF | 111.2 | 18.8 |
| $NaIO_3$ | 77.4 | | KCl | 130.0 | |
| $KNO_3$ | 145.0 | 34.9 | HCl | 426.2 | 4.9 |
| $LiNO_3$ | 110.1 | | $HNO_3$ | 421.3 | |
| KOH | 271.5 | 34.8 | LiCl | 115.0 | 4.9 |
| LiOH | 236.7 | | $LiNO_3$ | 110.1 | |

**Applications of Kohlrausch's law :**

**(i) Determination of ionic conductance of ions :** The transference number is the fraction of the current by any ion and therefore it gives fraction of the total conductance of the ion.

$$\Lambda_o^+ = t_o^+ \, \Lambda_o \qquad \qquad \dots \text{(i)}$$

$$\Lambda_o^- = t_o^- \, \Lambda_o \qquad \qquad \dots \text{(ii)}$$

where $t_o^+$ and $t_o^-$ are the transference numbers at infinite dilution of cation and anion of the electrolyte respectively, and $\Lambda_o$ is the equivalent conductance of the electrolyte at infinite dilution.

Equations (i) and (ii) permit ready calculation of the limiting ionic conductances from transference numbers and $\Lambda_o$ values of strong electrolytes.

For example, $\Lambda_o$ for $HNO_3$ is 421.3 at 25°C and transference numbers of $H^+$ and $NO_3^-$ are 0.821 and 0.170 respectively.

Then, $\qquad (\Lambda_o^+)_{H^+} = 0.821 \times 421.3 = 349.90$

$$(\Lambda_o^-)_{NO_3^-} = 0.170 \times 421.3 = 71.60$$

**(ii) Determination of equivalent conductance at infinite dilution of strong and weak electrolytes :** The equivalent conductances at infinite dilution of the different electrolytes can be determined by adding ionic equivalent conductances of ions composing the electrolyte using table of ionic conductances.

For example,

$$(\Lambda_o)_{NH_4OH} = (\Lambda_o^+)_{NH_4^+} + (\Lambda_o^-)_{OH^-}$$

$$= 73.4 + 198$$

$$= 271.4 \text{ ohm}^{-1} \text{cm}^2$$

The equivalent conductances at infinite dilution may also be determined by addition and subtraction of $\Lambda_o$ values of appropriate electrolytes. $\Lambda_o$ of $NH_4OH$ is determined by addition of $\Lambda_o$ of $NaOH$ and $NH_4Cl$ and subtracting $\Lambda_o$ of $NaCl$.

$$(\Lambda_o)_{NH_4OH} = (\Lambda_o)_{NaOH} + (\Lambda_o)_{NH_4Cl} - (\Lambda_o)_{NaCl}$$

$$= (\Lambda_o^+)_{Na^+} + (\Lambda_o^-)_{OH^-} + (\Lambda_o^+)_{NH_4^+} + (\Lambda_o^-)_{Cl^-} - (\Lambda_o^+)_{Na^+} - (\Lambda_o^-)_{Cl^-}$$

$$= (\Lambda_o^+)_{NH_4^+} + (\Lambda_o^-)_{OH^-}$$

$$= (\Lambda_o)_{NH_4OH}$$

This method of determination of $\Lambda_o$ values is particularly useful for weak electrolytes whose transport numbers and equivalent ionic conductances are not available.

**(iii) Calculation of the solubility of sparingly soluble salts :** Substances like AgCl or $PbSO_4$ which are ordinarily called insoluble do possess a definite value of solubility in water. This can be determined from conductance measurements of their saturated solutions. Since a very small amount of solute is present, it must be completely dissociated into ions even in a saturated solution so that the equivalent conductance kV is equal to equivalent conductance at infinite dilution. This according to Kohlrausch's law is the sum of the ionic mobilities.

i.e. $$kV = \Lambda_o = \Lambda_o^+ + \Lambda_o^-$$

Knowing k and $\Lambda_o$, V can be found out which is the volume in ml containing 1 gm. eq. wt. of the electrolyte.

**(iv) Calculation of the degree of dissociation or conductance ratio :** The apparent degree of dissociation, $\alpha$, of an electrolyte at the dilution V is given by, $\alpha = (\Lambda_o)_V / \Lambda_o$, where $(\Lambda_o)_V$ is the equivalent conductance of the electrolyte at the dilution V, and $\Lambda_o$ is its equivalent conductance at infinite dilution. This according to Kohlrausch's law is the sum of $\Lambda_o^+$ and $\Lambda_o^-$.

**(v) Calculation of the ionic product of water :** The observed specific conductance of the purest water at 25°C is $5.54 \times 10^{-8}$ mhos. The conductance of one litre of water containing 1 gm eq. wt. of it would be

$$(\Lambda_o)_{H_2O} = 5.54 \times 10^{-8} \times 1000 = 5.54 \times 10^{-5} \text{ mhos}$$

At the same temperature, the conductances of $H^+$ ions and $OH^-$ ions are,

$$(\Lambda_o)_{H^+} = 349.8 \text{ mhos}$$

$$(\Lambda_o)_{OH^-} = 198.5 \text{ mhos}$$

According to Kohlrausch's law,

$$(\Lambda_o)_{H_2O} = (\Lambda_o)_{H^+} + (\Lambda_o)_{OH^-}$$

$$= 349.8 + 198.5 = 548.3 \text{ mhos}$$

One molecule of water gives one $H^+$ ion and one $OH^-$ ion.

$$H_2O = H^+ + OH^-$$

Assuming that ionic concentration is proportional to conductance, we have,

$$[H^+] = [OH^-] = \frac{5.54 \times 10^{-5}}{548.3} = 1.01 \times 10^{-7} \text{ g ion litre}^{-1}$$

The ionic product of water is then,

$$K_W = [H^+] [OH^-]$$

$$= 1.02 \times 10^{-14} \text{ at } 25^oC$$

For most purposes, the value of $K_W$ is taken to be $10^{-14}$.

## 5.12 OSTWALD'S DILUTION LAW

**Ostwald's dilution law** is applicable to weak electrolytes only. Acetic acid is a weak acid and its ionisation in aqueous solution is represented as

$$CH_3COOH \rightleftharpoons H^+ + CH_3COO^-$$

Similarly, $NH_4OH$ is a weak base and its ionisation in aqueous solution is represented as

$$NH_4OH \rightleftharpoons NH_4^+ + OH^-$$

In general, weak acids and weak bases are regarded as weak binary electrolytes as BA. Ostwald noticed that the law of mass action can be satisfactorily applied to weak electrolytes and obtained an expression known as Ostwald's dilution law. It gives the relation between degree of dissociation and dissociation constant.

Let the initial concentration of the electrolyte BA be one mole in V dm³ of the solution and let $\alpha$ be its degree of dissociation. The dissociation equilibrium can be represented as :

|  | BA $\rightleftharpoons$ | B⁺ + | A⁻ |
|---|---|---|---|
| Initial moles | 1 | 0 | 0 |
| Moles at equilibrium | $1 - \alpha$ | $\alpha$ | $\alpha$ |
| Conc. at equilibrium | $1 - \alpha$ | $\alpha$ | $\alpha$ |
| (mole dm⁻³) | $\dfrac{1-\alpha}{V}$ | $\dfrac{\alpha}{V}$ | $\dfrac{\alpha}{V}$ |

Applying law of mass action,

$$K = \frac{[B^+] [A^-]}{[BA]}$$

where K is known as dissociation constant.

On substitution,

$$K = \frac{\frac{\alpha}{V} \times \frac{\alpha}{V}}{\frac{1-\alpha}{V}}$$

$\therefore$

$$K = \frac{\alpha^2}{V(1-\alpha)} \qquad \qquad ... (1)$$

When one mole is present in V dm³, concentration of the solution in one dm³ is 1/V mole and it is represented as C. Thus, C is reciprocal of V.

$\therefore$

$$\boxed{K = \frac{\alpha^2 \times C}{(1-\alpha)}} \qquad \qquad ... (2)$$

Equations (1) and (2) are called **Ostwald's Dilution Law**.

From above equation, law can be stated as "The degree of dissociation varies with concentration in such a way that value of dissociation constant remains constant at given temperature".

Ostwald's law is applicable to dilute solutions of weak electrolytes.

(a)  If BA is an acid, then K is represented as $K_a$.

$$K_a = \frac{\alpha^2}{V(1-\alpha)} = \frac{\alpha^2 \times C}{(1-\alpha)}$$

where $K_a$ is dissociation constant of an acid.

$\therefore \qquad \qquad K_a = \alpha^2 \cdot C \qquad \qquad (\because 1 - \alpha \approx 1,\ \text{as } \alpha \text{ is very small})$

$\therefore \qquad \qquad \alpha = \sqrt{K_a/C}$

$\therefore \qquad \qquad [H^+] = \alpha \cdot C = \sqrt{K_a \cdot C} \qquad \qquad ... \text{for an acid}$

(b)  If BA is a base, then K is represented as $K_b$.

$$K_b = \frac{\alpha^2 \times C}{(1-\alpha)} \text{ where } K_b \text{ is dissociation constant of a base.}$$

$\qquad \qquad K_b = \alpha^2 \cdot C \qquad \qquad (\because 1 - \alpha \approx 1,\ \text{as } \alpha \text{ is very small})$

$\therefore \qquad \qquad \alpha = \sqrt{K_b/C}$

$\therefore \qquad \qquad [OH^-] = \alpha \cdot C = \sqrt{K_b \cdot C} \qquad \qquad ... \text{for a base}$

For weak electrolytes, Ostwald's formula becomes

$\qquad \qquad K = \alpha^2 \cdot C \qquad \qquad ... \text{as } 1 - \alpha \approx 1$

$\therefore \qquad \qquad \alpha = \sqrt{K/C} \text{ or } \sqrt{K \cdot V}$

Since K is constant at given temperature,

$$\alpha \propto \frac{1}{\sqrt{C}} \text{ or } \alpha \propto \sqrt{V}$$

Thus, if dissociation constant (K) and initial concentration per $dm^3$ are known, then degree of ionisation can be calculated.

Thus for a weak acid or a weak base,

$$\alpha \propto \frac{1}{\sqrt{C}} \text{ or } \alpha \propto \sqrt{V}$$

*Thus, Ostwald's dilution law implies that the degree of dissociation of a weak electrolyte is directly proportional to the square root of dilution (V) or inversely proportional to the square root of concentration (C).*

Strong acids and strong bases are dissociated almost completely. Hence, $[H^+]$ for HCl or $HNO_3$ is practically the initial concentration of acid, i.e. C.

## SOLVED PROBLEMS ON OSTWALD'S DILUTION LAW

**Problem 5.14 :**

*Dissociation constant of acetic acid is $1.8 \times 10^{-5}$. Calculate its degree of dissociation in 0.1 M solution and percentage ionisation.*

**Solution :**

$$\alpha = \sqrt{\frac{K_a}{C}} = \sqrt{\frac{1.8 \times 10^{-5}}{0.1}} = \sqrt{1.8 \times 10^{-4}}$$
$$= 1.342 \times 10^{-2}$$

Hence, degree of dissociation ($\alpha$) = $1.342 \times 10^{-2}$.

Percentage ionisation = $1.342 \times 10^{-2} \times 100 = 1.342$.

**Problem 5.15 :**

*At 300 K a solution of ammonium hydroxide is 2% ionised in 0.1 M solution. Calculate its dissociation constant.*

**Solution :**

As the solution is 2% ionised, $\alpha = 2/100 = 2 \times 10^{-2}$.

Given : $\alpha = 2 \times 10^{-2}$, C = 0.1, $K_b$ = ?

But $\qquad \alpha = \sqrt{\frac{K_b}{C}}$ ($K_b$ is dissociation constant of $NH_4OH$, a base)

$\therefore \qquad \alpha^2 \times C = K_b$

$$\therefore \qquad K_b = (2 \times 10^{-2})^2 \times 0.1$$
$$= 4 \times 10^{-4} \times 0.1 = 4 \times 10^{-5}$$

Therefore, dissociation constant of base $NH_4OH = 4 \times 10^{-5}$.

### Problem 5.16 :

*Dissociation constant of a monobasic acid is $1.8 \times 10^{-5}$. Find (i) its degree of dissociation and (ii) $H^+$ ion concentration of the decinormal solution of the acid.*

### Solution :

Given : $K_a = 1.8 \times 10^{-5}$, $C = 0.1$, $\alpha = ?$, $[H^+] = ?$

Formula to be used is

$$\alpha = \sqrt{\frac{K_a}{C}}$$

$$\alpha = \sqrt{\frac{1.8 \times 10^{-5}}{0.1}} = \sqrt{1.8 \times 10^{-4}}$$

(As acid is monobasic, its normal solution is the same as molar solution. Hence, 0.1 N = 0.1 M.)

$$\therefore \alpha = \sqrt{1.8 \times 10^{-4}} = 1.342 \times 10^{-2}$$

But $\quad [H^+] = C \times \alpha = 0.1 \times 1.342 \times 10^{-2}$
$$= 1.342 \times 10^{-3} \text{ mol dm}^{-3}$$

## 5.13 ACIDS AND BASES

### (1) Arrhenius Theory of Acids and Bases (Water ion concept) :

In 1887, Arrhenius, the brilliant Swedish chemist, proposed the theory of ionisation to account for the properties of aqueous solutions of electrolytes.

**Definition :** According to Arrhenius theory.

**Acid :** *An acid is a hydrogen compound which in water (aqueous) solution gives hydrogen ions.*

For example,

$$HCl_{(aq)} \rightleftharpoons H^+_{(aq)} + Cl^-_{(aq)}$$

$$H_2SO_{4(aq)} \rightleftharpoons 2H^+_{(aq)} + SO_4^{--}{}_{(aq)}$$

$$CH_3COOH_{(aq)} \rightleftharpoons CH_3COO^-_{(aq)} + H^+_{(aq)}$$

**Base :** *Base is a hydroxide compound which in water (aqueous) solution produces hydroxide ions.*

For example, $NaOH_{(aq)} \rightleftharpoons Na^+_{(aq)} + OH^-_{(aq)}$

$NH_4OH_{(aq)} \rightleftharpoons NH_4^+_{(aq)} + OH^-_{(aq)}$

In general, for acids, equilibrium is :

$HA_{(aq)} \rightleftharpoons H^+_{(aq)} + A^-_{(aq)}$

and for bases, equilibrium is

$BOH_{(aq)} \rightleftharpoons B^+_{(aq)} + OH^-_{(aq)}$

For the sake of simplicity, ions are shown without solvation. The solvation means the combination of ion with solvent molecule ($H_2O$).

Properties of acids are due to the properties of $H^+$ ions and hence there are common properties of acids. Similarly, properties of bases are due to the properties of $OH^-$ ions and hence there are common properties of bases. Bases which are highly soluble in water are known as alkalies and those which are practically insoluble are known as mere bases.

**Neutralisation :** *The reaction between an acid and an alkali (soluble base) in equivalent amounts to form salt and water is known as neutralisation.*

Thus, when sodium hydroxide reacts with hydrochloric acid, sodium chloride (salt) and water are formed.

$NaOH + HCl \longrightarrow NaCl + H_2O$

Above reactions can be explained on the basis of ionic theory. First, molecules of sodium hydroxide and hydrochloric acid get ionised. Thus

$NaOH \longrightarrow Na^+ + OH^-$ (ionisation)

$HCl \longrightarrow H^+ + Cl^-$ (ionisation)

When the solution of sodium hydroxide containing a known fraction or multiple of its gram-equivalent is mixed with a solution of hydrochloric acid containing the same fraction or multiple of its gram-equivalent, then the resulting solution remains neutral in character and in the mixture we have ionised sodium chloride and unionised water.

By ionic theory,

$Na^+ + OH^- + H^+ + Cl^- \longrightarrow Na^+ + Cl^- + H_2O$

Disregarding the common ions, the net reaction is

$H^+ + OH^- \longrightarrow H_2O$

This is true in all types of neutralisation. In this process, the acidic and basic properties which are due to $H^+$ and $OH^-$ ions are lost. *Neutralisation, therefore, can be defined as a process in which $H^+$ ions (protons) of an acid combine with the hydroxyl ions ($OH^-$) of a alkali to form unionised molecules of water.*

This theory explains strength of acids and bases, neutralisation, hydrolysis, buffers. However, there are limitations of Arrhenius theory.

**Limitations of Arrhenius Theory :**

1. Acids and bases have been defined in terms of their aqueous solutions and not, in terms of substances themselves. Thus, the theory is applicable to aqueous solutions only.

2. Substance like HCl is regarded as an acid only when it is dissolved in water but in other solvents like benzene or other organic solvents or in the gaseous state, it is not considered as an acid.

3. According to Arrhenius theory, a base must be a hydroxy compound. However, there are many organic substances as well as ammonia which are known to show basic properties, though they are not hydroxy compounds.

4. According to Arrhenius theory, a bare proton, $H^+$, exists in aqueous solution. However, in aqueous solution, $H^+$ ion is always hydrated. The hydration energy of $H^+$ ion has been calculated to be as high as 1071.1 kJ $mol^{-1}$ i.e. $H^+ + H_2O \rightarrow (H_3O)^+$. So this ion can exist only in the hydrated form $(H_3O)^+$.

   Actually, the existence of hydronium ion, $H_3O^+$, in solutions of strong acids was proved conclusively in 1951 by means of infra-red spectroscopy. However, behaviour of $H^+$ ions and $H_3O^+$ ions is chemically similar.

5. It does not explain acidic nature of salts like $FeCl_3$ or basic character of $Na_2CO_3$.

6. The ionic compounds can exist as ions even in the crystalline state.

7. This theory cannot explain acid-base reaction (neutralisation) in non-aqueous medium. For example, a reaction between $NH_{3(g)}$ and $HCl_{(g)}$ to form solid $NH_4Cl$.

Inspite of these serious limitations to Arrhenius theory of acids and bases, it is quite adequate because of its simplicity, for an elementary approach, and chemists still use much of the terminology that Arrhenius established.

**(2) Bronsted-Lowry Concept (Protonic concept) :**

In 1923, Lowry in England and Bronsted in Denmark proposed almost simultaneously a more general definition of acids and bases to overcome the limitations of Arrhenius theory.

**Definition : Acid :** *An acid is any substance (molecule or ion) which can donate a proton (H⁺ ion).*

Thus acid is a proton donor. (Protogenic).

For example :

    (i)    $CH_3COOH \rightleftharpoons CH_3COO^- + H^+$

    (ii)    $HSO_4^- \rightleftharpoons H^+ + SO_4^{--}$

**Base :** It is a substance (molecule or ion) which can accept a proton.

Thus base is a proton acceptor. (Protophilic).

For example,

    (i)       $NH_3 + H^+ \longrightarrow NH_4^+$

    (ii)      $H_2O + H^+ \longrightarrow H_3O^+$

## (3) Conjugate Acid and Base Pairs :

In terms of Bronsted-Lowry theory, if the ionisation of an acid is carried out in water, there are two acid-base pairs.

$$HCl + H_2O \rightleftharpoons H_3O^+ + Cl^-$$

    $acid_1$  $base_2$      $acid_2$  $base_1$

Hydrogen chloride donates a proton to water. Hydrogen chloride is an acid. Water accepts the proton and forms hydronium ion ($H_3O^+$) and hence it is a base. In the reverse reaction, hydronium ion ($H_3O^+$) donates a proton to chloride ion and hence $H_3O^+$ ion acts as an acid and $Cl^-$ ion acts as a base.

Here, $acid_1$ and $base_1$ form a conjugate pair and $base_2$ and $acid_2$ form another conjugate pair.

In terms of Bronsted-Lowry theory, ionisation of an acid is an equilibrium reaction involving an acid-base pair. Thus,

$$HCl \rightleftharpoons H^+ \text{ (proton) } + Cl^-$$

$$Acid_1 \rightleftharpoons H^+ \text{ (proton) } + Base_1$$

In forward reaction, acid HCl produces $Cl^-$ ion as a base by loss of proton ($H^+$ ion).

In backward reaction, $Cl^-$ ion accepts the proton and forms the acid HCl. Here $Cl^-$ is conjugate base of acid HCl. Thus when acid loses a proton, residual part has tendency to gain the proton and thus acts as a base.

Similarly,      $H_2O + H^+ \rightleftharpoons H_3O^+$

              $base_2$          $acid_2$

In this way, every acid has its self generated base i.e. conjugate base and every base has its self generated acid i.e. conjugate acid.

So *an acid-base pair, members of which can be formed from each other mutually by the gain or loss of the proton is called as conjugate acid-base pair.* Thus, any acid-base reaction involves two acids and two bases. An acid-base pair that differs by a proton is also called as conjugate acid-base pair.

Since Bronsted has done much more work than Lowry, the concept or theory is known as Bronsted theory.

According to Bronsted theory, all negative ions are classified as bases since they combine with protons. Strength of a base is measured by its ability to capture protons. Similarly, strength of an acid is measured by its ability to donate a proton. HCl is a strong acid since it tends to give up proton readily, while the chloride ion must necessarily be a weak base since it has little tendency to hold on to proton. Thus, the stronger an acid, the weaker is its conjugate base and the stronger a base, the weaker is its conjugate acid.

**Conjugate pairs of acids and bases :**

In general, $Acid_1 + Base_2 \rightleftharpoons Acid_2 + Base_1$

| $Acid_1$ | | $Base_2$ | | $Acid_2$ | | $Base_1$ |
|----------|---|----------|---|----------|---|----------|
| $HSO_4^-$ | + | $H_2O$ | $\rightleftharpoons$ | $H_3O^+$ | + | $SO_4^{--}$ |
| $HCO_3^-$ | + | $H_2O$ | $\rightleftharpoons$ | $H_3O^+$ | + | $CO_3^{--}$ |
| $NH_4^+$ | + | $H_2O$ | $\rightleftharpoons$ | $H_3O^+$ | + | $NH_3$ |

**Amphoteric Nature of Water :** Water can accept a proton and can act as a base. Similarly, it can give up a proton and can act as an acid. Thus, it has dual nature depending upon the other substance with which it combines.

**Water as a Base :** Water can function as a base in the presence of acids stronger than itself. Here water is a proton acceptor.

For example,   $HCl + H_2O \rightleftharpoons H_3O^+ + Cl^-$
  acid      base

**Water as an Acid :** Water can function as an acid in the presence of base stronger than itself. Here water is a proton donor.

For example,  $H_2O + NH_3 \rightleftharpoons NH_4^+ + OH^-$
  acid                        base

From the above illustrations, it is evident that $H_2O$ can behave as a base or as an acid. Thus, it has amphoteric (amphiprotic) nature.

According to Bronsted theory, products of neutralisation are not salt and water, but they are conjugate base and acid respectively of the reacting acid and base.

**(4) Lewis Theory of Acids and Bases (Electronic concept) :**

In 1923, G. N. Lewis widened the definition of acids and bases. He formulated his concept on the electronic theory of valency. He went into its details in 1938.

Lewis concept of acids and bases is much broader than that of Bronsted, and it is explained not in terms of ionic reactions but in terms of bond formation. In Lewis sense, the fundamental acid-base reaction is the formation of a co-ordinate covalent bond between an acid and a base.

**Definition :** *An acid is any species (molecule, ion or atom) that is capable of accepting a pair of electrons to establish a co-ordinate bond.* For example, $BF_3$, $AlCl_3$, $ZnCl_2$, $SO_2$, $SO_3$, $Ag^+$, $Cu^{++}$, $Ba^{++}$. *A base is any species that is capable of donating a pair of electrons to form such a co-ordinate bond.* For example,

$:NH_3$, $H_2O$, $R - O - H$, $CN^-$, $Cl^-$, $Br^-$, $I^-$, $OH^-$, $NO_3^-$, $S^{-2}$.

For example, formation of $BF_3 \cdot NH_3$ compound.

| Acid | Base | | Co-ordination compound |

$BF_3$ is an electron deficient molecule and in $NH_3$, nitrogen has a lone pair of electrons. Thus acid boron trifluoride accepts an electron pair from the base ammonia to form co-ordinate compound $BF_3 \cdot NH_3$. Thus, **Lewis acid is an electron pair acceptor while Lewis base is an electron pair donor**. The process of neutralisation is simply co-ordination in which co-ordinate bond is denoted by an arrow pointing from Lewis base to Lewis acid.

For *Lewis acid, there must be at least one available unfilled or vacant orbital in the valence shell of the atom* in the species. This is the only requirement for a substance to be called as an acid. Lewis acids are therefore of various types.

## Types of Lewis Acids :

**1.    Simple Cations :** Theoretically, almost all simple cations are potentially Lewis acids as they accept electron pairs from other molecules like $H_2O$, $NH_3$ or ions like $CN^-$.

| Acid | | Base | | Co-ordinated complex |
|------|--|------|--|----------------------|
| $Ag^+$ | + | $2NH_3$ | $\rightarrow$ | $[Ag(NH_3)_2]^+$ |
| $Al^{+++}$ | + | $6H_2O$ | $\rightarrow$ | $[Al(H_2O)_6]^{+++}$ |
| $Fe^{+++}$ | + | $6CN^-$ | $\rightarrow$ | $[Fe(CN)_6]^{---}$ |

**2.  Electron Deficient Molecules :** Important Lewis acids are compounds whose central atoms have less than a full octet of electrons. The octet is completed by co-ordination.

(i)    $BF_3$, boron trifluoride, (ii) Aluminium trichloride, $AlCl_3$,

(iii) Sulphur trioxide, $SO_3$, (iv) Trimethyl boron, etc.

In these compounds, elements B, Al, S have less than eight electrons and hence, they can take up a pair of electrons.

## Types of Lewis Bases :

**1.    Simple Anions :** All the anions are Lewis bases because they donate electron pair. For example,

$$Ni^{2+} + 4 : Cl^- \rightarrow [Ni(Cl)_4]^-$$

acid        base

**2.  Electron Rich Compounds :** The compounds which donate lone pair of electron are known as Lewis bases. The compounds of the elements present in group 15 are Lewis bases,

$H_2\ddot{O}$ :, : $CO$, : $NH_3$, : $PH_3$, : $N(CH_3)_3$.

## 5.14 CONCEPT OF pH AND pOH

**Hydrogen Ion Concentration :** It can be readily seen that in any aqueous solution, the equilibrium

$$H_2O \rightleftharpoons H^+ + OH^-$$

will shift backward and forward according to the nature of solute but the equilibrium constant will remain constant at a fixed temperature, so that the ionic product of water, $K_W$, will also remain constant.

$$K_W = [H^+][OH^-] = 10^{-14}$$

In pure water, we have seen that $[H^+]$ equals $[OH^-]$ and this equality indicates that pure water is neutral. It is but quite obvious that in an acid solution, $[H^+]$ will be greater than $[OH^-]$ and in an alkaline solution, $[OH^-]$ will be greater than $[H^+]$.

Taking $[H^+] = [OH^-] = 10^{-7}$ mole dm$^{-3}$ in neutral water or in neutral solution, we have

In acidic solution,

$$[H^+] > [OH^-] \text{ and hence}$$

$$[H^+] > 10^{-7} \text{ and } [OH^-] < 10^{-7} \text{ mol/dm}^3$$

In alkaline solution, $[OH^-] > [H^+]$ and hence, $[OH^-] > 10^{-7}$ mol dm$^{-3}$ and $[H^+] < 10^{-7}$ mol dm$^{-3}$. Thus, we can see that there is a very wide range from strongly acidic solution with $H^+$ ion concentration of about 1 mole per dm$^3$ to a strongly alkaline solution with $H^+$ ion concentration of about $10^{-14}$ mole per dm$^3$.

**Definition of pH :** *pH of a solution is defined as the negative logarithm to the base 10 of molar concentration of hydrogen ions or pH is the logarithm of the reciprocal of $H^+$ ion concentration as mol dm$^{-3}$.*

In symbol, pH of the solution, 'p' stands for *potenz*, meaning strength and pH indicates the strength of hydrogen ion concentration expressed in mol dm$^{-3}$ in the solution. From the definition of pH, we have,

$$pH = -\log_{10}[H^+] = \log_{10}\frac{1}{[H^+]}$$

Above relation helps us to find out pH if $[H^+]$ is known and vice versa.

**Definition of pOH :** Just as pH is negative logarithm to the base 10 of $[H^+]$, *pOH is defined as the negative logarithm to the base 10 of $[OH^-]$, when the concentration is expressed in mol dm$^{-3}$.*

$$\therefore \qquad pOH = -\log_{10}[OH^-] = \log_{10}\frac{1}{[OH^-]}$$

**pH scale as a measure of Acidity and Alkalinity :**

The method of expressing $H^+$ ion or $OH^-$ ion concentration is very inconvenient to handle as it involves the negative power of 10. To decide the acidic or alkaline nature of a solution, it is necessary to express the hydrogen ion concentration $[H^+]$ on a convenient scale. Such a scale was suggested by Sorensen in 1909 and it is known as pH scale or Sorensen scale (Refer Fig. 5.10).

If $\qquad [H^+] = 1 \times 10^{-7}$ mol/dm$^3$, then

$$pH = -\log_{10}[1 \times 10^{-7}] = -(0-7) = +7$$

$\therefore \qquad pH = 7$

Thus, for a neutral solution with $[H^+] = [OH^-] = 10^{-7}$ mol/dm$^3$, the pH is 7.

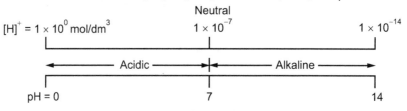

**Fig. 5.10 : pH scale**

For an acid solution, $[H^+] > 10^{-7}$ mol/dm$^3$, the pH is less than 7. For alkaline solution with $[H^+] < 10^{-7}$ mol/dm$^3$, the pH is greater than 7. Variation in pH both for acidic and alkaline solutions can be shown diagrammatically as in Fig. 5.10. Thus from pH scale, nature of solution can be determined whether it is acidic, basic or neutral.

**Derivation of pH + pOH = 14 :**

In every aqueous solution,

At 298 K, $\qquad [H^+][OH^-] = 1 \times 10^{-14}$

Taking logs,

$\therefore \qquad \log[H^+] + \log[OH^-] = \log[1 \times 10^{-14}]$

Changing signs,

$$-\log[H^+] + (-\log[OH^-]) = -(-14)$$

$\therefore \qquad\qquad pH + pOH = 14$

$$(\because pH = -\log_{10}[H^+] \text{ and } pOH = -\log_{10}[OH^-])$$

Hence, $\qquad\qquad pOH = 14 - pH$

The following Table 5.4 gives the relation between hydrogen ion concentration per dm$^3$ and pH and between hydroxyl ion concentration per dm$^3$ and pOH. Nature of the solution is also indicated.

## Table 5.4

| [$H^+$] | pH | [$OH^-$] | pOH | Ionic product | Nature of solution |
|---|---|---|---|---|---|
| $1 \times 10^0$ | 0 | $1 \times 10^{-14}$ | 14 | $1 \times 10^{-14}$ | Acidic |
| $1 \times 10^{-1}$ | 1 | $1 \times 10^{-13}$ | 13 | $1 \times 10^{-14}$ | Acidic |
| $1 \times 10^{-3}$ | 3 | $1 \times 10^{-11}$ | 11 | $1 \times 10^{-14}$ | Acidic |
| $1 \times 10^{-6}$ | 6 | $1 \times 10^{-8}$ | 8 | $1 \times 10^{-14}$ | Acidic |
| $1 \times 10^{-7}$ | 7 | $1 \times 10^{-7}$ | 7 | $1 \times 10^{-14}$ | Neutral |
| $1 \times 10^{-9}$ | 9 | $1 \times 10^{-5}$ | 5 | $1 \times 10^{-14}$ | Alkaline |
| $1 \times 10^{-11}$ | 11 | $1 \times 10^{-3}$ | 3 | $1 \times 10^{-14}$ | Alkaline |
| $1 \times 10^{-13}$ | 13 | $1 \times 10^{-1}$ | 1 | $1 \times 10^{-14}$ | Alkaline |
| $1 \times 10^{-14}$ | 14 | $1 \times 10^0$ | 0 | $1 \times 10^{-14}$ | Alkaline |

*$\log_{10}$ [$H^+$] or $\log_{10}$ [$OH^-$] is commonly written as log [$H^+$] or log [$OH^-$] respectively.

In calculating pH of an aqueous solution, $H^+$ ions contributed by the dissociation of water should be ignored since their concentration is negligible when compared with that of $H^+$ ions contributed by the acid. Same is true for pOH value.

## SOLVED PROBLEMS ON pH AND pOH

### Problem 5.17 :

*Calculate pH of a solution which contains $4 \times 10^{-4}$ moles of $H^+$ ions dm$^{-3}$.*

**Solution :**

$$pH \ = \ - \log_{10} [H^+]$$

On substitution,  $$pH \ = \ - \log_{10} [4 \times 10^{-4}]$$

$$= \ - [0.6021 - 4] = 4 - 0.6021 = 3.3979$$

### Problem 5.18 :

*Calculate pOH and pH values of 0.0016 M KOH solution assuming complete ionisation.*

**Solution :**

In 0.0016 M KOH solution, concentration of $OH^-$ ions is $1.6 \times 10^{-3}$ mole dm$^{-3}$.

$$pOH \ = \ - \log_{10} [OH^-] = - \log_{10} [1.6 \times 10^{-3}]$$

∴  $$pOH \ = \ (0.2041 - 3) - 3 - 0.2041 = 2.7959$$

But  $$pH + pOH \ = \ 14$$

∴  $$pH \ = \ 14 - 2.7959 = 11.2041$$

**Problem 5.19 :**

Calculate pH of 0.001 M $H_2SO_4$ solution, assuming complete dissociation.

**Solution :**

$H_2SO_4$ is a dibasic acid. It ionises as,

$$H_2SO_4 \longrightarrow 2H^+ + SO_4^{--}$$

$$\begin{array}{ccc} 0.001 & 0.002 & 0.001 \\ \text{mole} & \text{mole} & \text{mole} \end{array}$$

$$pH = -\log_{10}[0.002]$$
$$= -\log_{10}[2 \times 10^{-3}] = -(0.3010 - 3) = 2.6990$$

**Problem 5.20 :**

Calculate pH of 0.1 M acetic acid which is 1% dissociated.

**Solution :**

$$[H^+] = \alpha \times C$$

Here,     $\alpha = 0.01$ and C = 0.1

∴     $[H^+] = 0.01 \times 0.1 = 0.001$ mol/dm³

$$pH = -\log_{10}[H^+]$$
$$= -\log_{10}[1 \times 10^{-3}] = -(0 - 3) = 3$$

**Problem 5.21 :**

Find the values of [H⁺], [OH⁻], pH and pOH of 0.001 N solution of a monobasic acid. Assume that the acid is completely dissociated. $K_w = 1 \times 10^{-14}$ at 298 K.

**Solution :**

(i)     $[H^+] = \alpha \times C$

$$= 1 \times 0.001$$
$$= 1 \times 10^{-3} \text{ mol dm}^{-3}$$

(ii)  [OH⁻] ion concentration

We have,   $[H^+][OH^-] = 1 \times 10^{-14}$ at 298 K

∴     $[1 \times 10^{-3}][OH^-] = 1 \times 10^{-14}$

∴     $[OH^-] = \dfrac{1 \times 10^{-14}}{1 \times 10^{-3}} = 1 \times 10^{-11} \text{ mol dm}^{-3}$

(iii) pH of the solution

$$pH = -\log[H^+]$$
$$= -\log[1 \times 10^{-3}]$$
$$= -(0 - 3) = 3$$

∴     $pH = 3$

(iv) pOH of the solution

We have,    pH + pOH = 14

∴              3 + pOH = 14

∴                  pOH = 14 – 3 = 11

# 5.15 BUFFER SOLUTIONS

For many purposes, we have to maintain an aqueous solution at constant and specified pH value. There are many biological systems (e.g. blood) whose pH must not be allowed to vary considerably. The pH of human blood in a normal person is approximately 7.4. An increase or decrease of as much as 0.4 is likely to be fatal. For proper productivity of crops, the soil should have the proper pH. We need a solution that resists any tendency to change its pH.

**Definition :** *A solution which has a definite pH and which resists the sudden change in its pH even when a small amount of strong acid or base is added to it is known as buffer solution, or buffer.*

A buffer solution is also known as regulator solution or solution of reserve acidity and alkalinity.

**Types of Buffer Solution :** There are two types of buffers :

(1)   Acidic buffer

(2)   Basic buffer.

**Preparation of Buffer Solution :**

**(1)   Acidic Buffer :** Its pH is less than 7. It is prepared by dissolving in water a weak acid and its salt of strong base. Thus, following pairs of compounds can be used for preparing acidic buffers. (a) $CH_3COOH$ and $CH_3COONa$. (b) $HCOOH$ and $HCOONa$. (c) $C_6H_5COOH$ and $C_6H_5COONa$. (d) $HCOOH$ and $HCOOK$.

**(2)   Basic Buffer :** Its pH is more than 7. It is prepared by dissolving in water a weak base and its salt of strong acid. Such a pair of compounds is $NH_4OH$ and $NH_4Cl$.

**Preparation of a Buffer Solution of a desired pH :** Consider a buffer solution containing a weak acid HA and its salt with a strong base.

The weak acid HA ionises as

$$HA \rightleftharpoons H^+ + A^-$$

By the law of mass action, we have,

$$K_a = \frac{[H^+]\,[A^-]}{[HA]}$$

$$[H^+] = \frac{K_a\,[HA]}{[A^-]} \qquad\qquad ... (i)$$

Here,              $K_a$ = dissociation constant of acid HA.

On addition of a salt with anion A⁻, the ionisation of acid is suppressed and the concentration of the anion is practically equal to that of the added salt. Therefore in the above equation.

[HA] = concentration of weak acid

and [A⁻] = concentration of salt

$$\therefore \qquad [H^+] = \frac{K_a\,[acid]}{[salt]}$$

$$\therefore \qquad \log_{10}[H^+] = \log_{10}K_a + \log_{10}\frac{[acid]}{[salt]}$$

$$\therefore \qquad -\log_{10}[H^+] = -\log_{10}K_a - \log_{10}\frac{[acid]}{[salt]}$$

$$\therefore \qquad pH = pK_a + \log_{10}\frac{[salt]}{[acid]} \qquad\qquad ... (ii)$$

This equation is known as **Henderson Equation**. A buffer solution of a desired pH can be prepared by taking the definite ratio of salt to acid. It is now possible to prepare Universal Buffer mixture by making suitable mixtures of acids and salts.

Suppose we wish to prepare a buffer of pH 5 using acetic acid ($K_a = 1.75 \times 10^{-5}$) and sodium acetate.

Now, $\qquad\qquad K_a = 1.75 \times 10^{-5}$

$$\therefore \qquad pK_a = -\log K_a = 4.757$$

According to Henderson equation,

$$pH = pK_a + \log_{10}\frac{[salt]}{[acid]}$$

$$\therefore \qquad 5 = 4.757 + \log_{10}\frac{[salt]}{[acid]}$$

$$\therefore \qquad \log_{10}\frac{[salt]}{[acid]} = 5 - 4.757 = 0.243$$

$$\therefore \text{ antilog}\left(\log_{10}\frac{[salt]}{[acid]}\right) = \text{antilog } 0.243$$

$$\therefore \qquad \frac{[salt]}{[acid]} = 1.75 \text{ i.e. } 1.75:1$$

Therefore, to prepare a buffer solution of pH 5, sodium acetate and acetic acid are to be used in the above ratio in moles.

$$pOH = pK_b + \log_{10}\frac{[salt]}{[base]} \qquad \text{... (iii)}$$

where,             $K_b$ = Dissociation constant of a base.

But          pH + pOH = 14

∴              pH = 14 – pOH                               ... (iv)

**Mechanism of Buffer Action :** The property of the buffer solution to resist change in its pH value on addition of small amount of acid or base is known as buffer action.

**Acidic Buffer :** Consider a solution of $CH_3COOH$ and $CH_3COONa$. The salt, $CH_3COONa$ is almost completely ionised giving large concentration of $CH_3COO^-$ ions and $Na^+$ ions. The weak acid, $CH_3COOH$ is slightly ionised.

$$CH_3COOH \rightleftharpoons CH_3COO^- + H^+$$

$$CH_3COONa \longrightarrow CH_3COO^- + Na^+$$

The ionisation of $CH_3COOH$ is much reduced due to common $CH_3COO^-$ ions (common ion effect).

**1.   Addition of acid :** When small quantity of an acid (even strong acid as HCl) is added to this solution, $H^+$ ions from acid combine with $CH_3COO^-$ ions producing practically unionised $CH_3COOH$.

$$H^+ + CH_3COO^- \longrightarrow CH_3COOH$$

Thus, $H^+$ ions are used up and pH of the solution is not practically changed. The addition of acid is neutralised by $CH_3COO^-$ ions. Thus, this buffer has reserve basicity due to presence of $CH_3COO^-$ ions. The resistance to change in pH of a buffer on addition of small amount of acid is known as *reserve basicity*.

**2.   Addition of alkali :** When small quantity of an alkali (even strong as NaOH) is added to the solution, $OH^-$ ions from alkali combine with $H^+$ ions of acetic acid dissociating more and more of undissociated molecules of $CH_3COOH$ and forming $H_2O$.

$$OH^- + CH_3COOH \longrightarrow CH_3COO^- + H_2O$$

Thus, $OH^-$ ions are used up and pH of the solution remains practically unchanged. The addition of alkali is neutralised by acetic acid. *This buffer solution has reserve acidity due to $CH_3COOH$.* The resistance to change in pH of a buffer on addition of small amount of base or alkali is known as *reserve acidity*.

Thus, the same buffer solution has reserve acidity as well as reserve alkalinity.

**Basic Buffer :** Consider a solution of $NH_4OH$ and $NH_4Cl$. $NH_4Cl$ is almost completely ionised giving large concentration of $NH_4^+$ ions and $Cl^-$ ions. The weak base, $NH_4OH$ is slightly ionised.

$$NH_4OH \rightleftharpoons NH_4^+ + OH^-$$

$$NH_4Cl \longrightarrow NH_4^+ + Cl^-$$

The ionisation of $NH_4OH$ is much reduced due to common $NH_4^+$ ions (common ion effect).

1.    **Addition of base :** If a base (even strong like NaOH) is added, then $OH^-$ ions from a base combine with $NH_4^+$ ions producing practically unionised $NH_4OH$.

$$OH^- + NH_4^+ \longrightarrow NH_4OH$$

Thus, $OH^-$ ions are used up and pH of the solution remains practically unchanged. The addition of base is neutralised by $NH_4^+$ ions in buffer. This buffer solution has reserve acidity due to $NH_4^+$ ions.

2.    If an acid (even strong like HCl) is added, then $H^+$ ions from an acid combine with $OH^-$ ions of $NH_4OH$ dissociating more and more of the undissociated molecules.

$$H^+ + NH_4OH \longrightarrow NH_4^+ + H_2O$$

Thus, $OH^-$ ions are used up and pH of the solution remains practically unchanged. The addition of an acid is neutralised by $NH_4OH$. This buffer solution has reserve basicity due to $NH_4OH$.

**Properties of Buffer Solutions :**
1.    It maintains its pH even when diluted with water.
2.    It retains its pH even when kept for a long time.
3.    It does not change its pH even when a small amount of strong acid or strong base is added to it.
4.    It always has a definite pH.
5.    It has few $H^+$ or $OH^-$ ions.

**Applications of Buffer Solutions :**

Buffer solutions have numerous applications in various fields, such as analytical, industrial, pharmaceutical and biological systems. Following are some of the examples :

(1)  Citric acid when added to milk of magnesia, magnesium citrate is formed and it acts as a buffer to stabilize milk of magnesia.

(2)  Penicillin preparations are stabilized by the addition of sodium citrate which acts as a buffer.

(3)  The uptake of oxygen by blood and its transport and distribution from lungs to various parts of the body is done at the pH of about 7.4. The electrolytes present in the blood act as a buffer solution to maintain the desired value of pH of the blood. Any alternation in the pH of blood would lead to serious condition of a patient.

(4)  In the laboratory, many chemical reactions can be achieved only at a definite pH value of the solution, e.g. the precipitation of ZnS from $ZnCl_2$,

$$ZnCl_2 + H_2S \longrightarrow ZnS + 2HCl$$

is not very efficient, since the $H^+$ ions formed accumulate in the solution and make the reaction to shift towards left. However, if $H_2S$ is passed through $ZnCl_2$ solution in presence of sodium acetate, whole amount of zinc precipitates as sulphide.

$$ZnCl_2 + H_2S \longrightarrow ZnS + 2H^+ + 2Cl^-$$

$$2CH_3COO^- + 2H^+ \longrightarrow 2CH_3COOH$$

Here, $CH_3COO^-$ ions react with $H^+$ ions to produce slightly dissociated $CH_3COOH$ molecules and the solution now contains a buffer of acetic acid and sodium acetate. This prevents the back reaction of $H^+$ ions on ZnS.

(5)  Sodium benzoate is added as a buffer to preserve jellies and jams.

# 5.16 SOLUBILITY PRODUCT

**Expression for Solubility and Solubility Product :** The solubility of a substance is the maximum amount of a substance which can be dissolved in a given amount of solvent at given temperature. Concentration of a substance in its saturated solution is known as its solubility at a given temperature and denoted by 'S'. Solubility is expressed as kg per litre or mol per litre or $dm^3$ at that temperature.

Substances like AgCl, $BaSO_4$, $PbSO_4$ have negligible solubility in water at ordinary temperature. Such substances which are practically insoluble are known as sparingly soluble substances. A very small amount of such a substance when shaken in water, most of it remains undissolved and whatever little amount of it goes in solution makes the solution saturated. In this saturated solution, the salt is almost completely dissociated into its ions. Other sparingly soluble salts are $CH_3COOAg$, $Mg(OH)_2$, $Al(OH)_3$, $Ag_2CrO_4$, $Ag_2CO_3$ etc.

**Solubility product :** The following two equilibria exist when a sparingly soluble electrolyte (solute) say BA is in contact with its saturated solution. Thus

$$BA \text{ (solid)} \rightleftharpoons BA \text{ (dissolved)} \rightleftharpoons B^+ + A^-$$

The mass law equation of the equilibrium is

$$K = \frac{[B^+][A^-]}{[BA]}$$

As the electrolyte in saturated solution is in contact with the solid, the concentration of the unionised molecules must be constant. Hence, [BA] = constant, say K'.

$\therefore$ $\qquad$ $K \times K' = [B^+][A^-]$

$\therefore$ $\qquad$ $\boxed{K_{sp} = [B^+][A^-]}$ $\qquad\qquad$ $(\because K \times K' = K_{sp})$

where $K_{sp}$ is also a constant known as solubility product.

**Definition :** *In a saturated solution of a sparingly soluble salt (electrolyte), the numerical product of the molar concentration of ions raised to a suitable power is constant at a constant temperature. This constant '$K_{sp}$' is known as the solubility product.*

For example, AgCl is sparingly soluble in water. When a small amount of it is shaken with water, most of it remains undissolved and the supernant solution is saturated with the dissolved AgCl which in its turn is ionised.

Thus, we have

$$AgCl_{(solid)} \rightleftharpoons AgCl_{(dissolved)} \rightleftharpoons Ag^+ + Cl^-$$

This is the condition of finding out the solubility product of a substance at a given temperature. The solubility product of AgCl is $[Ag^+][Cl^+]$ under this condition.

Hence, $\qquad$ $K_{sp} = [Ag^+][Cl^-]$

The solubility equilibrium of AgCl is written as follows :

$$AgCl \rightleftharpoons Ag^+ + Cl^-$$

(solid) $\qquad$ (in solution)

**Expression of Solubility Product ($K_{sp}$) and its relation with solubility for different types of sparingly soluble salts :**

(a) In the case of sparingly soluble salts like $BaSO_4$, $CH_3COOAg$ and $PbSO_4$ giving only two ions : $(B^+, A^-)$ in water, the solubility product of such salts can be expressed as follows. If S is the solubility in mol dm$^{-3}$, then

$$K_{sp} = [B^+][A^-] \text{ (General form)} = S \times S = S^2$$

$$K_{sp} = [Ba^{++}][SO_4^{--}] = S^2$$

$$K_{sp} = [Ag^+][CH_3COO^-] = S^2$$

$$K_{sp} = [Pb^{++}][SO_4^{--}] = S^2$$

(b) If there is a sparingly soluble salt which gives more than two ions, the solubility equilibrium of such salts [$PbBr_2$, $Al(OH)_3$, etc.] having a general formula BxAy is given by the equation. Let S be solubility in mol $dm^{-3}$.

$$BxAy \rightleftharpoons xB^+ + yA^- \text{ (in solution)}$$

(solid)

and the solubility product is given by

$$K_{sp} = [B^+]^x [A^-]^y$$

(i)    For the salt $PbBr_2$,

$$PbBr_2 \rightleftharpoons Pb^{++} + 2Br^-$$

$$\quad\quad\quad S \quad\quad 2S$$

∴                    $K_{sp} = [Pb^{++}] [Br^-]^2 = S \times (2S)^2 = 4S^3$

(ii)    For the salt $Al(OH)_3$,

$$Al(OH)_3 \rightleftharpoons Al^{+++} + 3OH^-$$

$$\quad\quad\quad S \quad\quad 3S$$

$$K_{sp} = [Al^{+++}] [OH^-]^3 = S (3S)^3 = S \times 27S^3 = 27S^4$$

*It should be noted that the concentrations of the ions must be expressed in mol $dm^{-3}$. (i.e. mol/$dm^3$)*

## Saturation, Unsaturation and Precipitation :

The precipitation of a substance depends upon the values of ionic product and solubility product.

In a solution when

Ionic product   = solubility product ($K_{sp}$)    ... it is a saturated solution

Ionic product   < $K_{sp}$                               ... it is unsaturated solution

Ionic product   > $K_{sp}$                               ... precipitate is obtained

## Applications of Solubility Product :

**(i)   Prediction of Precipitation :** With the knowledge of solubility product of a sparingly soluble salt, we can predict whether under certain given conditions, the salt would be precipitated or not. According to the solubility product principle, the precipitation occurs only when the ionic product i.e. the product of concentrations of its ions in solution, exceeds the value of the solubility product of the salt.

e.g.      AgCl has $K_{sp} = 1 \times 10^{-10}$

Hence, the precipitate of AgCl is obtained only when the ionic product of AgCl exceeds $1 \times 10^{-10}$ i.e.

$$[Ag^+] \times [Cl^-] > 1 \times 10^{-10}$$

Similarly, if $[Ag^+] \times [I^-] > 1 \times 10^{-14}$, then precipitation of AgI occurs because $K_{sp}$ for AgI is $1 \times 10^{-14}$.

**(ii) In Qualitative Analysis of basic radicals :** In qualitative analysis, a salt is precipitated if the product of the ionic concentrations exceeds the solubility product of the salt. In other words, when the product of ionic concentrations is more than the solubility product, the salt is precipitated. Typical cases of the precipitation of hydroxides and sulphides are considered here.

In qualitative analysis, cations are placed in different groups depending upon the concept of solubility product.

**(a) In precipitation of IIIA group cations ($Al^{+3}$, $Fe^{+3}$, $Cr^{+3}$) :** IIIA group cations are precipitated in the form of their hydroxides in an alkaline medium by addition of $NH_4Cl$ and $NH_4OH$ solution to original solution (O.S.). The solubility product values of IIIA group hydroxides are low, hence low concentration of $OH^-$ ions is required for their precipitation.

In presence of ammonium chloride, degree of dissociation of $NH_4OH$ is suppressed due to common ion effect. As a result, $OH^-$ ion concentration becomes considerably low. In presence of even low concentration of $OH^-$ ions, ionic product of IIIA group hydroxides becomes greater than solubility product. Hence, only IIIA group hydroxides are precipitated and not other group hydroxides (IIIB, IV, V) as they have comparatively higher solubility product values. (See Table 5.5).

**Table 5.5 : $K_{sp}$ for some Hydroxides**

| Substance | Solubility Product | Substance | Solubility Product |
|-----------|-------------------|-----------|-------------------|
| $Fe(OH)_3$ | $1.1 \times 10^{-36}$ | $Ni(OH)_2$ | $8.7 \times 10^{-19}$ |
| $Cr(OH)_3$ | $2.9 \times 10^{-29}$ | $Zn(OH)_2$ | $1.0 \times 10^{-18}$ |
| $Al(OH)_3$ | $8.5 \times 10^{-23}$ | $Mg(OH)_2$ | $1.5 \times 10^{-11}$ |

**(b) In precipitation of II group cations ($Cu^{+2}$, $Cd^{+2}$) :** II group cations are precipitated in the form of their sulphides in an acidic medium by addition of dil HCl and $H_2S$ gas to O.S. The solubility product values of II group sulphides are low, hence low $S^{-2}$ concentration is required for their precipitation.

In presence of HCl, dissociation of $H_2S$ (weak acid) is suppressed due to common ion effect. As a result, sulphide ion concentration becomes low. In presence of such low concentration of $S^{-2}$ ions, ionic product of II group sulphide exceeds the solubility product. Hence, only II group cations are precipitated as sulphides. Here IIIB group sulphides are not precipitated as they have higher solubility product values, hence higher concentration of $S^{-2}$ ion is required for their precipitation (See Table 5.6).

**(c)  In precipitation of IIIB group cations (Co$^{+2}$, Ni$^{+2}$, Zn$^{+2}$) :** IIIB group cations are precipitated as sulphides in presence of $NH_4Cl$, $NH_4OH$ and $H_2S$ gas. The solubility product values of IIIB group sulphides are higher, hence higher concentration of $S^{-2}$ ion is required for their precipitation. Therefore, IIIB group cations are not precipitated at the time of precipitation of II group cations as a sulphides.

Here also group reagent is $H_2S$ gas but in alkaline medium, $NH_4OH$ is added before passing $H_2S$ gas.

$$NH_4OH \rightleftharpoons NH_4^+ + OH^-$$

$$H_2S \rightleftharpoons 2H^+ + S^{-2}$$

$$\therefore \qquad K = \frac{[H^+]^2\,[S^{-2}]}{[H_2S]}$$

$$H^+ + OH^- \longrightarrow H_2O$$

$H^+$ ions combine with $OH^-$ ions from $NH_4OH$ to form $H_2O$. To keep the value of K constant, $S^{-2}$ ion concentration is increased by greater dissociation of $H_2S$. In presence of such high concentration of $S^{-2}$, ionic product of IIIB group sulphides exceeds the solubility product. Thus only IIIB group cations are precipitated in the form of sulphides.

### Table 5.6 : K$_{sp}$ for some Sulphides

| Group II | | Group III B | |
|---|---|---|---|
| Substance | Solubility Product | Substance | Solubility Product |
| PbS | $3.4 \times 10^{-28}$ | MnS | $1.4 \times 10^{-16}$ |
| CdS | $3.5 \times 10^{-29}$ | ZnS | $1.2 \times 10^{-22}$ |
| CuS | $8.5 \times 10^{-45}$ | NiS | $1.4 \times 10^{-24}$ |
| HgS | $4.2 \times 10^{-54}$ | CoS | $3.2 \times 10^{-26}$ |

## SOLVED PROBLEMS ON SOLUBILITY PRODUCT

**Problem 5.22 :**

*The solubility product of AgCl is $1 \times 10^{-10}$ at 298 K. Calculate the solubility of AgCl in (i) mol dm$^{-1}$, (ii) gdm$^{-3}$ at 298 K.*

**Solution :**

Let the solubility of AgCl be S mol dm$^{-3}$.

AgCl dissociates in saturated solution as :

$$1\ AgCl \rightleftharpoons 1\ Ag^+ + 1\ Cl^-$$
$$\text{S moles} \qquad \text{S moles} \quad \text{S moles}$$

Now,          $[Ag^+] [Cl^-] = K_{sp}$

$\therefore$                    $S \times S = 1 \times 10^{-10}$

                         $S^2 = 1 \times 10^{-10}$

$\therefore$                      $S = 1 \times 10^{-5}$

Solubility of AgCl is $1 \times 10^{-5}$ mol dm$^{-3}$ at 298 K.

        Molecular weight of AgCl $= 108 + 35.5 = 143.5$

Thus,                1 mole of AgCl $= 143.5$ g

$\therefore$  $1 \times 10^{-5}$ mol of AgCl in g dm$^{-3} = 0.001435$ g at 298 K

$\therefore$     Solubility of AgCl is 0.001435 g at 298 K.

### Problem 5.23 :

Solubility of lead sulphate (PbSO$_4$) in water at 298 K is 0.99 $\times 10^{-4}$ mol dm$^{-3}$. What is the solubility product of PbSO$_4$ at 298 K ?

### Solution :

PbSO$_4$ dissociates in saturated solution as

$$1\ PbSO_4 \rightleftharpoons 1\ Pb^{++} + 1\ SO_4^{--}$$

        S moles          S moles       S moles

Now,  $[Pb^{++}] [SO_4^{--}] = K_{sp}$

$\therefore$                  $S \times S = K_{sp}$

Solubility of PbSO$_4$ is $0.99 \times 10^{-4}$ mol dm$^{-3}$ and this corresponds to S.

$\therefore$           $(0.99 \times 10^{-4}) \times (0.99 \times 10^{-4}) = K_{sp}$

$\therefore$                    $0.98 \times 10^{-8} = K_{sp}$

$\therefore$     Solubility product of PbSO$_4$ at 298 K $= 0.98 \times 10^{-8} = 9.8 \times 10^{-9}$.

## 5.17 REDOX REACTIONS

The following terms are involved in redox reactions :

**(i) Oxidation :** Any process or reaction, in which there is a loss of electrons by atoms or ions takes place, is known as oxidation. Therefore, oxidation is a de-electronation reaction.

        e.g. Fe (II) $\rightarrow$ Fe (III) + 1e$^-$

**(ii) Reduction :** Any process or reaction, in which there is a gain of electrons by atoms or ions takes place, is known as reduction. Therefore, reduction is an electronation reaction.

        e.g. Ce (IV) + 1e$^-$ $\rightarrow$ Ce (III)

**(iii) Oxidising agent :** The substance which gains electrons and forces another substance to loose electrons is known as oxidising agent or oxidant. While oxidising other substance, an oxidising agent itself gets reduced.

**(iv) Reducing agent :** The substance which loses electrons and forces another substance to gain electrons is called a reducing agent or reductant. While reducing other substance, a reducing agent itself gets oxidised.

**(v) Oxidation state :** Oxidation state is also known as oxidation number, which is defined as the numerical charge (positive or negative) which we assign to the atom of the element in a compound by considering the charges present on the other atoms in that compound.

**Principle :** Redox reactions are generally associated with transfer of electrons. During redox reactions, oxidising agent gains electrons and itself gets reduced.

Conversely, the reducing agent during redox reactions, loses electrons and gets itself oxidised. The ability of gaining of electrons of various oxidising agents varies with the chemical nature among themselves. Similarly, the ability of losing electrons of various reducing agents varies among themselves in strength.

The principle of redox reactions can be well understood from the reactions of $Fe^{3+}$ ions with $Cl^-$ ions, and $MnO_4^-$ ions with $Cl^-$ ions. From the experimental observations, we see that $Fe^{3+}$ ions can oxidise $Sn^{2+}$ but not $Cl^-$ ions. On the other hand, $MnO_4^-$ can oxidise both $Sn^{2+}$ and $Cl^-$. From these reactions, it is clear that permanganate ion is a stronger oxidising agent than the $Fe^{3+}$ ion. Both the oxidising as well as reducing agents differ themselves in strength i.e. tendency of gaining of electrons and tendency of losing of electrons. The strength of these different oxidising and reducing agents can be best expressed quantitatively in terms of reduction potential. The oxidation potential is the quantity which gives quantitative measure of the ability of an oxidising agent to gain electrons. Similarly, the reduction potential is the physical quantity which gives quantitative measure of the ability of an reducing agent to lose electrons.

## 5.18 ELECTRODE POTENTIAL

Electrode potential can be explained on the basis of *Nernst Theory*.

**Single Electrode :** An electrode or a half cell is produced by dipping a metal rod in the solution of its own ions. Such an arrangement is also called as couple of metal and its ionic solution. A couple is also produced from a gas and the solution of its ions.

| | |
|---|---|
| Zinc couple : | $Zn^{++}$ (aq) \| Zn |
| Copper couple : | $Cu^{++}$ (aq) \| Cu |
| Hydrogen couple : | Pt, $H_2$ (g) \| $H^+$ (aq) |

**Origin or Development of Single Electrode Potential :** Single electrode potential is also known as *half-cell potential*. When an active metal rod like Zn is placed in its salt solution, it has a tendency to ionise and pass into the solution.

$$Zn \longrightarrow Zn^{++} + 2e^-$$

In this process, electrons are removed from metal atoms and hence the process is called *de-electronation or oxidation*. Zn rod acquires negative charge.

At the same time, there is opposite tendency of the metal ions from the solution to deposit on the metal electrode and gain the electrons from the metal electrode and change into atoms.

$$Zn^{++} + 2e^- \longrightarrow Zn$$

Thus, ions are removed from the solution. In this process, electrons are added to the ions and therefore the process is called *electronation or reduction*.

Thus, when a zinc couple is produced, there are both tendencies of *de-electronation and electronation*.

$$Zn \rightleftharpoons Zn^{++} + 2e^-$$

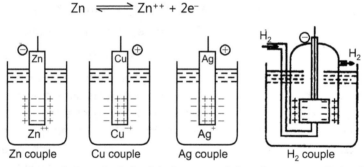

Zn couple     Cu couple     Ag couple     H$_2$ couple

**Fig. 5.11 : Formation of electrical double layer and development of single electrode or half cell potential**

It is a reversible process. When $Zn^{++}$ ions are produced, electrons remain behind on the electrode. At the same time, $Zn^{++}$ ions thus formed produce a layer of positive ions in the solution. *Hence, an electrical double layer is developed. Here the potential developed is because of oxidation. It is called oxidation potential.* The potential produced can be positive or negative. At the electrode, both the processes take place simultaneously and an equilibrium is reached. The potential developed at the time of equilibrium is called *single electrode potential* or half cell potential. *Thus, the potential difference between the electrode and the solution around it at equilibrium is called the single electrode potential or half-cell potential.*

In the case of copper couple, the tendency here is more of electronation, i.e.

$$Cu^{++} + 2e^- \rightleftharpoons Cu$$

At equilibrium, copper plate acquires positive charge while a layer of negative charges is in the solution, near the electrode, forming an electrical double layer. The positive charge developed on copper plate is due to *reduction or electronation*.

In a similar manner, it can be explained about a negative charge developed on platinum plate in the hydrogen couple due to oxidation or de-electronation while a positive charge is developed on silver plate in silver couple, due to reduction or electronation.

**Nernst Theory of Electrode Potential :** W. Nernst in 1889, suggested the mechanism of establishment of difference of potential in a cell. His theory is based on the theory of electrolytic dissociation and his ideas of solution pressure are also known as theory of electronation and de-electronation.

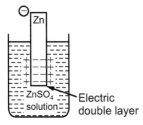

**Fig. 5.12 (a) : $P_s > P_o$**

**1.    De-electronation :** According to Nernst, all metals and hydrogen have a tendency to pass into the solution in the form of positive ions. This property of the metals is due to **solution pressure ($P_s$)** and metals widely differ in their **solution pressures**. This process is known as **de-electronation** as electrons are removed when a positive ion is formed and this is oxidation.

As a result, solution acquires positive charge due to excess of cations whereas metal rod acquires negative charge due to excess of electrons. This forms electric double layer across metal surface which gives rise to electrode potential. For example, zinc electrode ($Zn \rightarrow Zn^{+2} + 2e^-$).

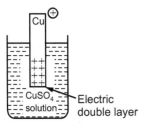

**Fig. 5.12 (b) : $P_s < P_o$**

**2.    Electronation :** The solution pressure tendency is opposed by reverse tendency of metal cations to get deposited on metal by accepting the electrons from metal.

The tendency of metal cations to get deposited as a neutral atom by accepting electrons is known as osmotic pressure ($P_o$). The process of gain of electrons is electronation and this is reduction.

As a result, solution acquired negative charge due to lack of cations and rod acquires positive charge due to lack of electrons. This forms electric double layer which gives rise to electrode potential. For example, copper electrode ($Cu^{+2} + 2e^- \rightarrow Cu$).

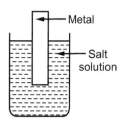

**Fig. 5.12 (c) : P$_s$ = P$_o$**

**3. Null electrode :** When rate of de-electronation is equal to the rate of electronation (P$_S$ ≈ P$_O$), metal rod acquires neither positive charge nor negative charge. Such electrode is known as null electrode and has zero potential. Example is rare.

Obviously, the magnitude and sign of potential difference between the metal and the solution is determined by the relative magnitudes of the solution pressure (P$_S$) of the metal and the osmotic pressure (P$_O$) of the positive metallic ions. The following three cases are possible.

(i) **P$_s$ > P$_o$ [Refer Fig. 5.12 (a)] :** In such a case, positive ions pass into the solution more rapidly leaving the electrode negatively charged. The solution acquires positive charge. Zinc metal dipping in the solution of zinc ions behaves in this way.

(ii) **P$_s$ < P$_o$ [Refer Fig. 5.12 (b)] :** In this case, ultimately the positive ions of the dissolved salt are deposited on the electrode making it positively charged. The solution acquires a negative charge. Copper metal dipping in the solution of copper ions behaves in this way.

(iii) **P$_s$ = P$_o$ [Refer Fig. 5.12 (c)] :** No action will take place and no potential difference will be established between the metal and the solution. Such a system is called a 'null electrode'.

The above discussion of solution pressure holds equally well in the case of substances capable of producing negative ions.

The formation of electrical double layer is responsible in giving electrode potential. *The resultant potential of the metal is then equal to the difference between its solution pressure and the osmotic pressure of the ions.*

**Expression for the Potential of Single Electrode (Nernst Equation) :**

The difference of potential between the electrode and its solution around it in equilibrium is called as single electrode potential or half-cell potential.

Single electrode potential and cell potential are determined by three factors : (i) the nature of the constituents of the electrodes, (ii) the temperature and (iii) the activities or concentration of the solutions surrounding the electrodes.

Now the standard electrode potential can be determined only under specific standard conditions viz. temperature = 298 K, salt solution = 1 M ion concentration or for gas 1 atm. pressure. However, it is not always possible to maintain all these conditions. The potential observed at any condition other than standard condition, is called **observed or formal electrode** potential. Nernst gave the following fundamental electrode relation between the observed potential and standard electrode potential for redox reactions.

**Nernst equation for potential of single electrode :**

The general expression for potential of electrode or cell is given by

$$E = E^O - \frac{2.303 \, RT}{nF} \log \frac{a_{products}}{a_{reactants}}$$

where,     E – Electrode/cell potential

$E°$ – Standard electrode/cell potential

R – Gas constant

T – Absolute temperature

n – Number of electrons transferred in the half reaction

F – Faraday (96,500 C)

$a_{reactants}$ – Activity or concentration of reactants

$a_{products}$ – Activity or concentration of products

(I)    For metal M with its valency 'n' immersed in a solution containing its own metal ions $M^{n+}$, electrode reaction can be written as follows :

$$M(s) \rightarrow M^{n+} (aq) + ne^- \text{ (oxidation)}$$

For above reaction, oxidation electrode potential is given by using Nernst equation,

$$E_{oxi} = E^o_{oxi} - \frac{2.303 \, RT}{nF} \log \frac{a_{M^{n+}}}{a_M}$$

But $a_M$ i.e. [M], activity of pure metal is unity.

$\therefore$        $$E_{oxi} = E^o_{oxi} - \frac{2.303 \, RT}{nF} \log a_{M^{n+}}$$

Here factor $\frac{2.303 \, RT}{F}$ is constant, at 298 K it is equal to 0.059.

(R = 8.368 J, T = 298 K, F = 96,500 C, $\therefore \frac{2.303 \times 8.368 \times 298}{96,500} = 0.059$)

$\therefore$        $$E_{oxi} = E^o_{oxi} - \frac{0.059}{n} \log a_{M^{n+}}$$

or        $$\boxed{E_{oxi} = E^o_{oxi} - \frac{0.059}{n} \log [M^{n+}]}$$

e.g. for zinc electrode, $Zn (s) \rightarrow Zn^{++} (aq) + 2e^-$

n = 2, $\therefore$      $$E_{Zn} = E^o_{Zn} - \frac{0.059}{2} \log [Zn^{++}]$$

(II) For metal M with valency 'n' immersed in a solution containing its own metal ion $M^{n+}$, reduction can be written as

$$M^{n+}_{(aq)} + ne^- \rightarrow M(s) \text{ (Reduction)}$$

Nernst equation for reduction electrode potential for above reaction can be written as,

$$E_{red} = E^o_{red} - \frac{0.059}{n} \log \frac{[M]}{[M^{n+}]}$$

Since [M] = 1,

$$\therefore \qquad E_{red} = E^o_{red} - \frac{0.059}{n} \log \frac{1}{[M^{n+}]}$$

$$\therefore \qquad \boxed{E_{red} = E^o_{red} + \frac{0.059}{n} \log [M^{n+}]}$$

e.g. for copper electrode, $Cu^{++}$ (aq) + $2e^- \rightarrow$ Cu (s)

$$n = 2, \qquad E_{Cu} = E^o_{Cu} - \frac{0.059}{2} \log \frac{1}{[Cu^{++}]}$$

(III) For cell potential,

$$E_{cell} = E_{oxi} \text{ (LHE)} + E_{red} \text{ (RHE)} = E_{red} \text{ (RHE)} - E_{red} \text{ (LHE)}$$

$\therefore$   Nernst equation for cell potential is given by

$$E_{cell} = E^o_{cell} - \frac{0.059}{n} \log \frac{[\text{Oxidised state}]}{[\text{Reduced state}]}$$

e.g. for cell Zn (s) | $Zn^{2+}$ (aq) || $Cu^{2+}$ (aq) | Cu (s),
Nernst equation can be written as

$$n = 2, \therefore \quad \boxed{E_{cell} = E^o_{cell} - \frac{0.059}{2} \log \frac{[Zn^{2+} \text{(aq)}]}{[Cu^{2+} \text{(aq)}]}}$$

Thus for a given electrode, its potential depends upon (i) the temperature, (ii) the activity of its own ions in solution in which metal is dipped.

## 5.19 CONCENTRATION CELL

In a concentration cell, there is no net chemical reaction. The electrical energy in a concentration cell arises from the transfer of a substance from the solution of a higher concentration to the solution of lower concentration. A concentration cell consists of two half cells having identical electrodes, identical electrolyte, except that the concentrations of the reactive ions at the two electrodes are different. The salt bridge is used to join the two half cells.

| $^-$Ag | $AgNO_3$ ($C_1$) (dilute) | Salt bridge of saturated $NH_4NO_3$ | $AgNO_3$ ($C_2$) (conc.) | $Ag^+$ |
|---|---|---|---|---|

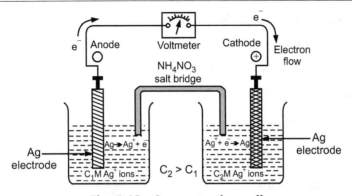

**Fig. 5.13 : Concentration cell**

# 5.20 REFERENCE ELECTRODES

(1) **Standard Hydrogen Electrode :** This is a primary reference electrode and conventionally its potential is arbitrarily taken zero at all temperatures. All other electrode potentials are expressed on the basis of hydrogen electrode as standard electrode and are called potentials on hydrogen scale.

**Construction :** It consists of a piece of platinized platinum foil immersed in a solution of hydrochloric acid with unit activity of $H^+$ ions and pure and dry hydrogen gas at exactly one atmospheric pressure is bubbled at the surface of the platinum foil. Hydrogen gas is adsorbed at the surface of the foil and is in contact with $H^+$ ions from the solution. Following oxidation reaction takes place at the surface of the electrode :

$$H_2 (g) \ (1 \text{ atm}) \longrightarrow H^+ (aq) \ (a_{H^+} = 1) + e^-$$

Slight negative potential is developed at the platinum electrode. However, for all practical purposes, e.m.f. developed at the electrode is arbitrarily taken as 0.000 V standard hydrogen electrode. The standard hydrogen electrode is shown in Fig. 5.14.

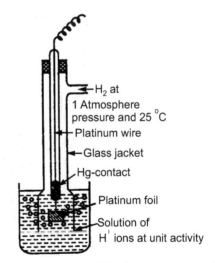

**Fig. 5.14 : Standard hydrogen electrode**

**Drawbacks of standard hydrogen electrode :**

(i)   It is not possible to maintain the pressure of $H_2$ gas at 1 atmosphere all the time.

(ii)  It is not possible to maintain unit activity of $H^+$ ions in the solution.

(iii) Impurities and oxidising agents alter the potential of the electrode.

(iv) The $H_2$ gas is poisoned by absorption of impurities and become inactive.

**(2) Calomel Reference Electrode :** Since the standard hydrogen electrode is difficult to prepare and maintain in practice, secondary reference electrodes, whose potentials with reference to the standard hydrogen electrode are exactly known and reproducible, are used. One type is the calomel electrode. The cell reaction is :

$$Hg_2Cl_2\,(s) + 2e^- \rightleftharpoons 2\,Hg\,(l) + 2Cl^-\ (C = X)$$

The values of X being different in different cells of the type. For the 0.1 N and 1 N calomel electrodes, X = 0.1 N and 1 N respectively. Potassium chloride is actually used as a source of $Cl^-$ ions and a saturated solution of KCl is used for the saturated calomel electrode.

A common form of calomel electrode is shown in Fig. 5.15. This consists of a glass vessel G with two side arms; side arm A for making electrical contact, and side arm B for insertion into a suitable solution into which also dips the second electrode whose potential is to be determined. Into the bottom of G, a platinum wire is seated and then a layer of specially purified mercury is poured into it. Above this is a layer of a paste of mercury and calomel and on top is the solution of potassium chloride of appropriate strength (depending on the type of calomel electrode required) saturated calomel whose solution also fills the side arm B. In the saturated calomel electrode, some crystals of potassium chloride are also placed just above the mercury-mercurous chloride paste. This ensures saturation at all temperatures.

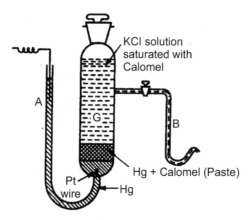

**Fig. 5.15 : The calomel electrode**

**(3) Metal-Metal ion Electrode :** Electrodes of this type involve a metal in equilibrium with a solution of its ions. The electrodes consist of metal bar or strip immersed in a solution of its own ions. The electrodes operate on the general reaction :

$$M\ (s) \rightleftharpoons M^{n+} + ne^-$$

where n is the valency of the metal.

The electrode potential equation is given by,

$$\boxed{E_M = E_M^o - \frac{2.303\ RT}{nF} \log a_{M^{n+}}}$$

Examples of this type are $Zn\ |\ Zn^{2+}$ electrode, $Cu\ |\ Cu^{2+}$ electrode, $Mg\ |\ Mg^{2+}$ electrode, $Ag\ |\ Ag^+$ electrode.

e.g.          $Mg\ (s)\ \rightarrow Mg^{2+} + 2e^-$

e.m.f. of metal electrode depends upon temperature and the activity of metal ions in the solution.

**(4) Amalgam Electrode :** When a pure metal, in metal-ion electrode, is highly reactive, then it is mixed with mercury to form alloy, called as amalgam. The amalgam electrode is constructed by dipping amalgam of a desired metal in its solution. These electrodes are useful to establish equilibrium between metals and their respective ions, more rapidly than to the pure metals.

Amalgamation dilutes the impurities in the metals, so that they practically do not affect the behaviour of electrodes and yield satisfactory results.

Cadmium amalgam dipped in cadmium sulphate solution is an example of amalgam electrode.

The oxidation electrode representation is,

$$Cd\ (Hg)^-\ |\ Cd^{2+}\ (a_{Cd^{2+}})$$

The oxidation electrode reaction is,

$$Cd\ (Hg) \longrightarrow Cd^{2+}\ (a_{Cd^{2+}}) + 2e^-$$

For lead amalgam electrode, the oxidation electrode representation is,

$$Pb\ (Hg)^-\ |\ Pb^{2+}\ (a_{Pb^{2+}})$$

and the oxidation electrode reaction is,

$$Pb\ (Hg) \longrightarrow Pb^{2+}\ (a_{Pb^{2+}}) + 2e^-$$

The e.m.f. $E_a$ developed at the amalgam electrode is given by the Nernst equation :

$$E_a = E_{Pb}^o - \frac{RT}{2F} ln \frac{a_{Pb^{2+}}}{a_{Pb}} \qquad \qquad ...\ (i)$$

where $E_{Pb}^o$ is standard electrode potential of pure lead electrode, $a_{Pb^{2+}}$ is activity of lead ion in solution and $a_{Pb}$ is activity of metal lead in amalgam.

The equation (i) may be rearranged and written as,

$$E_a = \left( E^o_{Pb} + \frac{RT}{2F} \ln a_{Pb} \right) - \frac{RT}{2F} \ln a_{Pb^{2+}} \qquad \text{... (ii)}$$

Substituting $E^o_{Pb} + \frac{RT}{2F} \ln a_{Pb} = E^o_a$ , the equation (ii) becomes,

$$\boxed{E_a = E^o_a - \frac{RT}{2F} \ln a_{Pb^{2+}}} \qquad \text{... (iii)}$$

where $E^o_a$ is the standard potential of the given amalgam electrode and depends upon composition of the amalgam.

**(5) Gas Electrode :** They are constructed by bubbling the gas through solution of its ion. Some inert metal is used. The function of inert metal is to establish the equilibrium between ions and atoms rapidly.

The important gas electrodes are hydrogen electrode, chlorine electrode and oxygen electrode.

**(a) Hydrogen electrode :**
The electrode is represented as,

$^-$ Pt | $H_2$ (g) $(P_{H_2})$ | $H^+$

Reversible with $H^+$ ions,

$$\frac{1}{2} H_2 (P) \rightleftharpoons H^+ (a_{H^+}) + e^-$$

e.m.f. developed at the electrode depends on activity of $H^+$ ions and pressure of hydrogen gas, and is given by,

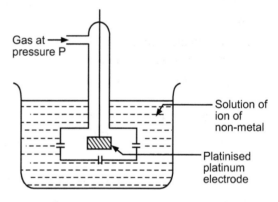

Gas at pressure P

Solution of ion of non-metal

Platinised platinum electrode

**Fig. 5.16 : Non-metal electrode**

$$\boxed{E_{H_2} = E^o_{H_2} - \frac{RT}{F} \ln \frac{a_{H^+}}{P_{H_2}^{1/2}}}$$

$$E_{H_2} = 0.05916 \ pH$$

**(b) Chlorine electrode :** The chlorine electrode is represented as,

$$Pt \mid Cl_2 (g) \ (P_{Cl_2}) \mid Cl^-$$

Reversible with $Cl^-$ ions,

$$\frac{1}{2} Cl_2 (P) + e^- \rightarrow Cl^- (a_{Cl^-})$$

$$\boxed{E_{Cl_2} = E_{Cl_2}^o - \frac{RT}{F} \ln \frac{a_{Cl^-}}{P_{Cl_2}^{1/2}}}$$

$E_{Cl_2}^o = 1.3595$ volts at 25°C

**(c) Oxygen electrode :** The oxygen electrode is represented as,

$$Pt^+ \mid O_2 (g) (P_{O_2}) \mid OH^-$$

Reversible with $OH^-$ ions,

$$H_2O + \frac{1}{2} O_2 + 2e^- \longrightarrow 2\,OH^- (a_{OH^-})$$

The e.m.f. developed at oxygen electrode is given by,

$$\boxed{E_{O2} = E_{O_2}^o - \frac{RT}{2F} \ln \frac{a_{OH^-}^2}{a_{O_2}^{1/2}}}$$

**(6) Metal-Insoluble Salt Electrode :** The electrode is prepared by immersing a metal bar or thick wire in a solution of sparingly soluble salts and this salt is in contact with a solution containing common ion.

Following are the examples of metal-insoluble salt-electrodes :

**(a) Pb – PbSO₄ electrode :** Reversible with $SO_4^{2-}$ ions,

$$Pb (s) + SO_4^{2-} (a) \rightarrow PbSO_4 (s) + 2e^-$$

$$\boxed{E (oxi) = E^o - \frac{2.303\,RT}{nF} \log \frac{1}{a_{SO_4}^{2-}}}$$

$E^o (oxi) = 0.3588$ V

**(b) Calomel electrode :** The electrode is represented as,

$$Hg \mid Hg_2Cl_2 (s), Cl^- (a_{Cl^-})$$

Reversible with $Cl^-$ ions,

$$\frac{1}{2} Hg_2Cl_2 + e^- \longrightarrow Hg\,(l) + Cl^- (a_{Cl^-})$$

$$\boxed{E_C (red) = E_C^o - \frac{2.303}{F} RT \log a_{Cl^-}}$$

$E_C^o (red) = 0.2676$ V

**(c) Ag – AgCl electrode :** The electrode is represented as,

$$Ag \mid AgCl\ (s) \mid Cl^-$$

Reversible with $Cl^-$ ions,

$$AgCl\ (s) + e^- \rightarrow Ag\ (s) + Cl^-\ (a_{Cl^-})$$

$$E\ (red) = E^o_{Ag-AgCl} - \frac{2.303\ RT}{F}\ log\ a_{Cl^-}$$

$$E^o_{Ag-AgCl} = 0.2225\ V$$

**(7) Oxidation-Reduction Electrode :** Oxidation-reduction electrode designates electrodes in which e.m.f. of the electrodes result from the pressure of ions of a substance in two different oxidation states like ferrous and ferric or cerrous and cerric, etc.

In general, any oxidation-reduction reaction is given by,

$$M^{n_1}\ (a_1) \rightarrow M^{n_2}\ (a_2) + ne^-$$

where $n_1$ is the lower oxidation state and $n_2$ the higher, so that $n_2 - n_1 = n$. The e.m.f. developed on platinum electrode is given by,

$$E_{M^{n_1}/M^{n_2}} = E^o_{M^{n_1}/M^{n_2}} - \frac{RT}{nF}\ ln\ \frac{a_2}{a_1}$$

For example, the ferrous-ferric oxidation-reduction electrode is represented as,

$$Pt \mid Fe^{++}\ (aq)\ (a_1),\ Fe^{+++}\ (aq)\ (a_2)$$

A typical reversible reaction for oxidation is given by,

$$Fe^{++}\ (aq)\ (a_1) \rightarrow Fe^{+++}\ (aq)\ (a_2) + e^-$$

The e.m.f. developed on platinum electrode is given by,

$$E_{Fe^{++}/Fe^{+++}} = E^o_{Fe^{++}/Fe^{+++}} - \frac{RT}{F}\ ln\ \frac{a_2}{a_1}$$

## SOLVED PROBLEMS ON REFERENCE ELECTRODES

**Problem 5.24 :**

Write the cell reaction and calculate the e.m.f. of the cell at 25°C :

$$H_2\ (g)\ (0.4\ atm)\ /HCl,\ (a = 3.0),\ AgCl\ (s)\ /Ag$$

if $E^o_{Ag-AgCl} = -0.2225\ V$.

**Solution :**

Following reactions take place at two electrodes :

L.H.S. :  $\quad \frac{1}{2} H_2\ (g) \longrightarrow H^+ + e^-$

and e.m.f. developed is,

$$E_{H_2} = E^o_{H_2} - \frac{RT}{F} \ln \frac{a_{H^+}}{P_{H_2}^{1/2}}, E^o_{H_2} = 0$$

R.H.S. :     $AgCl\ (s) + e^- \longrightarrow Ag\ (s) + Cl^-$

and e.m.f. developed is,

$$E_{Ag\text{-}AgCl} = -E^o_{Ag\text{-}AgCl} - \frac{RT}{F} \ln a_{Cl^-}$$

The net cell reaction is given as,

$$\frac{1}{2} H_2\ (g) + AgCl\ (s) \rightarrow H^+ + Ag\ (s) + Cl^-$$

and          $E_{cell} = E_{H_2} + E_{Ag\text{-}AgCl}$

$$= -E^o_{Ag\text{-}AgCl} - \frac{RT}{F} \ln \frac{a_{H^+} \cdot a_{Cl^-}}{P_{H_2}^{1/2}}$$

$$= 0.2225 - 0.05916 \log \frac{a_{HCl}}{P_{H_2}^{1/2}} \qquad (\because a_{H^+} \cdot a_{Cl^-} = 1)$$

Hence,     $E_{cell} = 0.2225 - 0.05916 \log \dfrac{3}{0.4^{1/2}}$

$$= 0.2225 - 0.0753 = 0.1472\ V$$

---

### Problem 5.25 :

*The potential of the cell :*

*$Hg\ (l)\ /\ Hg_2Cl_2\ (s),\ KCl\ (satd)\ /\ Cl_2\ (g)\ (P = 0.283\ atm)$*

*was found to be 1.0758 volts if $E^o$ of saturated calomel electrode is 0.268 V for reduction. Estimate $E^o$ for chlorine electrode.*

### Solution :

Following reactions take place in the cell :

L.H.S. : The electrode to the left is saturated calomel electrode and oxidation takes place at calomel electrode as,

$$Hg\ (l) + Cl^-\ (aq) \rightarrow \frac{1}{2} Hg_2\,Cl_2\ (s) + e^-$$

and          $E_{Cal} = -E^o_{Cal} - \dfrac{RT}{F} \ln \dfrac{1}{a_{Cl^-}}$

R.H.S. : $\frac{1}{2} Cl_2\ (g) + e^- \rightarrow Cl^-\ (aq)$

and          $E_{Cl_2} = -E^o_{Cl_2} - \dfrac{RT}{F} \ln \dfrac{a_{Cl^-}}{P_{Cl_2}^{1/2}}$

Hence,       $E_{cell} = E_{Cal} - E_{Cl_2}$

$$= -0.268 - E_{Cl_2}^o - \frac{RT}{F} \ln \frac{a_{Cl^-}}{a_{Cl^-} \cdot P_{Cl_2}^{1/2}}$$

$$1.0758 = -0.268 - E_{Cl_2}^o - \frac{RT}{F} \ln \frac{1}{0.283^{1/2}}$$

$$1.0758 = -0.268 - \frac{0.05916}{2} \log \frac{1}{0.283}$$

$$= -0.268 - 0.0162$$

$$= -0.2842 - E_{Cl_2}^o$$

∴              $E_{Cl_2}^o = 1.36 \text{ V}$

---

**Problem 5.26 :**

Find the e.m.f. of the cell at 25°C :

$$Cd \,/\, Cd^{2+} \,(a = 0.05) \,//\, Fe^{2+} \,(a = 0.002),\, Fe^{3+} \,(a = 0.2) \,/\, Pt$$

Write the cell reaction, if $E_{Cd}^o$ (oxi) = 0.4 V and $E_{redox}^o$(red) = – 0.77 V.

**Solution :**

Reactions :       $Cd\,(s) \rightarrow Cd^{2+} + 2e^-$

$$2\,Fe^{3+} + 2e^- \rightarrow Fe^{2+}$$

i.e.      $Cd\,(s) + 2\,Fe^{3+} \rightarrow Cd^{2+} + Fe^{2+}$

$$E_{Cd}\,(oxi) = E_{Cd}^o\,(oxi) - \frac{0.059}{n} \log a_{Cd^{2+}}$$

$$= 0.4 - \frac{0.059}{2} \log 0.05$$

$$= 0.4 + 0.038 = 0.438 \text{ V}$$

$$E_{redox}\,(red) = E_{redox}^o\,(red) - \frac{0.059}{2} \log \left(\frac{a_{Fe^{2+}}}{a_{Fe^{3+}}}\right)^2$$

$$= 0.77 + 0.118 = 0.888 \text{ V}$$

$$E_{cell} = E_{Cd}\,(oxi) + E_{redox}\,(red)$$

$$= 0.438 + 0.888 = 1.326 \text{ V}$$

---

## 5.21 POLARIZATION

Nernst gave the equation of electrode potential as

$$E = E^O + \frac{0.0592 \text{ V}}{n} \log [M^{n+}]$$

where E is the electrode potential, $E^O$ the standard electrode potential and $[M^{n+}]$ is the metal ion concentration surrounding the electrode surface at equilibrium.

On passage of electric current, due to continuous reduction of the metal ions to metal atoms, the value of $[M^{n+}]$ in the vicinity of the electrode surface decreases.

Hence,                    $M^{n+} + ne^- \longrightarrow M$

Similarly, the value of the electrode potential also changes. However, as the metal ions from the bulk of the solution diffuse towards the electrode, due to existence of a concentration gradient between the bulk of the solution and around the electrode surface, there is re-establishment of equilibrium. But the rate of diffusion is usually slow and hence there is variation in electrode potential. The electrode under this condition, is said to be polarized. Therefore, polarization is defined as the process where there is a variation of electrode potential due to inadequate diffusion of species from the bulk of the electrolytic solution to the vicinity of the electrode. Due to polarization, there is accumulation of charge on the electrode. Hence, polarized galvanic cells develop smaller potential than theoretically predicted.

On following factors, the extent of polarization depends :

(1) **Temperature :** By increasing the temperature, polarization effects are minimized, as rate of diffusion of ions increases.

(2) **Concentration of electrolyte :** Polarization effects get decrease because of low concentration of electrolyte.

(3) **Size of electrode :** Polarization effects get decrease because of large surface area.

(4) **Stirring of the electrolytic solution :** Polarization effects get minimized because of stirring.

(5) **Nature of electrode surface :** Smooth surface of electrode possesses higher polarization effects than rougher surface.

## 5.22 DECOMPOSITION POTENTIAL

During the process of electrolysis, products of electrolysis accumulate around the electrodes. Due to this, there is change in concentration around the electrodes and production of an opposing e.m.f., called back e.m.f. For example, when a voltage is applied between two platinum electrodes dipping in dilute sulphuric acid solution, at once the electrolysis of water starts evolving hydrogen and oxygen. After some time electrolysis stops, because of back e.m.f. greater than the applied voltage. The electrolysis will proceed smoothly if we increase the applied voltage slowly, when the applied voltage just exceeds the back e.m.f. Refer Fig. 5.17.

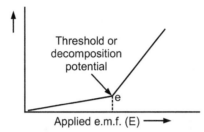

**Fig. 5.17 : Decomposition potential**

Hence, decomposition potential is defined as the minimum potential which must be applied between the two electrodes immersed in the given electrolytic solution in order to bring about continuous electrolytic decomposition. Hence, decomposition potential is equal to back e.m.f.

$$E_d = E_b = E_{cathode} - E_{anode}$$

For dilute acids and bases using bright platinum electrodes, the decomposition potential is 1.7 volts.

**Merits of Decomposition potential :**

    (1)   In electroplating processes.

    (2)   In separation of metal ions mixture by electrolysis.

    (3)   In refining of metals.

## 5.23 OVERVOLTAGE

For electrolysis to occur, the applied voltage should atleast overcome the back e.m.f. or decomposition potential. In few cases, it is observed that electrolysis does not occur, eventhough a potential higher than the theoretical decomposition potential is applied. This is seen in case of electrolysis of dilute $H_2SO_4$ solution. The theoretical decomposition potential value for the electrolysis of dil. $H_2SO_4$ solution with platinum electrodes is 1.229 V but actual decomposition takes place at a potential value of 1.70 V.

Hence, overvoltage is defined as the difference between the potential of the electrodes at which the electrolysis actually proceeds continuously and the theoretical decomposition potential for the same solution.

**Factors affecting overvoltage value :** Following factors affect the overvoltage value :

    (1)   Temperature.

    (2)   pH of electrolytic path.

    (3)   Presence of inhibitors.

    (4)   Current density.

(5)   Nature of substance deposited.

(6)   Nature and physical state of electrode metal.

(7)   Rate of stirring of the electrolyte.

## 5.24 CONDUCTOMETRIC TITRATIONS

Conductometric titration is a method of volumetric analysis based on the change in conductance of the solution, at the equivalence point or end point during titration. This method of titration depends upon following factors :

(1)   Mobility or speed of the ions.

(2)   The number of free ions in the solution.

(3)   The charge on the free ions.

Conductance measurements may be used to determine the end points of various titrations. Consider first the titration of a strong acid like hydrochloric with a strong base like sodium hydroxide. Before the base is added, the acid solution has a high content of the highly mobile hydrogen ions which give the solution a high conductance.

As alkali is added, the hydrogen ions are removed to form water, and their place is taken by the much slower cations of the base. Consequently, the conductance of the solution decreases and keeps on falling with the addition of base until the equivalent point is reached. Further addition of alkali introduces now an excess of the fast hydroxyl ions, and these cause the conductance to rise again. When this variation of the conductance of the solution is plotted against the volume of alkali added, the result is curve ABC as shown in Fig. 5.18.

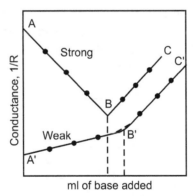

**Fig. 5.18 : Conductometric titration of strong acid with a strong base**

The descending branch of this curve gives the conductances of mixtures of acid and salt, the ascending branch conductances of mixtures of the salt and excess base. At the minimum, point B, there is no excess present of either acid or base, and hence it is the end point.

Titration curves of this type are obtained only on neutralization of strong acids by strong bases. When the acid is weak (say, acetic acid) and the base is strong, the titration curve has the general form of A'B'C', as shown in Fig. 5.18. Because the acid is weak, its conductance is correspondingly low. As the base is added, the poorly conducting acid is converted to highly ionized salt, and consequently the conductance goes up along A'B'. Once the acid is neutralized, addition of excess base causes another sharp increase in conductance, and the curve rises along B'C'. The equivalence point is again the intersection of the two straight lines. Actually the intersection of A'B' and B'C' is not as sharp as shown but has the form indicated by the dotted lines. This rounding of the intersection is due to hydrolysis of the salt formed during the neutralization reaction. However, this rounding introduces no particular difficulty, for the straight-line portions of the curve may be extended, as shown in Fig. 5.18, to give the correct end point.

When the relative strengths of acid and base are changed, the titration curves also change. Thus, it is concluded that many titrations can be run conductometrically in water or mixed solvents which would be difficult or impossible with indicators, and that the method can be applied to mixtures of weak and strong acids, weak and strong bases, precipitation, oxidation-reduction, and other types of reactions.

## 5.25 BATTERIES

Batteries are the storehouses for electrical energies on demand. They range in size from large house-sized batteries for utility storage, cubic meter-sized batteries, for automotive starting, lighting, ignition and sophisticated controls down to tablet-sized batteries for hearing aids and paper-thin batteries for memory protection in electronic devices, compact rechargeable batteries for lap tops and mobile telephones.

In bulk chemical reactions, an oxidizer (electron acceptor) and fuel (electron donor) react to form products resulting in direct electron transfer and the release or absorption of energy as heat. By special arrangement of reactants in batteries, it is possible to control the rate of reaction and to accomplish the direct release of chemical energy in the form of electrical energy instead of heat energy on demand.

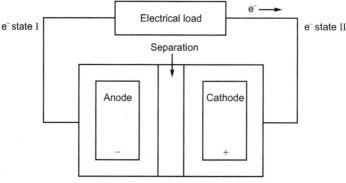

**Fig. 5.19 : Battery system**

Fig. 5.19 represents simple electrochemical reactor in which the chemical energy stored in the electrodes is manifested directly as a voltage and current flow. The electrons involved in the chemical reactions are transferred from active materials (undergoing oxidation) to the oxidising agent by means of an external circuit. The passage of electron through this external circuit generates an electric current providing a direct means for energy utilization.

Faraday established the relationship between the current flow and chemical reactions, as the amount of chemical charge was directly proportional to the quantity of charge passed and to the equivalent weight of the reacting material.

$$g = \frac{MIt}{nF}$$

where,    g  $\rightarrow$ Mass of material in grams that reacts during electrolysis

M  $\rightarrow$ Molecular weight

n  $\rightarrow$ Number of charges transferred in the reaction

t  $\rightarrow$ Time of electrolysis

F  $\rightarrow$ Faraday's constant

I  $\rightarrow$ Current in amperes

In Fig. 5.19, anode is a negative electrode from which an electron leaves the cell and oxidation occurs. Cathode is a positive electrode of the cell from which electron enters the cell and reduction occurs.

Separator is a physical barrier between positive and negative electrodes, it prevents electrical shorting. Separator is a porous inert material permeable to ions. It also can be a gelled electrolyte.

A simple voltaic cell (See Fig. 5.20) is composed of three parts, a pair of dissimilar metal plates called electrodes, a dilute acid solution called electrolyte and non-conducting container called a cell.

Many different combinations of materials are used in such cells. When a voltmeter is connected to the two terminals of the cell, the pointer indicates the difference of potential in volts, this is called the electromotive force (emf).

**Definition** : Battery is a collection of two or more electrochemical cells, connected in series, having terminals, to produce electrical energy. The battery potential is the sum of individual cell potentials (See Fig. 5.21). The purpose of connecting two or more cells in series is to get higher e.m.f. than that available with one cell alone. Battery is also called electrochemical transducer.

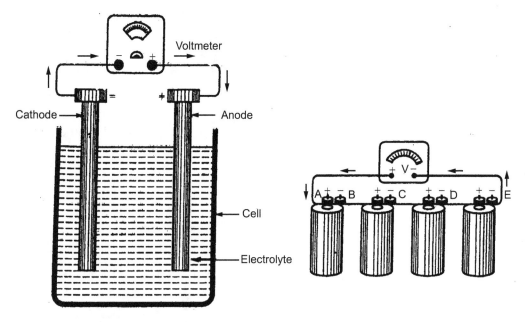

**Fig. 5.20 : The emf of a voltaic cell is measured with a voltmeter**

**Fig. 5.21 : Four dry cells connected in series form a 6 volt battery**

## 5.26 TYPES OF BATTERIES

The batteries are classified into two major classes, as primary batteries and secondary batteries. They are manufactured in two common forms as 'dry cells' and 'wet cells'.

## 5.26.1 Primary Cells or Batteries

These are electrolytic cells or group of cells which are intended to generate electrical energy from chemical energy. These can be used until exhausted and then are discarded. Primary batteries are manufactured in different shapes and sizes and are composed of dry cells. They are also called Leclanche cell, a cell invented by Leclanche in 1868. It can be represented as

$$Zn_{(s)} \mid Zn^{2+}_{(Aq)}, \ NH_4Cl_{(Aq)} \mid MnO_{2\,(s)}, \ Mn_2O_{3\,(s)} \mid C_{(s)}$$

The reaction of dry cells is given as

$$Zn + 2\,NH_4Cl + 2\,MnO_2 \rightleftharpoons Zn(NH_3)_2Cl_2 + Mn_2O_3 + H_2O$$

Carbon-zinc batteries having round carbon rod as a cathode and zinc as anode are commonly found primary batteries. Aqueous solution of ammonium chloride is used as liquid electrolyte. In many cells, paste of ammonium chloride and zinc chloride in water is also used. By using different electrolytes and variety of cathodes, many types of primary cells are manufactured. Few of them are discussed below.

## 1. Zinc-manganese dioxide batteries :

The dry cell is the outgrowth of Laclanche cell. The carbon rod cathode is surrounded by a thick layer of $MnO_2$, mixed with small amount of graphite to increase the conductivity. High purity cylindrical zinc container acts as anode. The electrolyte is an aqueous solution of $ZnCl_2$ and $NH_4Cl$. The cell reaction may be given as

$$Zn_{(s)} + 2\ MnO_{2\ (s)} + H_2O \longrightarrow Zn^{2+} + Mn_2O_3 + 2\ OH^-$$

Above aqueous electrolyte solution is gelled with starch or agar so that the cell is 'dry'. A paper lining separates the $MnO_2$ from aqueous electrolyte. The newly prepared cell has an open circuit potential of about 1.55 volts. Above cell reaction increases pH of the solution, which is buffered by ammonium chloride. The cell reaction is partially reversible, so dry cell cannot be recharged. Zinc ions get precipitated as hydroxide or oxychloride or remain in solution as ammine complex. These cells are inexpensive so widely used, but have short shelf life. Shelf life is the time at 25°C which a given battery retains 90 % of its original energy content. It is reduced by high temperature because of side chemical reactions within the cells, moisture loss and corrosion of zinc anode.

Cylindrical cells (See Fig. 5.22) are used to power flashlights (See Fig. 5.23) and photoflash. They are used for radio applications and also for general purposes like electric clocks, torches.

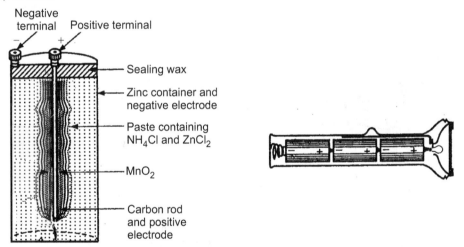

**Fig. 5.22 : Cross-section diagram of a dry cell or 'flashlight" battery, showing the essential elements**

**Fig. 5.23 : Cross-section of a 3-cell flashlight**

## Modification :

By replacing ammonium chloride by alkali like NaOH or KOH, primary alkaline cells are developed. The electrolyte is not gelled and it is more corrosive than $NH_4Cl$, so packing becomes difficult. This increases cost of the cell. In this alkaline cell, zinc anode has high surface area and electrolyte is potassium hydroxide. Manganese dioxide of high density acts as a cathode. The shelf life of alkaline $Zn–MnO_2$ cell is longer than that of the cell having ammonium chloride as an electrolyte.

Alkaline cells are employed for camera cranking, radio controlled model planes, radios and tape recorders. Miniature alkaline cells-small button shaped are used in watches, calculators, hearing aids and in many other miniature devices. Alkaline cells operate over a wide temperature range and they withstand mechanical shocks and high pressure.

**2.  Alkaline zinc-mercury cells :**

These cells were developed by U.S. army during World War II (1940). Since its development, it is fundamentally unchanged, but new sizes have been marketed.

It is represented as,

$$Zn - Hg \mid Zn(OH)_{2\,(s)} \mid KOH_{(Aq)}, Zn(OH)_4^{2-}{}_{(Aq)} \mid HgO_{(s)} \mid Hg$$

There are two basic designs, one having a rolled anode and the other having a pressed-powder anode. The cell consists of mercuric oxide (mixed with little graphite to improve conductivity), cathode, an anode of pure amalgamated zinc and aqueous potassium hydroxide as electrolyte. Cathode is pressed into the bottom of a nickel-plated steel case, above this electrolyte is kept in adsorbent material. Anode is pressed into the cell top. (See Fig. 5.24). This cell has energy density of 165 watt hour/kg and open cell potential of 1.35 volts.

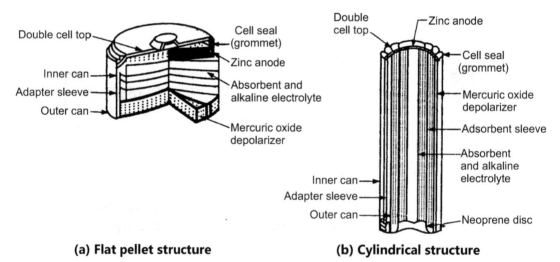

**(a) Flat pellet structure**          **(b) Cylindrical structure**

**Fig. 5.24 : Cross-sectional view flat and cylindrical type mercury cells**

The cell reaction is

$$Zn + HgO + H_2O \longrightarrow Hg + Zn(OH)_2$$

As the electrolyte is not consumed by the cell reaction, the cell potential is constant during the discharge. So it has long shelf life. But it cannot be used below 10°C and disposal creates environmental problem. These cells are used to power transistor radios, watches, hearing aids, electronic computers, voltage recorders, and similar equipment.

**3.   The silver batteries :**

A close relative of mercury cell is zinc-silver oxide alkali cell. In this basic system, electrolytically formed silver peroxide serves as one electrode i.e. cathode and zinc as the other electrode i.e. anode. Anode is in the form of pellet or zinc powder. Cathode is also in the form of pellet. An electrolyte is a solution of potassium hydroxide.

The cell can be represented as,

$$Zn_{(s)} \mid Zn(OH)_{2\ (s)} \mid KOH_{(Aq)}, Zn(OH)_4^{2-}{}_{(Aq)} \mid Ag_2O_{2\ (s)} \mid Ag_{(s)}$$

The active materials are separated from each other by semipermeable membranes such as cellophane. It has open circuit potential of about 1.5 volts. It has high energy density of 200 watt-hours/kg. This cell operates successfully even at significantly lower temperatures. The reaction taking place is

$$2\ Zn + Ag_2O_2 + 2\ KOH \rightleftharpoons 2\ Ag + 2\ KHZnO_2$$

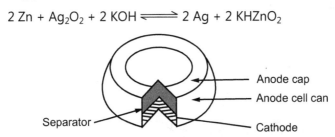

**Fig. 5.25 : Cutaway view of silver oxide cell**

**Applications :**

These cells are used in hearing aids, watches, in the guidance system of rockets, and in photoelectric exposure devices.

Typical silver oxide button cell is shown in Fig. 5.25. It has applications in electronic systems and instruments.

# 5.26.2 Secondary Cells or Batteries

These are electrolytic cells or group of cells which are intended to store electrical energy as chemical energy and can supply electrical energy on demand. These batteries after being discharged may be restored to its original charged condition by an electric current flowing in the direction opposite to the flow of current when the cell was discharged.

Discharging and recharging are equally important parts of the operational cycle. Secondary batteries must be capable of many charge-discharge cycles with high energy efficiency. The lead-acid battery can be charged 250 times in its life. There should not be any side reaction converting the component into some other chemical form which is not at all useful. The energy available per unit weight of the cell should be large. These batteries are also called storage batteries.

## 1.  Lead-acid battery :

The lead-acid cell because of its use in automobile storage batteries is familiar since 1859. The cell can be represented as

$$Pb_{(s)} \mid PbSO_{4\,(s)} \mid H_2SO_{4\,(Aq)} \mid PbSO_{4\,(s)},\ PbO_{2\,(s)} \mid Pb_{(s)}$$

Lead storage batteries are made in a wide range of sizes and capacities by connecting two or more lead-acid storage cells in series. One of the electrodes of the cell is made of lead grills filled with spongy lead and other electrode is made of lead dioxide into lead grids. Number of lead plates acting as negative electrodes and lead dioxide plates acting as positive electrodes are connected in parallel such that lead plates fit in between lead dioxide plates. These plates are separated from the neighbouring one by insulating material like perforated rubber, plastic, strips of wood or glass fibre. This entire assembly is then immersed in dilute sulphuric acid having density 1.2 to 1.3. When acid concentration is 2 M, the cell potential is about 2 volts. So battery having six cells will provide potential of 12 volts. (See Fig. 5.26)

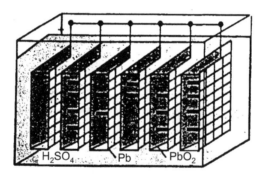

**Fig. 5.26 : The cell of a storage battery has a number of plates**

The half-cell reactions are

$$Pb_{(s)} + SO_4^{2-} \longrightarrow PbSO_{4\,(s)} + 2\ e^- \qquad\qquad \text{... (i) at anode}$$

$$PbO_{2\,(s)} + 4\ H^+ + SO_4^{2-} + 2\ e^- \longrightarrow PbSO_{4\,(s)} + 2\ H_2O \qquad\qquad \text{... (ii) at cathode}$$

**Discharging :** When a galvanic cell is supplying electrical energy, it is said to be discharging. In lead-acid battery, at anode [equation (i)], oxidation of lead takes place, and the lead ions formed combine with sulphate ions to form lead sulphate.

i.e. $Pb_{(s)} \rightarrow Pb^{2+} + 2\ e^-$

Electrons released in the above equation migrate towards cathode. Cathode is made of $PbO_2$, by accepting two electrons, it also forms lead ions. These $Pb^{2+}$ ions on reacting with $SO_4^{2-}$ ions form lead sulphate [equation (ii)]. Thus, lead sulphate gets precipitated at both the electrodes and the cell ceases to function. The net reaction during discharge is,

$$Pb + PbO_2 + 4\,H^+ + 2\,SO_4^{2-} \longrightarrow 2\,PbSO_4 \downarrow + 2\,H_2O + Energy$$

Discharge of cell reduces the concentration of sulphuric acid.

**Charging :** To recharge the lead-storage cell, the reactions taking place during discharging are reversed by passing an external e.m.f. greater than two volts, from a generator. For recharging, positive pole of the generator is attached to the positive pole of the battery, so the reverse reaction takes place. The net reaction during charging is

$$2\,PbSO_4 + 2\,H_2O + Energy \longrightarrow Pb + PbO_2 + 4\,H^+ + 2\,SO_4^{2-}$$

Charging of cell increases concentration of sulphuric acid.

As excessive discharge would rupture the lead grids, so lead-acid battery is operated so that about 30% of available energy is withdrawn before charging.

## 2. Nickel-cadmium cell or batteries :

Edison in 1910 developed alkaline iron-nickel cell as a power source for electric vehicles having cell potential of about 1.37 volts. It can be represented as

$$Fe_{(s)} \mid NiO_{2\,(s)},\ Ni_3O_{4\,(s)} \mid KOH_{(Aq)},\ Fe_3O_{4\,(s)} \mid Fe_{(s)}$$

The total cell reaction can be given as,

$$6\,NiO_{2\,(s)} + 3\,Fe_{(s)} \rightleftharpoons Fe_3O_{4\,(s)} + 2\,Ni_3O_{4\,(s)}$$

As electrolyte is not consumed in the reaction, a small volume is required to build a cell. So cell is more compact and lighter in weight than lead acid cell. When iron and $Fe_3O_4$ are replaced by cadmium and $Cd(OH)_2$, the cell developed is called nickel-cadmium cell.

In nickel-cadmium cell, active material of the positive plate is nickel plated woven mesh of nickel hydrate with graphite while active material of the negative plate is cadmium sponge with additives to increase conductivity. The electrolyte is aqueous solution of potassium hydroxide.

The cell can be represented as

$$Cd_{(s)} \mid Cd(OH)_{2\,(s)} \mid KOH_{(Aq)},\ Ni(OH)_{3\,(s)} \mid Ni_{(s)}$$

The total cell reaction (charge-discharge reaction) can be written as (See Fig. 5.27),

$$Cd + 2\,Ni(OH)_3 \rightleftharpoons 2\,Ni(OH)_2 + Cd(OH)_2$$

The reaction can be explained with the help of Fig. 5.27.

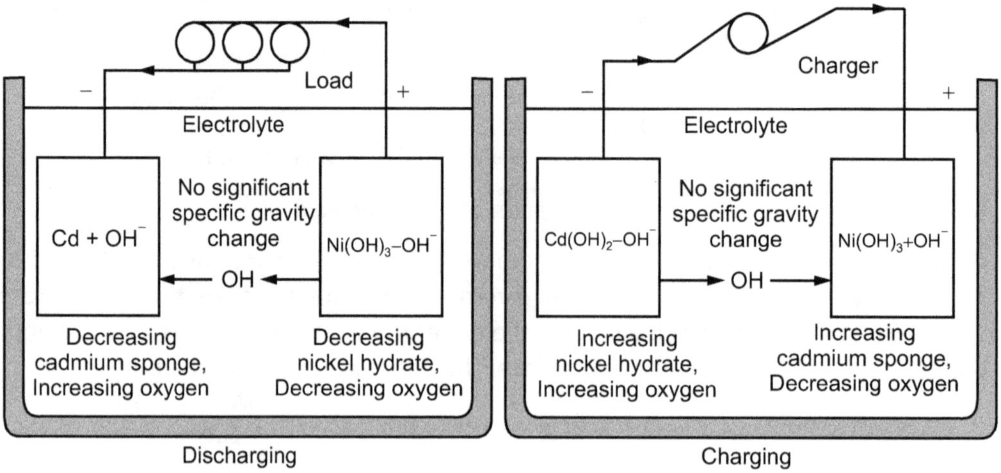

**Fig. 5.27 : Chemical action in a nickel-cadmium storage battery**

It has cell potential of 1.25 volts, so more cells per battery are required. As basic solution is less corrosive than concentrated acid used in lead-acid battery, the electrodes are less susceptible to damage by complete discharging. Nickel is more expensive than lead, so initial cost of batteries is more. The cell has long shelf life and longer service life than lead acid cell, it may be cheaper in long run. It is not giving satisfactory results for turning starting motors of internal combustion engines.

Small rectangular batteries can be used in transistor radios, tape recorders, pocket calculators. These cells are available in button shape and cylindrical shape also. Sintered vented battery (See Fig. 5.28) is used in jet engines, sealed rechargeable batteries are used in electronic photoflash, dictating machines, electric shavers, alarm systems, lap-tops, portable cameras, hearing aids, amplifiers and in appliances. Cross-section of button cell and pocket plate are shown in Fig. 5.29 and Fig. 5.30.

**Fig. 5.28 : Nickel-cadmium cell cover with vent**

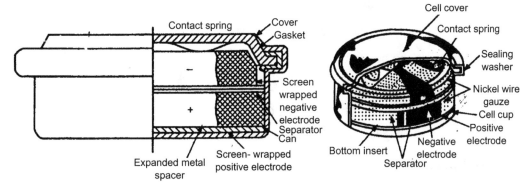

**Fig. 5.29 : Cutaway views of button cells of nickel-cadmium system**

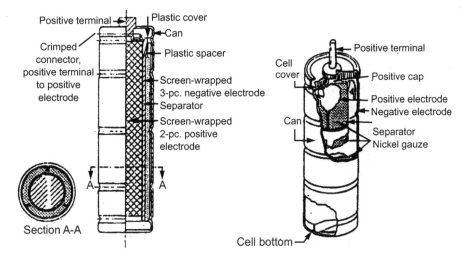

**Fig. 5.30 : Cutaway views of standard rate, pocket-plate cylindrical cells**

### 3. Nickel-zinc cell or batteries :

This combination has a high voltage of about 1.75 volts, which results in favourable energy density. These batteries are housed in moulded plastic cell jars of styrene or ABS material.

### Construction :

Cathode is made of nickel either sintered or pocket type. Nickel hydrate serves as active material mixed with graphite. (Active material is the material which generates electric current by means of a chemical reaction within the battery). It is mixed with inert organic binder like polyethylene or TFE. Then it is rolled into sheets, then pressed into electrodes as dry powder on nickel grid. Anode is fabricated zinc oxide. Binder TFE reduces solubility of electrode in aqueous potassium hydroxide.

The cell can be represented as,

$$Zn_{(s)} \mid ZnO_{(s)} \mid KOH_{(Aq)}, \, Ni-O-OH \mid Ni_{(s)}$$

The cell reaction can be written as

$$2 \, Ni\text{-}O\text{-}OH + Zn + 2 \, H_2O \rightleftharpoons Zn(OH)_2 + 2 \, Ni(OH)_2$$

OR

$$2 \, Ni(OH)_3 + Zn \rightleftharpoons Zn(OH)_2 + 2 \, Ni(OH)_2$$

(Nickel hydrate Ni-O-OH · $H_2O$ also can be written as $Ni(OH)_3$ in cell reactions.)

Nickel-zinc system is ideal for mobile applications such as electric bicycles, scooters. It provides lowest cost option for alkaline batteries.

## 5.27 FUEL CELLS

Fuel cells are electrochemical devices that convert chemical energy of a fuel directly into electrical and thermal energy. The thermal energy results from formation of water from its constituents in fuel cells which is an exothermic reaction releasing 286 kJ/mole of heat.

There are several types of fuel cells but most common are hydrogen - oxygen cells. Fundamentally, cell consists of two electrodes separated by an electrolyte. Hydrogen gas which is used as a fuel is supplied continuously to the anode / fuel electrode. By catalytic action of electrode, oxidation takes place at anode. Two molecules of hydrogen are ionised into four protons ($H^+$) and four electrons.

$$2 \, H_2 \rightarrow 4 \, H^+ + 4 \, e^- \text{ (Oxidation)}$$

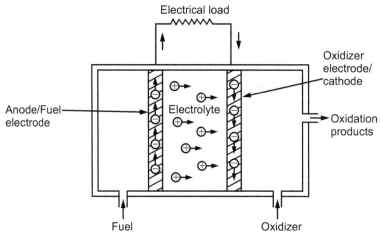

**Fig. 5.31 : A fuel cell**

The electrons pass through the external circuit, thus delivering electrical energy. The positive hydrogen ions pass through the electrolyte to cathode / oxygen electrode where gaseous oxygen or air is fed continuously. At cathode, reduction takes place as

$$4\,e^- + O_2 + 4\,H^+ \longrightarrow 2\,H_2O \quad \text{(Reduction)}$$

The overall net result is a spontaneous oxidation - reduction reaction. The combined action at the two electrodes can be obtained by adding two equations as,

$$2\,H_2 + O_2 \longrightarrow 2\,H_2O$$

The fuel electrode must provide proper catalytic action. It must be porous enough so that ample surface is provided for hydrogen to be ionised. The oxidizer electrode must be porous. Both electrodes must permit flow of electrons readily. The electrolyte, on other hand, must resist the passage of electrons but must readily conduct positive hydrogen ions. To ensure good performance, a fuel cell should operate at elevated temperature and pressure.

Besides direct production of electricity, heat is also produced in fuel cell, this heat can be effectively utilized in generation of additional electricity or for other purposes. The fuel cell theoretically has capability of producing electrical energy as long as the fuel and oxidant are fed to the electrodes. In reality, degradation or malfunction of components limit the practical operating life of fuel cells.

On the basis of electrolyte used, the important types of fuel cells are - phosphoric acid fuel cell (PAFC), molten carbonate fuel cell (MCFC) and solid oxide fuel cell (SOFC). These are used for electric power generation.

## Applications :

Fuel cells operating on pure $H_2$ and $O_2$ provide a useful power source in remote areas such as in space or under the sea where system weight and volume are important parameters. They can provide electricity to individual, building, industry, transportation, etc.

## General Characteristics :

(1) A very high fuel to electricity efficiency is expected.

(2) The fuel cells are quiet (produce no noise).

(3) They also produce useful heat.

(4) They do not contribute to air pollution or global warming like fossil fuels.

(5) They provide power source located close to the end user (distributed generation) which will avoid the cost of long transmission lines together with line losses.

(6) The fuel cells are almost self-contained, can be operated remotely.

(7) The efficiency of fuel cells is independent of their size.

### The problems with fuel cell :

(1) One of the major problem of fuel cell is that of fuel. Although hydrogen gas is a satisfactory fuel, since it is not a primary fuel, it has to be derived from some primary fuel source such as from coal gasification, from natural gas, etc. The efficiency of getting hydrogen by electrolysis of water has to be improved.

(2) Initial cost of fuel cell is very high.

(3) It does not have a reliable life.

## 5.28 SOLAR BATTERY

Solar battery takes solar energy (i.e. energy obtained from the sun) by conversion to electrical energy directly using photovoltaic cell.

Fig. 5.32 shows a photovoltaic or solar cell in which a p-type semiconductor is in contact with an n-type semiconductor. Between the two types of semiconductors, due to close contact, a limited extent of electrons from n-type semiconductor and positive holes from p-type semiconductor can cross the boundary or junction. As they tend to produce separation of charges, such migrations are very limited. For example, due to the presence of immobile B ions, when a positive hole leaves the p-type semiconductor, a build up of negative charge occurs.

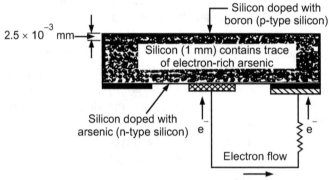

**Fig. 5.32 : Photovoltaic or solar cell using silicon-based semiconductors**

Suppose the outer layer of p-type semiconductor is struck by a beam of light from the sun. The electrons in the valence band in this layer can absorb some of this incident light energy and get promoted to conduction band. Since conduction electrons can easily cross p-n junction into the n-type semiconductor, hence a potential difference between two layers is created, and flow of electrons is set up. The potential difference and hence current increase as more solar energy falls on the surface of outer layer and excites more electrons. Hence, when terminals attached to p and n layers are connected to on external circuit, electrons flow from n-layer to p-layer, thereby generating an electric current. Hence the photovoltaic cell is a device which converts directly the solar energy to electrical energy. On the other hand, a array of a large number of interconnected photovoltaic cells is called a solar battery.

## EXERCISE

1.  Define the following terms :

    (1)  Electrochemistry            (2)  Conductor

    (3)  Insulator                   (4)  Electrolyte

    (5)  Non-electrolyte             (6)  Anion

    (7)  Cation                      (8)  Ionisation

(9)  Degree of ionisation
(10)  Strong electrolyte
(11)  Weak electrolyte
(12)  Electrolytic cell or voltameter
(13)  Poles of battery
(14)  Electrodes
(15)  Anode
(16)  Cathode
(17)  Current density
(18)  Electrolysis
(19)  Electronation
(20)  De-electronation
(21)  Primary stage of electrolysis
(22)  Secondary stage of electrolysis
(23)  Discharge potential
(24)  Coulomb
(25)  Ampere
(26)  E.C.E.
(27)  Faraday
(28)  Polarization
(29)  Overvoltage value
(30)  Decomposition potential
(31)  Conductometric titration

2.  Distinguish between :
  (a)  Electrolyte and Non-electrolyte
  (b)  Atom and Ion
  (c)  Cation and Anion
  (d)  Metallic conductors and Electrolytic conductors
  (e)  Strong electrolyte and Weak electrolyte

3.  State the mathematical relationship between chemical equivalent and electrochemical equivalent.

4.  State Faraday's laws of electrolysis and give their mathematical forms.

5.  How are metals refined on the principle of electrolysis ? Give the labelled diagram.

6.  Explain the mechanism of electrolysis by drawing a suitable diagram.

7.  State whether the process of electrolytic dissociation is reversible or irreversible. Why ? Give two examples in support.

8.  By which law of electrolysis equivalent weight of a metal can be calculated ? State the law and derive it mathematically.

9.  What are the products formed at the electrodes, due to the electrolysis of fused sodium
chloride ? Give chemical reactions at the electrodes.

10.  Define ionisation and state the Arrhenius theory of electrolytic dissociation.

11.  Explain the mechanism of electrolysis of NaCl solution using Pt electrodes. What are the products of electrolysis ?

12.  What is ionisation ? Explain the different factors that affect the degree of ionisation.

13.  (a)  Define and explain the terms electrolytes and non-electrolytes.
  (b)  Explain the mechanism of electrolysis.

14. (a)  State the Faraday's laws of electrolysis.

    (b)  How Faraday's second law of electrolysis is used for finding out the equivalent weight of an element ?

15. (a)  State the postulates of Arrhenius theory.

    (b)  What do you understand by the term 'degree of ionisation' ? Explain the effect of solvent on it.

16. (a)  Define and explain the terms : (i) Coulomb, (ii) Faraday and (iii) E.C.E.

    (b)  An electric current is passed through two cells in series containing respectively solutions of $CuSO_4$ and $AgNO_3$. What weight of silver will be liberated while 1.25 gm of copper gets deposited ?

17. Define : (a) Electrolytic cell, (b) Current density, (c) Anode, (d) Cation, (e) Ampere, (f) Throwing power of bath, (g) Anode mud, (h) Anodizing.

18. (a)  What is the difference between metallic conductors and electrolytes ?

    (b)  Draw a labelled diagram to explain the mechanism of electrolysis.

19. What are Faraday's laws of electrolysis ? Discuss their importance.

20. What are strong electrolytes and weak electrolytes ? Give one example of each.

21. State and explain Kohlrausch's law of independent migration of ions.

22.  State and explain Ostwald's dilution law.

23. Explain the theories of acids and bases with examples.

24. Explain the concept of pH and pOH.

25. What are buffer solutions ? Give preparation and mechanism.

26. Explain solubility and solubility product.

27. Explain the terms involved in redox reactions.

28. Explain the concept of electrode potential.

29. Explain concentration cell.

30. Explain the various reference electrodes with examples.

31. What are batteries ? Explain primary and secondary batteries.

32. Write notes on :

    (a)  Leclanche cell.

    (b)  Lead-acid storage cell.

    (c)  Nickel-cadmium cell

    (d)  Solar battery.

◻◻◻

## 6.1 INTRODUCTION

Isomerism is a property which differentiates organic chemicals from inorganics. For organic molecules of same compound, different structures or spatial orientations are possible. And for same structural formula different chemical compound is also possible. The reason for isomerism lies in presence of tetrahedral carbon, it's bonding in various hybridization with other carbon atom or other heteroatoms. To explain stereochemistry of tetrahedral carbon compounds one needs (i) at least one carbon which is $sp^3$ hybridized, (ii) representation of molecules of 3D-objects.

For example :

A 2D drawing is not appropriate to differentiate between stereoisomers but a 3D view is essential.

In the present unit, the special arrangements of various organic molecules which give rise to different optical behaviours, different chemical activities and different biological activities will be discussed.

## 6.2 IMPORTANT TERMINOLOGIES

1.  **Isomers :** Compounds that have same molecular formula but are not identical are called as isomers.

2.  **Constitutional Isomers :** Compounds which have same molecular formula but the atoms in each compound are connected differently are called as constitutional isomers. For example : acetone

$$
\begin{array}{ccc}
\overset{\textstyle O}{\overset{\textstyle \|}{CH_3 - C - CH_3}} & \text{and} & \overset{\textstyle O}{\overset{\textstyle \|}{CH_3 - CH_2 - C - H}} \\
\text{Ketone} & & \text{Aldehyde} \\
\text{(acetone)} & & \text{(propionaldehyde)}
\end{array}
$$

are constitutional isomers.

**3. Structural Isomerism :** Compounds that have the same molecular formula but different structural formula. It can be manifested in five different ways namely :

1. Chain isomerism.

2. Position isomerism.

3. Functional isomerism.

4. Metamerism.

5. Tautomerism.

**Stereoisomerism :** When isomerism is caused by different arrangements of atoms or groups in space, the phenomenon is called as stereoisomerism. The stereoisomers have same formula and same connectivity but differ in the position of atoms in space. This means the compounds differ only in configuration.

It is observed in two types : (i) Geometrical or cis-trans isomerism and (ii) Optical isomerism.

In this unit, we will discuss both the types. Lets begin with optical isomerism.

## 6.3 OPTICAL ISOMERISM

**Historical perspective :**

**Optical activity :** Some organic compounds when taken in solution form (like dextrose sugar) are able to polarize the planes of light, the phenomenon of polarization is called as optical activity. Dutch astronomer mathematician and physicist Christian Huygens (1629-1695) discovered plane polarized light. In 1815, Jean Biot (1774-1862) noted that certain organic liquids rotate the plane or polarized light and detected optical activity in organic compounds. It can be symbolically shown in Fig. 6.1.

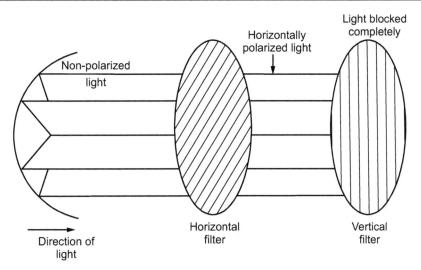

**Fig. 6.1 : Optical polarization**

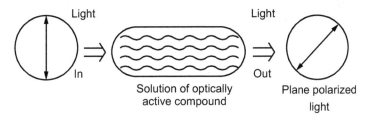

**Fig. 6.2 : Optical activity**

The optical polarization is observed in two directions clockwise and anticlockwise. The compounds which rotate the plane of polarized light in clockwise direction are called as 'Dextrorotatory' and represented by d or (+).

The compounds which rotate the plane of polarized light in anticlockwise direction are called Levorotatory and they are represented by *l* or (–).

Nicotine is levorotatory (–) and Methamphetamine is dextrorotatory (+).

Nicotine (–)                    Methamphetamine (+)

In 1819 Racemic Acid was discovered and had been assigned a formula. In 1832, it was observed that tartaric acid obtained from fermentation of grape juice also has same formula and it is dextrorotatory.

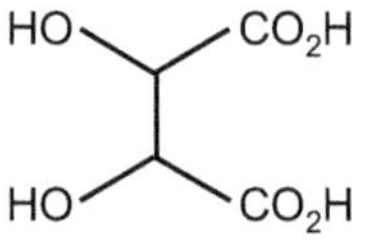

Racemic acid/
tartaric acid

Although Tartaric acid and Racemic acid have same formula in 1838 Biot noted that Racemic acid is not optically active like Tartaric acid. The reason for no optical activity in case of Racemic acid was found by Louis Pasteur in 1847, crystallization of sodium ammonium salts of Racemic acid gave two mirror image crystals which he could easily separate. The solutions made out of the separated crystals gave exactly equal but opposite optical rotation.

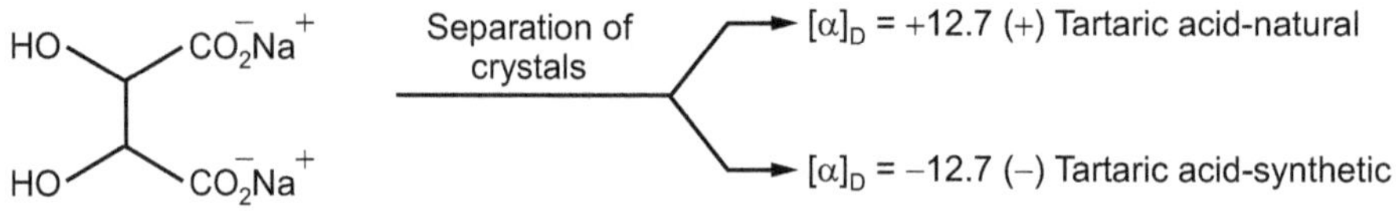

Racemic acid

Separation of crystals

$[\alpha]_D = +12.7$ (+) Tartaric acid-natural

$[\alpha]_D = -12.7$ (−) Tartaric acid-synthetic

In 1853, Pasteur studied Mesotartaric acid (same formula as Racemic acid and Tartaric acid) but it failed to separate into (+) and (−) crystals like Racemic acid, as discussed above. In 1854, he noted that certain plant mold metabolizes (+) tartaric acid but not (−) tartaric acid.

The notworthy point here is all organic compounds are not optically active. If a solution contains mixture of two optically active compounds with exactly opposite rotations the resultant mixture may be optically inactive. Such a mixture is called as **Racemic mixture** as Racemic acid does not show resultant optical activity though the constituents when separated from each other are optically active.

A carbon atom which is attached to four different substituents is called as **asymmetric carbon atom**, it is also called as **sterocentre**.

## 6.4 ENANTIOMERS

Stereoisomers of 2 chlorobutane.

A and B are stereoisomers which are non-superposable mirror images. Such pairs are called as enantiomers. The carbon atom marked with * is stereocentre. Equimolar mixture of A and B will be Racemic mixture. Molecules shown in A and B which are non-superposable with its mirror image are chiral molecules. The molecules which are superposable with its mirror image is achiral molecule.

A molecule having a tetrahedral carbon with four different substituents may exist as a pair of isomers i.e. enantiomers.

**Enantiomer configurations :**

In earlier sections, we have seen how a Racemic mixture contains enantiomers. How to decide and differentiate between two enantiomers. The Cahn - Ingold – Prelog (CIP) rule is used to assign R or S configurations to the two enantiomers.

These rules will be explained using the same example used earlier, i.e. 2 chlorobutane.

1.    Assign the priorities to the groups attached to the stereocentre (marked by * in the above figure). Priority is based on the atomic number, higher the atomic number higher the priority so we will get higher priority over H.

The other two substituents are ethyl and methyl, and the attachment of both is through carbon. In such case, the priority is assigned on the basic of heavier substituents attached to the carbon. In this case, one (methyl) carbon has three hydrogen substituents and second (ethyl) carbon has two hydrogen and one carbon substituent. Naturally, ethyl carbon is attached to heaviour substituents hence ethyl carbon will get priority over methyl carbon hence the priority sequence will be 1-chloro, 2-ethyl, 3-methyl, 4-hydrogen.

2.    Orient the molecule such that the group with lowest priority points away from the observer.

3.  Draw a circular arrow from the group of first priority to the group with second and second to third.

4.  If the circular motion is clockwise, the enantiomer is the 'R' enantiomer.

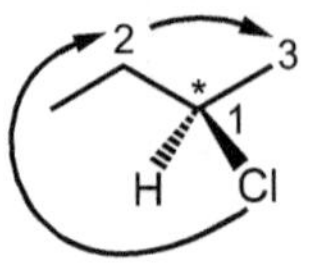

If it is anticlockwise, it is 'S' enantiomer. Thus, A is the 'R' enantiomer of 2 chlorobutane and 'B' is the 'S' enantiomer.

Organic molecules are many times long chain molecules. It is possible in such molecules to have multiple stereocentres. For molecules with one stereocentre it is possible to have two configurations, similarly in case of molecules with 'n' stereocentres there can be $2^n$ configurations or stereoisomers.

For example, lets take a case of tartaric acid where 2 stereocentres are present $2^2 = 4$ stereoisomers are possible in this case.

**Tartaric acid :**

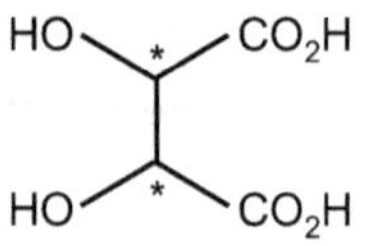

Tartaric acid

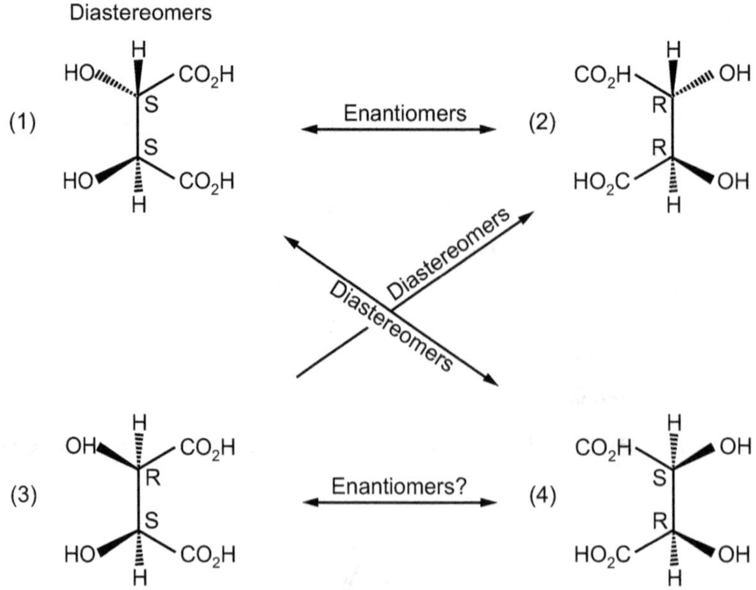

Diastereomers

(1)

Enantiomers

(2)

Diastereomers

Diastereomers

(3)

Enantiomers?

(4)

**Points to Remember :**

- Enantiomers are non-superposable mirror images.
- Diastereomers are stereoisomers that are not mirror images.

  (S, S) tartaric acid and (S, R) tartaric acid are distereomers.

  But (R, S) tartaric acid and (S, R) tartaric acid are not enantiomers as :

(a) they have same molecular formula.

(b) same connectivity.

(c) they look like mirror images but

(d) they are not non-superposable, they are superposable hence they are not enantiomers, they are achiral compound i.e. they are (refer to figure 3 and 4) identical.

**Mesoform – Not Enantiomers :**

A compound with at least two stereocentres is or may be achiral due to presence of plane of symmetry. The part 3 and 4 of earlier figure.

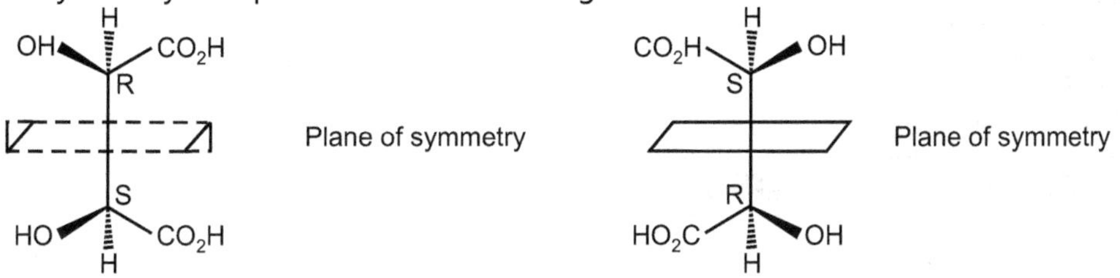

**Properties of Steroisomers :**

**1. Enantiomers :** Enantiomers have same chemical and physical properties in an achiral environment but they differ in the direction of rotation while exhibiting optical activity.

e.g. Epinephrine (Adrenaline).

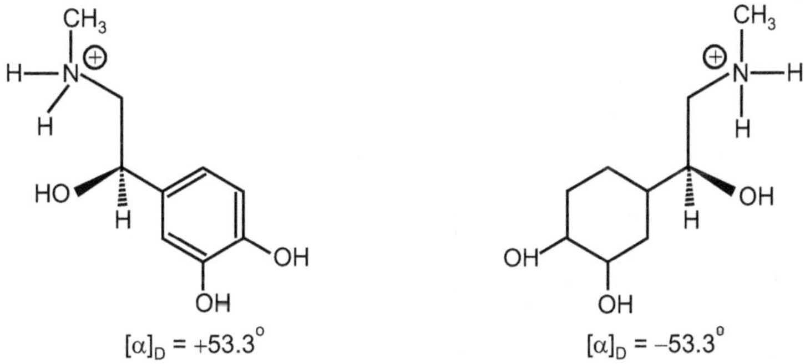

$$[\alpha]_D = +53.3^\circ \qquad\qquad [\alpha]_D = -53.3^\circ$$

Same M.P./B.P., same rate of reaction with achiral agents, same degree of rotation with plane polarized light hence difficult to separate.

**Properties of Diastereomers :**

Diastereomers have different chemical and physical properties in any type of environment.

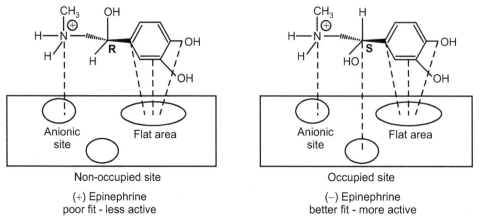

| | (S, S) Tartaric acid | Mesotartaric acid |
|---|---|---|
| $[\alpha]_D$ | – 12.7 | 0 achiral |
| M.P. °C | 171 – 174°C | 146-148 |
| Density g/cc | 1.75 | 1.66 |
| Solubility in $H_2O$ g/lit | 139 | 125 |

(S,S Tartaric acid)              Mesotartaric acid

**Physical and Chemical Properties :**

# 6.5 BIOLOGICAL SIGNIFICANCE OF CHIRALITY

Important biological fluids like amino acids, nucleosides, carbohydrates, phospholipids all have chiral molecules. Hence, they display different properties/reactivity in our body, for example, in a drug has two different enantimomers, one may have tight binding with an enzyme the other may have weak binding. Naturally, the enantiomer which shows tight binding will be more effective as a drug.

**Epinephrine Enantiomers :**

Why did the two enantiomers display different biological activity ?

Enantiomers differ in the arrangement of atoms in space. Therefore, the S enantiomer of epinephrine can fit the active site of a specific enzyme (like a key for a specific lock) producing the desired effect of drug. On the other hand, the R enantiomer cannot interact with same site due to a different enzyme active pocket, triggering a different biological response (toxic).

**Resolution of Enantiomers :**

Many a times it is observed that in synthetic organic molecules one isomer is a drug and other isomer is toxic. It is essential to separate them during synthesis of drug, stabilize the desired isomer so that it does not transform to a toxin. Enantiomers are temporarily converted into a pair of distereomers by adding a chiral reagent.

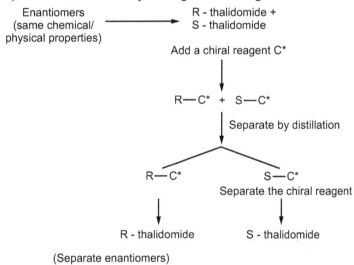

**Conclusions about Stereoisomers :**

- Some organic molecules possess one or more (n) stereocentres, thus several $2^n$ stereoisomers are possible for such molecules.

- Enantiomers and distereomers differ only in position of atoms in space but same molecular formula.

- Enantiomers have same chemical and physical properties in an achiral environment. Distereomers have different chemical and physical properties.

- In the human body (chiral environment), two enantiomers can be discriminated producing different biological responses.

## 6.6 CLASSIFICATION OF STEREOISOMERS

Stereoisomers differ in the way their atoms are arranged in space. There are types of stereoisomers conformational and configurational.

## 6.6.1 Conformational Isomers

Isomers can be easily interconverted at room temperature. Because they are easily interconvertible they cannot be separated. The inetrconversion is possible because of single bond. Saturated organic molecules are formed by single bond which allows rotation about the bond, for example,

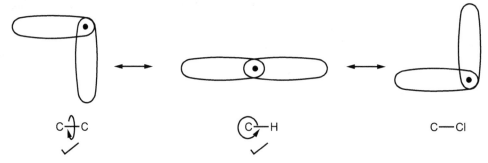

Conformational isomers result from rotation about carbon-carbon single bond. A carbon-carbon single bond arises due to overlap of two $sp^3$ hybridized carbon atoms.

Sigma bond is cylindrically symmetrical hence rotation of the axis of symmetry is possible. Different arrangements are possible due to the rotation giving rise to different conformations. A specific conformation is called as conformational isomer. Let's see how many conformations are possible for simplest saturated alkane i.e. ethane. A major problem one may come across while showing different conformations is how to show a 3-dimensional molecule on a 2-dimensional paper. Melvin Newman a professor from Ohio state university worked out a way to represent a 3D molecule on 2D plane. The representations are called as Newman projection formula. There are various ways to represent the molecules like perspective formula or wedge projection, sawhorse projection, Newman projection.

In perspective formula or wedge projection solid lines are used for bonds that lie in the plane of paper. Solid wedges are used for bonds protruding into the paper.

$$
\underset{H}{\overset{H}{\underset{\displaystyle H^{\prime}}{\bigvee}}}C\text{---}C\underset{H}{\overset{H}{\bigwedge}}H \quad \underset{60^\circ}{\rightleftharpoons} \quad \underset{H}{\overset{H}{\underset{\displaystyle H^{\prime}}{\bigvee}}}C\text{---}C\underset{H}{\overset{H}{\bigwedge}}H
$$

Wedge projection

**Sawhorse projection :** In the sawhorse projection, one observes carbon-carbon bond from an oblique angle.

**Newman projection :** In the Newman projection, one observes the length of a particular carbon-carbon bond. The front carbon is represented by a point and the rear carbon is represented by a circle. There are three line emerging from each carbon, which represent hydrogen atoms. As compared to earlier projections this represents more clearly the special arrangements of all the substituents on both the carbons.

Staggered
configuration

Eclipsed
conformation

If we see both these conformations it can be seen that in eclipsed form the electrons in carbon-hydrogen bond in front and back carbon are closest to each other. In such situation the electrons will repel each other hence stability of the conformation will be less. In the staggered conformation, the planes containing C-H shared electron are away from each other hence the repulsive force between electrons from front and rear carbon will be minimum, hence staggered conformation is more stable.

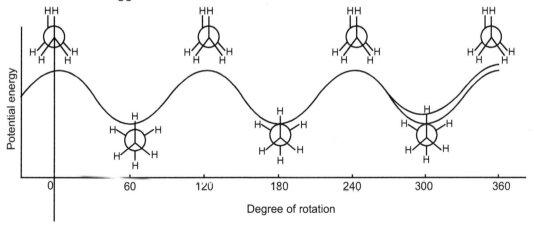

**Fig. 6.3**

Fig. 6.3 shows variation of potential energy in case of various conformations of ethane. All staggered conformations and eclipsed ones have to cross over an energy difference 12 kJ/mol.

When there is interchange from staggered to eclipsed to vice versa goes through different intermediates with different energy and different degree of repulsion.

## 6.6.2 Configurational Isomers (Geometrical Isomers)

Configurational isomers are of two types :

(i)  Cis trans isomers.

(ii)  Isomers with chirality centre.

In case of unsaturated molecules which contain π bonding between carbon atoms, it is difficult to rotate the C = C as the π bond is not labile. The configurational isomers do not readily interconvert and hence can be easily separated. There are two types of configurational isomers cis-trans and the others contain chiralty centres.

**Cis-trans Isomers :**

Cis-trans isomers result due to restricted rotation. There are two possibilities under which cis-trans isomers occur, one is unsaturated molecule with – C = C – in the structure and the other is a cyclic molecule where unsaturation is the form of ring.

2 pentene exists in two forms.

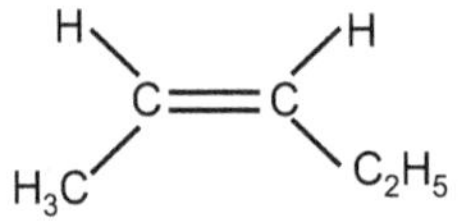

cis-2 pentene 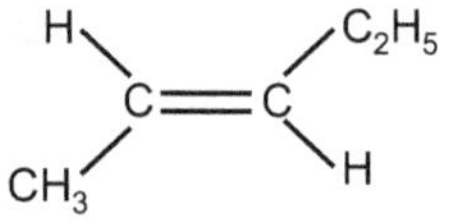                              trans-2 pentene

Cis-trans isomers can be separated. They have different chemical reactivity and stability. Most prominently these differences are seen in case of natural and synthetic rubber. Cis isomers have similar substituents on same side of the double bond and in transisomer same substituents are on opposite sides.

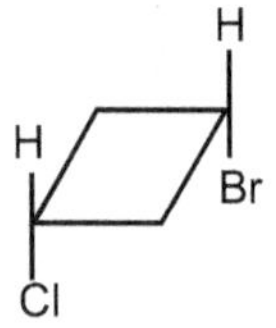

cis 1-bromo
3-chloro cyclobutane

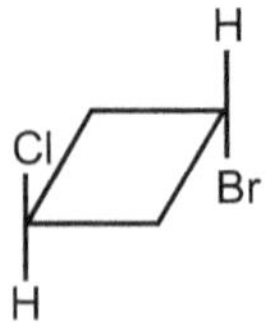

trans 1-bromo
3-chloro cyclobutane

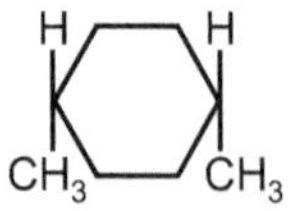

cis 1,4 dimethyl
cyclohexane

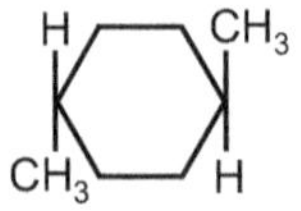

trans 1,4 dimethyl
cyclohexane

Isomers with one chirality centre. A carbon attached to four different groups is called as chiral centre. The chirality centre in each of the following compounds is indicated by asterisk. e.g. $4^{th}$ carbon of 4-octanol is a chiral centre, as it is bonded to H, OH, $CH_2$ – $CH_2$ – $CH_3$ and $C_4H_9$). Note that the difference in the groups bonded to chirality centre need not be directly attached to chiral centre.

e.g. 4-octanol.

In 4-octanol two substituents are carbon (same atom) but on one carbon the chain length is 3 and for other it is 4 hence it is different, hence it is an asymmetric carbon. Note that only $sp^3$ hybridized carbon has chiral centre and not $sp^2$ or sp as they do not have 4 substituents.

## E-Z isomers :

For a compound like 1 bromo 2 chloropropene the cis-trans system of nomenclature cannot be used, as there are four different substituents on the vinyl carbons. The E-Z isomer nomenclature was devised for such situations.

In order to name an E/Z isomer one has to decide priorities to the two substituents attached to vinyl carbon. If the high priority group are on the same side of C = C the configuration is called as 'Z' (Zuzamen – together in German) and if high priority groups are on opposite side the configuration is called as E (Engagen – opposite in German).

|  Z isomer | E isomer |
| --- | --- |

IUPAC prefers E/Z nomenclature as it can be used for all alkenes.

**Rule 1 :** The relative priority is higher for higher atomic number group, directly attached to $sp^2$ carbon. In above case, 1-bromo, 2-chloropropene one of the $sp^2$ carbons is bonded to bromine and other to hydrogen.

Bromine has greater atomic number than hydrogen, so bromine will get higher priority. The other carbon is bonded to chlorine and carbon. Chlorine has greater priority over carbon. (Here one uses atomic weight of carbon atom but not the formula weight of the entire group).

**Rule 2 :** If that two substituents on a $sp^2$ carbon have same atomic numbers then the atomic weights of other substituents are considered.

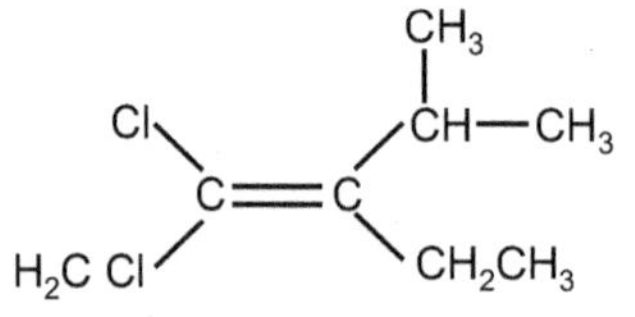

1,2 - dichloro 3 ethyl
4 methyl 2 pentene
(Z)

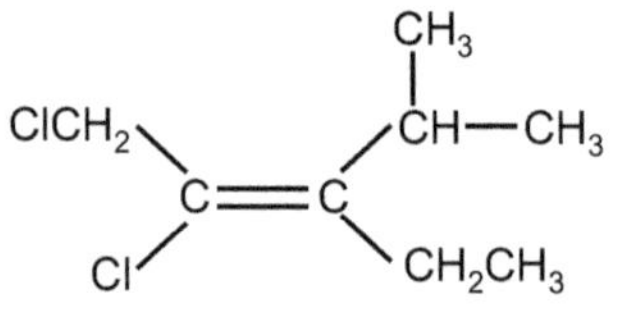

1,2 - dichloro 3 ethyl
4 methyl 2 pentene
(E)

**Rule 3 :** In case of more than one sites of unsaturation while deciding the priorities, the system is whereever there is a double bond the system treats it as if it is bonded to two of those atoms singly bonded to carbon.

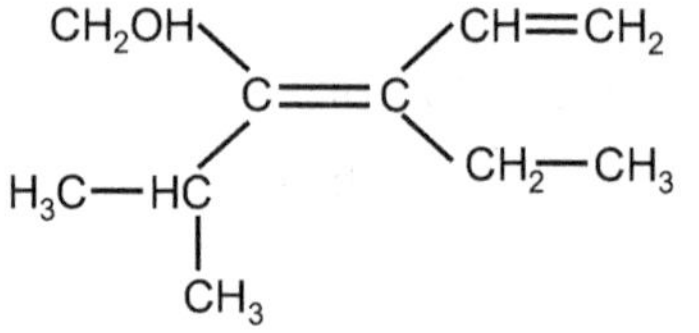

Here the carbon of vinyl group is bonded to an H. Therefore, the first carbon of the ethyl gap is considered to be

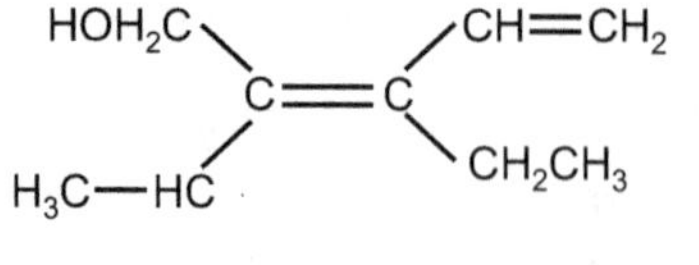

**Rule 4 :** In case of isotopes being present, on $sp^2$ carbon as substituents, higher priority is given to an isotope with higher mass number. In case of hydrogen and deuterium attached to $C_1$ duterium will get higher priority of hydrogen.

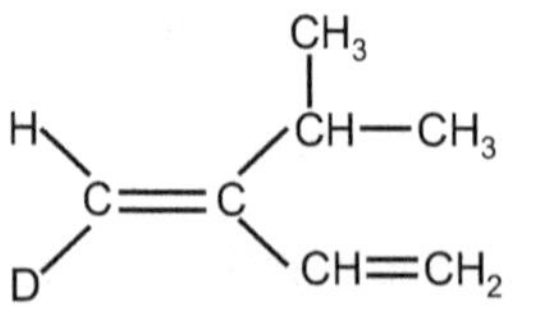

'Z' isomer

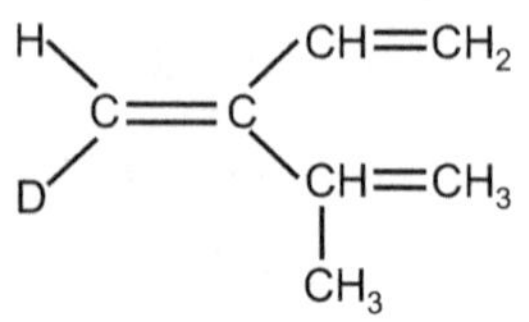

'E' isomer

## Conformations of n butane :

Butane has 3 carbon-carbon single bonds and the molecule can rotate about each of them.

For example, a staggered and eclipsed conformation can be drawn for rotation between $C_1$ and $C_2$. In Newman projection the carbon in front will be $C_1$.

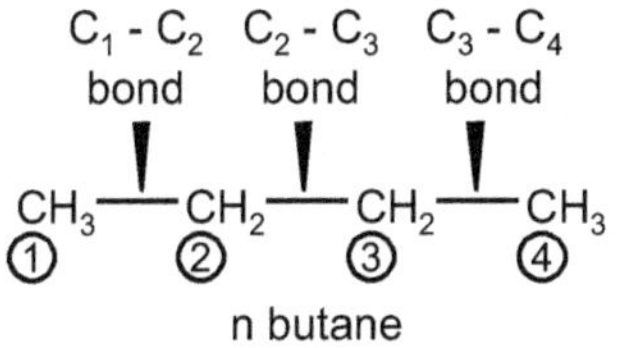

n butane

## Newman projection :

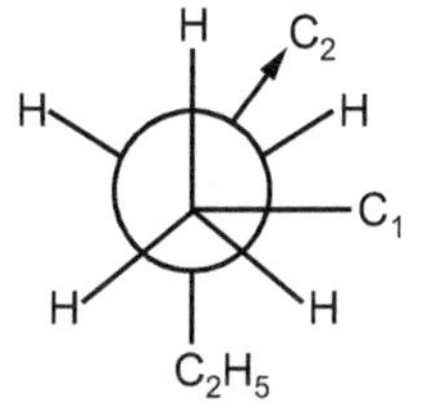

Staggered conformation
for rotation about $C_1$-$C_2$

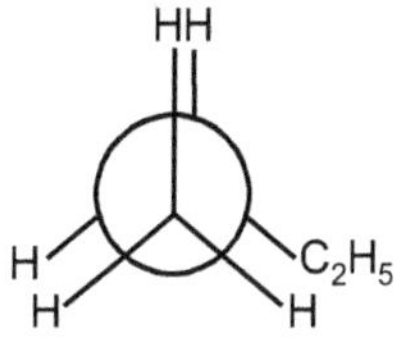

Eclipsed conformation
for rotation around $C_1$-$C_2$

Although the staggered configurations obtained by rotation about $C_1 - C_2$ will have same energy, the staggered conformation by rotations about $C_2$ and $C_3$ will not have same energy.

Newman projection with rotation of $C_2 - C_3$ will look like this.

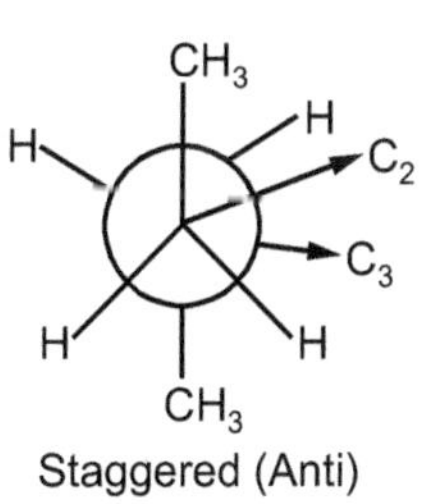

Staggered (Anti)

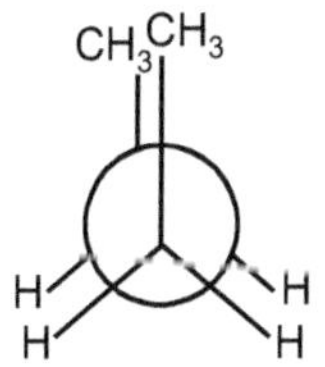

Eclipsed (Syn)

# EXERCISE

1. Explain optical activity with diagram.

2. Explain in brief types of geometrical isomerism.

3. Write in detail about enantiomers.

4. Write short notes on the following :

   (a) Optical isomerism.

   (b) Conformations of n-butane.

   (c) Conformations of ethane.

   (d) Chirality.

   (e) Fisher projection.

   (f) Newman projection.

❑❑❑

# SOLVED UNIVERSITY QUESTION PAPER

## December 2014

**Time : 2 Hours**                                                   **Max. Marks : 60**

**Instructions :**
1. *All questions are Compulsory.*
2. *Figure to the right indicate full marks.*
3. *Use to the non programmable Calculator is allowed*
4. *Neat diagram must be drawn wherever necessary.*
5. *Assume suitable data, if necessary.*

---

**1.** (a) What are the terms boiler corrosion and caustic embrittlement ? Give their causes, disadvantages and preventive measure. **[06]**

**Ans.:** Please Refer to Art 1.9.1 and 1.9.2 on Page 1.13 and 1.14.

    (b) A zeolite softner gets exhausted on softening 4000 lit. of hard water. Calculate hardness of water if the exhausted zeolite requires 10 lit. of 10% NaCl solution for regeneration. **[04]**

**Ans.:** Similar to Problem 1.3 on Page 1.28.

OR

**1.** What is meant by zeolites ? How zeolite is regenerated when it is exhausted ? Give the principle and working of phosphate conditioning. **[10]**

**Ans.:** Please Refer Art 1.11.3 on Page 1.21.

**2.** Derive Bragg's equation with suitable diagram. What are miller indices and Weiss indices ? Explain with suitable example. **[10]**

**Ans.:** Please Refer Art 2.4 , 2.11.1 on Page 2.9, 2.28.

OR

**2.** (a) Define cement and give chemistry, properties and applications of Portland cement. **[06]**

**Ans.:** Please Refer to Art 2.14 and 2.16 on Page 2.38 and 2.43.

    (b) The spacing between the principal planes of Nacl crystal is 2.82 A°, What is the wavelength of X-ray when the first order Bragg's reflection is observed at an angle 10° ? **[04]**

**Ans.:** Please Refer to Art 2.11.1 on Page 2.29.

**3.** (a) What is fuel ? How are fuels classified ? Give the importance of proximate and ultimate and ultimate analysis of coal. **[06]**

**Ans.:** Please Refer to Art 3.1, 3.3, 3.14 on Page 3.1, 3.2, 3.16 and 3.18.

    (b) A sample of certain variety of coal contains 60% carbon, 33% Oxygen, 6% hydrogran, 0.5% sulphur, 0.2% nitrogen and 0.3% ash. Calculate the gross and net calorific values of a coal sample. **[04]**

**Ans.:** Please Ref. Problem 3.5 on Page 3.24.

**OR**

**3.** Give the working of Bomb calorimeter. How correction factor can be determined in Bomb calcorimeter ? **[10]**

**Ans.:** Please Refer to Art 3.7 on Page 3.8.

**4.** (a) "Anodic metallic coatings provide better protection to metals than cathodic ones". **[06]**

**Ans.:** Please Refer to Art 4.6 (E) on Page 4.23.

(b) "Passivity is not a static but a dynamic phenomenon". Comment. **[04]**

**Ans.:** Please Refer to Art 4.4 on Page 4.19.

**OR**

**4.** (a) What is corrosion? Explain mechanism of atmospheric corrosion with examples. **[06]**

**Ans.:** Please Refer to Art 4.1 and 4.2.1 on Page 4.1 and 4.2.

(b) Write about concentration cell corrosion. **[04]**

**Ans.:** Please Refer to Art 4.2.4 on Page 4.13.

**5.** (a) Define reference electrode. Give construction and working of calomel electrode. **[06]**

**Ans.:** Please Refer to Art 5.20 on Page 5.55.

(b) Explain the concept of pH and pOH. **[04]**

**Ans.:** Please Refer to Art 5.14 on Page 5.35.

**OR**

**5.** (a) Define : **[06]**

(i) Specific conductance

(ii) Equivalent conductance

(iii) Molar conductance

**Ans.:** Please Refer to Art 5.3 on Page 5.2.

(b) How is buffer solution prepared ? Give mechanism of buffer action. **[04]**

**Ans.:** Please Refer to Art 5.15 on Page 5.39.

**6.** Define the terms of conformational isomers. Give the conformational isomerism in n-butane. **[10]**

**Ans.:** Please Refer to Art 6.6.1 and 6.6.2 on Page 6.10 and 6.15 .

**OR**

**6.** (a) How do you represent Newman projection formula of n-butane ?

**Ans.:** Please Refer to Art 6.6.2 on Page 6.15.

(b) Explain the following terms : **[04]**

(i) Geometrical isomerism

(iii) Optical isomerism

**Ans.:** Please Refer to Art 6.3 and 6.6.2 on Page 6.2 and 6.12.

CPSIA information can be obtained
at www.ICGtesting.com
Printed in the USA
LVHW100603180121
676779LV00035B/842